Credits

Acquisitions Editor
Aaron Black

Sr. Project Editor
Sarah Hellert

Technical Editor
Dennis R. Cohen

Copy Editor
Kim Heusel

Editorial Director
Robyn Siesky

Business Manager
Amy Knies

Sr. Marketing Manager
Sandy Smith

Vice President and Executive Group Publisher
Richard Swadley

Vice President and Executive Publisher
Barry Pruett

Project Coordinator
Katie Crocker

Graphics and Production Specialists
Ana Carrillo
Noah Hart
Andrea Hornberger
Jennifer Mayberry

Quality Control Technician
Jessica Kramer

Proofreader
Sossity R. Smith

Indexer
Potomac Indexing, LLC

About the Author

Guy Hart-Davis is the author of *Teach Yourself VISUALLY iPod touch*, *Teach Yourself VISUALLY iPhone 5*, *Teach Yourself VISUALLY Mac mini*, *Teach Yourself VISUALLY iMac*, 2nd Edition, *iMac Portable Genius*, 4th Edition, *iLife '11 Portable Genius*, and *iWork '09 Portable Genius*.

Author's Acknowledgments

My thanks go to the many people who turned my manuscript into the highly graphical book you are holding. In particular, I thank Aaron Black for asking me to update the book; Sarah Hellert for keeping me on track and guiding the editorial process; Kim Heusel for skillfully editing the text; Dennis Cohen for reviewing the book for technical accuracy and contributing helpful suggestions; and Andrea Hornberger and Jennifer Mayberry for laying out the book.

How to Use This Book

Who This Book Is For

This book is for the reader who has never used this particular technology or software application. It is also for readers who want to expand their knowledge.

The Conventions in This Book

① Steps

This book uses a step-by-step format to guide you easily through each task. **Numbered steps** are actions you must do; **bulleted steps** clarify a point, step, or optional feature; and **indented steps** give you the result.

② Notes

Notes give additional information — special conditions that may occur during an operation, a situation that you want to avoid, or a cross-reference to a related area of the book.

③ Icons and Buttons

Icons and buttons show you exactly what you need to click to perform a step.

④ Tips

Tips offer additional information, including warnings and shortcuts.

⑤ Bold

Bold type shows command names or options that you must click or text or numbers you must type.

⑥ Italics

Italic type introduces and defines a new term.

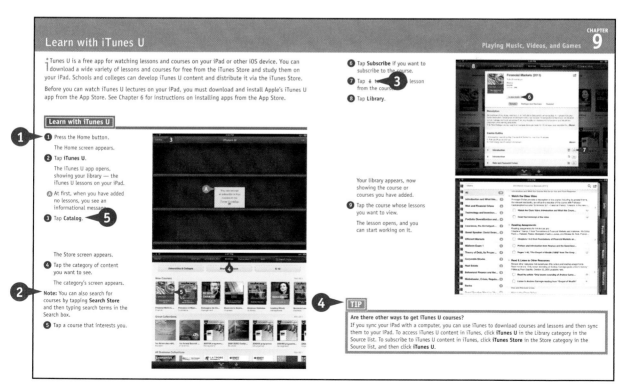

Table of Contents

Chapter 3 Working with Siri and Text

Chapter 4 Setting Up Mail, Contacts, and Calendar

Table of Contents

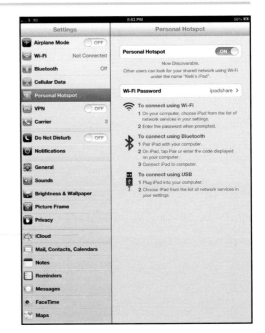

Table of Contents

Chapter 11 Using Maps and Clock

Chapter 12 Taking Photos and Videos

Table of Contents

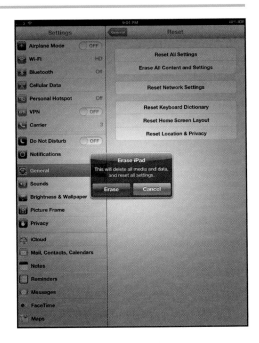

CHAPTER 1

Getting Started with Your iPad

The iPad is a powerful and extremely popular touch-screen tablet computer created by Apple Inc. You can use the iPad either as a full-powered computing device on its own or as a companion device to your Mac or PC. In this chapter, you set up your iPad, sync data to it, and learn to use the user interface.

Take a Look at the iPad and iPad mini

Apple's iPad is the most popular tablet computer on the market. Powerful, elegantly designed, and easy to use, the iPad can take over many of the tasks you normally perform on your desktop or laptop computer, such as surfing the web, exchanging e-mail messages, desktop publishing, and playing video games.

The iPad mini is a smaller iPad that packs almost all of the iPad's features into a smaller form factor.

The Difference Between iPad and iPad mini

The iPad has a 9.7-inch screen with 2048-×1536-pixel resolution at 264 pixels per inch, or ppi. The iPad mini has a 7.9-inch screen with 1024-×768-pixel resolution at 163 ppi.

Although the difference in diagonal measurements is less than 2 inches, the iPad mini's screen is only just over half the size of the iPad's screen, making the iPad mini much smaller and more easily portable.

The iPad measures 9.5 inches tall × 7.31 inches wide, whereas the iPad mini is 7.78 inches tall × 5.3 inches across.

The iPad weighs around one and one-third pounds. The iPad mini weighs less than three-quarters of a pound.

iPad Storage Capacity

Both the iPad and the iPad mini come in three capacities: 16GB, 32GB, and 64GB. Having more storage enables you to install more apps and carry more music, movies, and other files with you. The nearby diagram shows sample amounts of contents.

As usual, higher capacities command higher prices, so you must decide how much you are prepared to spend. Generally speaking, higher-capacity devices get more use in the long run.

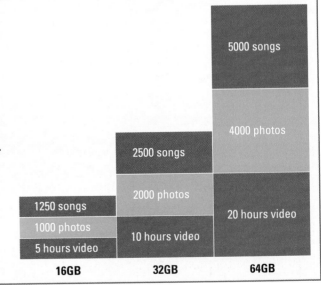

16GB	32GB	64GB
1250 songs	2500 songs	5000 songs
1000 photos	2000 photos	4000 photos
5 hours video	10 hours video	20 hours video

Wi-Fi Only or Cellular and Wi-Fi

Both the iPad and the iPad mini come in Wi-Fi–only and cellular-and–Wi-Fi models.

With a Wi-Fi–only iPad, you can connect to the Internet only through wireless networks, such as those at your home or workplace or wireless hotspots open to the public.

With a cellular-and–Wi-Fi iPad, you can connect both through the cellular network and through wireless networks, giving you Internet access no matter where you go. This option costs more both in the iPad's price and in paying cellular services fees on either a monthly plan or a pay-as-you-go plan.

Touch Screen

Each iPad model has a touch screen that takes up most of the space on the front of the tablet. You use the touch screen to access everything on the iPad with your fingers and to view content. The iPad's software uses gestures to scroll, rotate, and zoom in on objects on-screen.

Cameras

Each iPad has a camera on the front — the screen side — and another on the back.

The front camera is for FaceTime video calling and self-portraits, and can capture 1.2-megapixel photos and high-definition video at the 720p standard. 720p means 720 vertical lines using progressive scan, which gives a good-quality video picture.

The back camera is for taking photos and videos of other subjects, much as you would use a stand-alone digital camera. The back camera can capture 5-megapixel photos and high-definition video at the 1080p standard.

Unbox Your iPad and Charge It

Once you have your iPad, your first move is to unbox it, identify the components, and set the iPad to charge.

To get the best battery life out of your iPad, you should first fully charge the battery, even if it came partly charged. So no matter how eager you are to set up your iPad, sync it with iTunes or iCloud, and start using it, take a few hours to charge it fully.

Unbox Your iPad and Charge It

1 Open the iPad's box and remove its contents.

2 Make sure you have the iPad itself and the following components:

A The power adapter.

B The USB-to-Lightning cable.

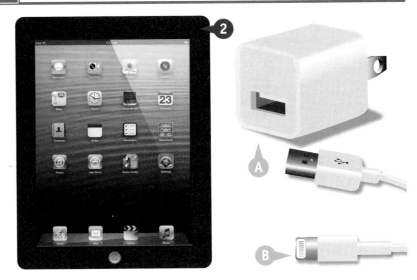

3 Peel the protective film off the front and back of the iPad.

4 Connect the USB end of the USB cable to the power adapter.

5 Plug the power adapter into a power socket.

6 Connect the Lightning end of the USB cable to the iPad.

Note: The Lightning connector is reversible, so it does not matter which way you plug in the connector.

A Charging readout appears on-screen.

7 Leave the iPad to charge until the battery readout shows that the battery is fully charged.

TIP

Can I charge the iPad from my computer's USB port instead of using the power adapter?
Yes, you can. Charging from the USB port offers the convenience of charging the iPad at the same time as syncing data with it. You must make sure that the USB port provides enough power to the iPad; some USB ports on keyboards, other external devices, and even some older computers do not provide enough.

For the first charge, using the power adapter is better than charging from a USB port. This is because the power adapter delivers a more consistent power feed, which charges the iPad as fast as possible.

Turn On Your iPad and Meet the Hardware Controls

After charging your iPad, turn it on and meet its hardware controls. For essential actions, such as turning on and controlling volume, the iPad has a Sleep/Wake button, a Volume Up button and a Volume Down button, and a Side Switch, together with the Home button below the screen.

If your iPad has cellular connectivity, it needs a SIM card. If the store or carrier that sold you the iPad has not inserted a suitable SIM card, you will need to insert one yourself before you can connect to the cellular network.

Turn On Your iPad and Meet the Hardware Controls

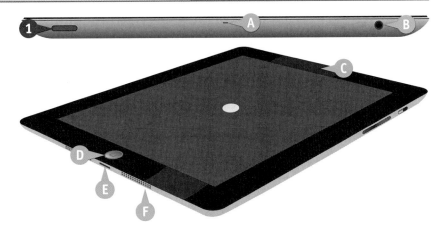

1 Press and hold the Sleep/Wake button on top of the iPad for a couple of seconds.

The top of the iPad also contains:

A The microphone.

B The headphone socket.

As the iPad starts, the Apple logo appears on the screen.

C Above the iPad's screen is the front-facing camera.

D Below the iPad's screen is the Home button, which you press to display the Home screen.

At the bottom of the iPad are:

E The Lightning Connector.

F The speaker or speakers.

Note: The iPad has one speaker at the bottom. The iPad mini has two speakers.

2 Turn the iPad so that you can see its right side.

3 Move the Side Switch down, so that an orange dot appears when you want to mute the iPad's notifications, alerts, and sound effects.

Note: You can configure the Side Switch to lock the screen rotation. To do so, choose **Settings**, **General**, **Side Switch**, and then **Lock Rotation**.

4 Press the Volume Up (+) button to increase the sound volume.

Note: When the Camera app is active, you can press the Volume Up (+) button to take a picture with the camera.

5 Press the Volume Down (−) button to decrease the volume.

6 When the lock screen appears, tap the **slide to unlock** slider, and then drag your finger to the right.

The iPad unlocks, and the Home screen appears.

TIP

How do I insert a SIM card in my iPad?
If you have a cellular iPad that does not yet contain a SIM card, get a suitable micro-SIM for the regular iPad or nano-SIM for the iPad mini. Then insert the SIM removal tool (Ⓐ) in the SIM hole (Ⓑ) at the top of the left side of the iPad. Push gently straight in until the tray (Ⓒ) pops out, and then pull it with your fingernails. Insert the SIM in the tray (Ⓓ), and then push the tray in fully.

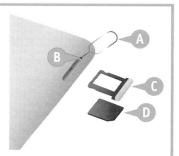

Download, Install, and Set Up iTunes

To sync your iPad with your computer, you use Apple's iTunes application. iTunes comes preinstalled on every Mac but not on PCs; to get iTunes for Windows, you download it from the Apple website and then install it on your PC.

If you do not have a computer, or you do not want to sync your iPad with your computer, you can set up and sync your iPad using Apple's iCloud service, as described later in this chapter.

Download, Install, and Set Up iTunes

1 On your PC, open the web browser, Internet Explorer in this example.

2 Click the Address box, type **www.apple.com/itunes/download**, and then press **Enter**.

The Download iTunes Now web page appears.

3 Click the check boxes (☑ changes to ☐) unless you want to receive e-mail from Apple.

4 Click **Download Now**.

The File Download – Security Warning dialog box opens.

5 Click **Save**.

The Save As dialog box appears.

6 Select the download location — for example, your Downloads folder — and then click **Save**.

The download starts.

7 In the Download Complete dialog box, click **Run**.

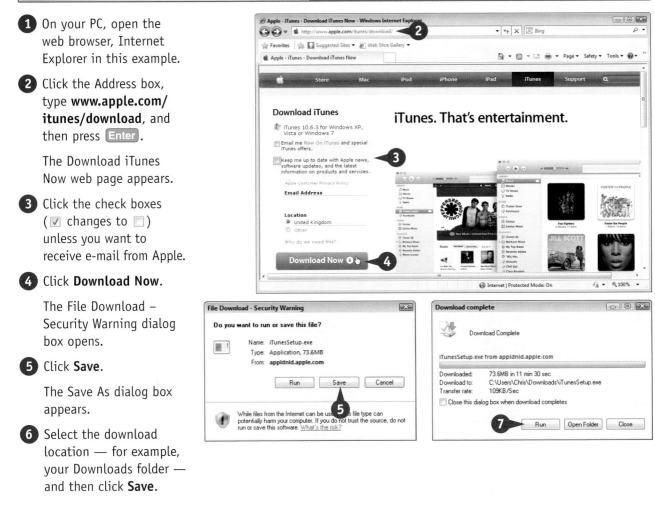

10

The iTunes Installer opens.

8 Click **Next**, and then follow the steps of the installer.

Note: You must accept the license agreement in order to install iTunes. In the Installation Options dialog box, click the **Add iTunes and QuickTime shortcuts to my desktop** check box (changes to ☐) unless you need these shortcuts.

When the installation finishes, the installer displays the Congratulations dialog box.

9 Click **Finish**.

The installer closes.

10 If the installer prompts you to restart your PC, restart it as soon as is convenient.

How do I set up iTunes on a Mac?
If you have not run iTunes already, click the **iTunes** icon (⊚) that appears on the Dock by default. If the Dock contains no iTunes icon, click **Launchpad** (⊛) on the Dock, and then click **iTunes** (⊚) on the Launchpad screen. The iTunes Setup Assistant launches. Follow the steps to set up iTunes.

Set Up Your iPad Using iTunes

Before you can use your iPad, you must set it up. You can set up the iPad through iTunes, as described in this task, or by using iCloud, as explained later in this chapter.

During setup, you choose which items to sync automatically with the iPad. You can choose other sync options as described in the next task.

Set Up Your iPad Using iTunes

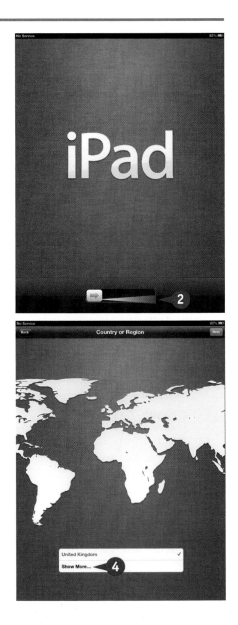

1 Turn on the iPad by pressing and holding the power switch for a couple of seconds until the Apple logo appears.

2 When the initial iPad screen appears, tap the slider and drag it to the right.

The iPad unlocks and begins the setup routine.

3 If the Language screen shows the language you want to use, tap ➡. Otherwise, tap **Show More**, tap the language on the screen that appears, and then tap ➡.

4 If the first Country or Region screen shows the right country or region, tap **Next**. Otherwise, tap **Show More**, tap the country or region on the second Country or Region screen, and then tap **Next**.

The Wi-Fi screen appears.

5 Tap **Connect to iTunes**.

6 Connect your iPad to your computer using the USB-to-Lightning cable.

The iTunes window appears.

7 On the Set Up Your iPad screen, change the name as needed.

8 Click **Automatically sync songs and videos to my iPad** (☐ changes to ☑) to sync songs and videos.

Note: To control which items you sync, click this check box (☑ changes to ☐) and see the next task.

9 Click **Automatically add photos to my iPad** (☐ changes to ☑) if you want to sync photos to your iPad.

10 Click **Automatically sync apps to my iPad** (☐ changes to ☑) to sync new apps automatically. Syncing apps automatically is usually helpful.

11 Click **Done**.

iTunes syncs your iPad.

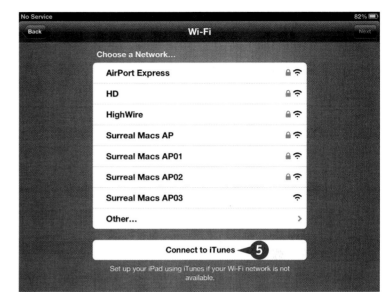

 TIP

What should I do if iTunes does not open when I connect my iPad?
If iTunes does not open automatically, launch iTunes manually. In OS X, click **iTunes** (🎵) on the Dock or in the Applications folder. In Windows, click **Start** and then **iTunes**.

Choose Which Items to Sync

After setting up your iPad, you can choose which items to sync to it. You can sync a wide range of items, ranging from your contacts, calendars, and e-mail accounts to your music, movies, books, and photos.

This task shows you how to choose exactly which items to sync. This task shows OS X screens; the Windows screens are similar, but some items have different names.

Choose Which Items to Sync

Connect Your iPad and Access the Control Screens

1 Connect your iPad to your computer.

The iTunes window appears.

2 Click your iPad.

Note: Your iPad appears in iTunes with the name you gave it.

The iPad's control screens appear.

Choose Which Contacts to Sync

1 Click **Info**.

The Info screen appears.

2 Click **Sync Contacts** (☐ changes to ☑).

Note: In Windows, click **Sync contacts with** (☐ changes to ☑). Then select the program that contains the contacts — for example, Outlook.

3 To sync only some contacts, click **Selected groups** (◯ changes to ◉).

4 Click the check box for each contacts group you want to sync (☐ changes to ☑).

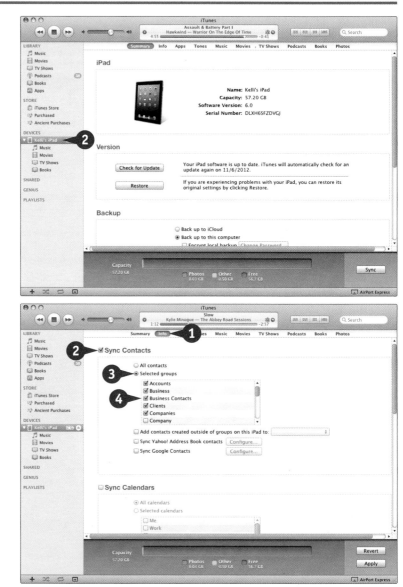

5 Click **Add contacts created outside of groups on this iPad to** (☐ changes to ☑).

6 Click ⬍ and then click the contacts group to which you want to add contacts created outside groups on your iPad.

7 If you need to sync Yahoo! contacts, click **Sync Yahoo! Address Book contacts** (☐ changes to ☑).

The Yahoo! Address Book dialog opens.

8 Type your Yahoo! ID.

9 Type your password.

10 Click **OK**.

The Yahoo! Address Book dialog closes.

11 If you need to sync Google contacts, click **Sync Google Contacts** (☐ changes to ☑).

The Google Contacts dialog opens.

12 Type your Google ID.

13 Type your password.

14 Click **OK**.

The Google Contacts dialog closes.

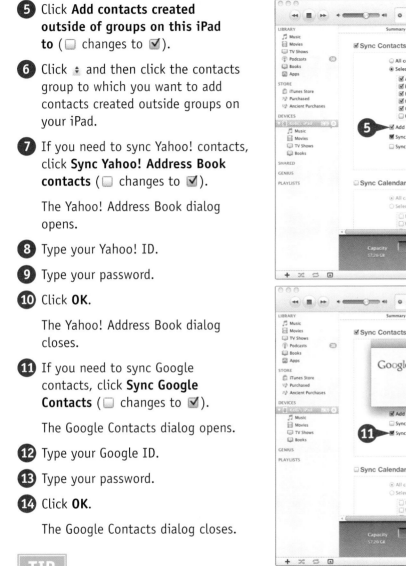

TIP

What happens if I change the same contact on my computer and my iPad?
If you change the same information on both your computer and iPad between syncs, you may create a sync conflict. iTunes then displays the Conflict Resolver dialog. Click **Review Now** to expand the Conflict Resolver dialog to see the details, and then click the correct version of each contact record that has a conflict. Click **Done** to close the Conflict Resolver dialog.

continued ►

By syncing your calendars with your iPad, you can ensure you always have up-to-date information about appointments and commitments both on your iPad and your computer.

You can also sync the details of your e-mail accounts to your iPad to quickly set up the accounts on the iPad. iTunes does not sync the folders and mailboxes with the iPad. After you sync the account details, your iPad communicates directly with the e-mail server, just as your computer's e-mail application does.

Choose Which Items to Sync (continued)

Choose Which Calendars to Sync

1 On the Info screen for your iPad, click **Sync Calendars** (☐ changes to ☑).

Note: In Windows, click **Sync calendars with** (☐ changes to ☑). You can then choose the program with which you want to sync — for example, Outlook.

2 To sync only some calendars, click **Selected calendars** (○ changes to ⦿).

3 Click the check box for each calendar you want to sync (☐ changes to ☑).

4 To limit the number of days of calendar data, click **Do not sync events older than _N_ days** (☐ changes to ☑). Leave the default number, 30, or type a different number in the box.

Note: The Do Not Sync Events Older than _N_ Days Option for calendars helps to limit the amount of data you sync between the iPad and your computer. Use this option to make sure your iPad is not wasting time syncing old appointments.

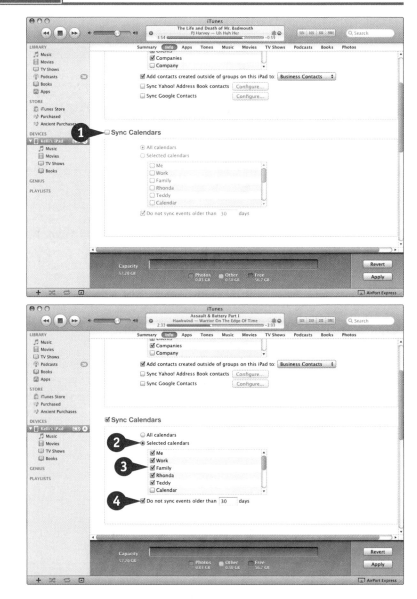

Choose Which E-Mail Accounts to Sync

1 On the Info screen for your iPad, click **Sync Mail Accounts** (☐ changes to ☑).

Note: In Windows, click **Sync selected mail accounts from** (☐ changes to ☑) and then click the program.

2 Click each mail account you want to sync (☐ changes to ☑).

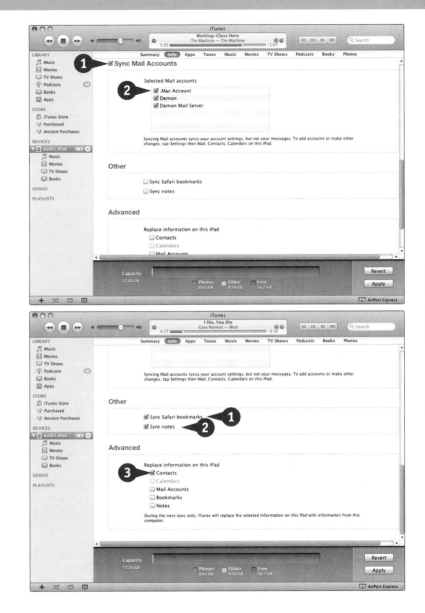

Choose Other Options and Advanced Options

1 On the Info screen for your iPad, click **Sync Safari bookmarks** (☐ changes to ☑).

2 Click **Sync notes** (☐ changes to ☑).

3 In the Advanced box, click any item (☐ changes to ☑) on the iPad you want to replace with information from your computer.

Note: Use the Advanced options only when data on your iPad has become corrupted. After the sync replaces the data, iTunes clears the Advanced check boxes (☑ changes to ☐) so that it does not overwrite the data again.

TIP

Can I add to the iPad an e-mail account that is not on my computer?
Yes. You can set an e-mail account directly on the iPad. See Chapter 4 for instructions on how to set up an e-mail account.

continued ▶ **17**

To add apps to your iPad, you can buy the apps from the App Store using either iTunes on your computer or the App Store app on your iPad. When you buy apps on your iPad and sync the iPad with your computer, iTunes copies the apps to your computer.

iTunes can sync apps to your iPad either automatically or manually. iTunes can automatically sync new apps, which is useful for making sure you have all your latest apps with you.

Choose Which Items to Sync (continued)

Choose Which Apps to Sync to Your iPad

1 Click **Apps**.

The Apps screen appears.

2 Click **Sync Apps** if you want to sync apps to your iPad.

3 Click ⬍.

4 Click the way you want to sort the apps: **Sort by Name**, **Sort by Kind**, **Sort by Category**, **Sort by Date**, or **Sort by Size**.

iTunes lists the apps in the order you chose.

Note: Optionally, click ⬍ and click **Show Only iPad Apps**. iTunes lists only the apps specifically designed for the iPad, hiding apps designed for the iPhone and iPod touch.

5 Click each app you want to sync (☐ changes to ☑).

Note: On a Mac, to select each check box (☑), ⌘+click a check box. In Windows, **Ctrl**+click a check box.

Ⓐ The app readout shows how many apps your iPad will have.

Ⓑ The Home screen preview shows how the icons will appear.

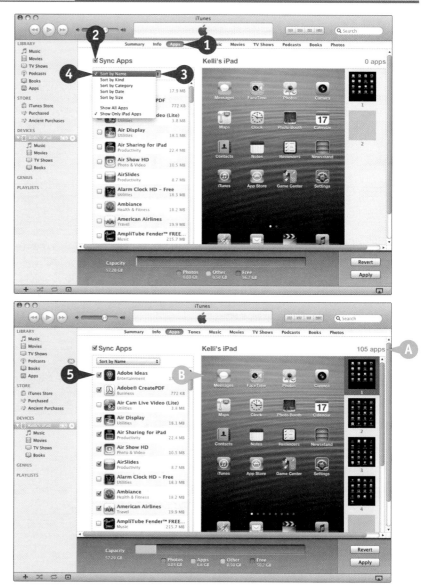

Choose Which Tones to Sync

1 Click **Tones**.

The Tones screen appears.

2 Click **Sync Tones** (☐ changes to ☑).

3 Click **All tones** (○ changes to ◉) if you want to sync all tones. Otherwise, click **Selected tones** (○ changes to ◉).

4 If you clicked **Selected tones**, click the check box (☐ changes to ☑) for each tone to sync.

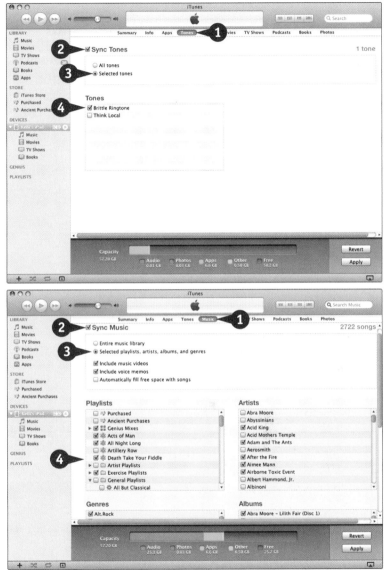

Choose Which Music to Sync

1 Click **Music**.

The Music screen appears.

2 Click **Sync Music** (☐ changes to ☑).

3 Click **Selected playlists, artists, albums, and genres** (○ changes to ◉).

4 Use the controls in the Sync Music box, Playlists box, Artists box, Genres box, and Albums box to specify which music to sync.

TIP

Can I sync all my music to my iPad?
This depends on how much music your library contains and how high your iPad's capacity is. Normally, it is best to click **Selected playlists, artists, albums, and genres** and specify which music you want. You can click **Automatically fill free space with songs** (☐ changes to ☑) to pack in as much music as possible, but your iPad may then lack space for shooting photos and videos or adding other content, such as e-books.

continued ▶

To make the most of your iPad's pin-sharp screen, you can sync your movies, TV shows, podcasts, iTunes courses, books, audiobooks, and photos to the device.

If you have only a few movies, TV shows, podcasts, audiobooks, and photos, you may decide to sync them all. If you have many, you will normally need to choose which to sync so you do not run out of space on your iPad. By contrast, most books have small file sizes, so you can easily fit a large library on your iPad.

Choose Which Items to Sync (continued)

Choose Which Movies to Sync

▶ Click **Movies**.

▶ On the Movies screen, click **Sync Movies** (☐ changes to ☑).

▶ To sync movies automatically, click **Automatically include** (☐ changes to ☑), click ⬍, and then choose which movies — for example, **All**, **5 most recent**, or **10 most recent unwatched**.

④ Click each movie (☐ changes to ☑) to sync.

Choose Which Books and Audiobooks to Sync

▶ Click **Books**.

▶ On the Books screen, click **Sync Books** (☐ changes to ☑).

▶ Click **All books** (○ changes to ◉) or **Selected books** (○ changes to ◉).

④ Choose which books to sync.

⑤ Scroll down to the Audiobooks area.

⑥ Click **Sync Audiobooks** (☐ changes to ☑).

▶ Choose which audiobooks to sync.

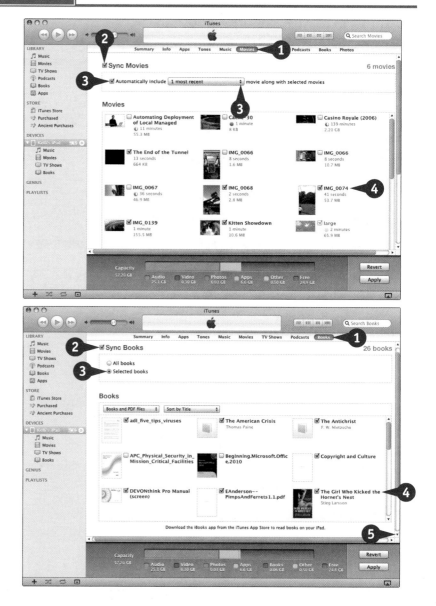

Choose Which Photos to Sync

1 Click **Photos**.

The Photos screen appears.

2 Click **Sync Photos from** (☐ changes to ☑).

3 In the pop-up menu, choose the source of the photos — for example, iPhoto.

4 Choose which photos to sync. For example, click **Selected albums, events, and faces, and automatically include** (○ changes to ●), and then choose which albums, events, and faces to include.

Perform the Sync

1 After choosing the items to sync, click **Apply**.

iTunes syncs the chosen items to your iPad.

A iTunes displays the sync status.

Note: If you decide you do not want to apply the sync changes, click **Revert**. iTunes restores the sync settings to how they were before and displays the Sync button in place of the Revert button and Apply button.

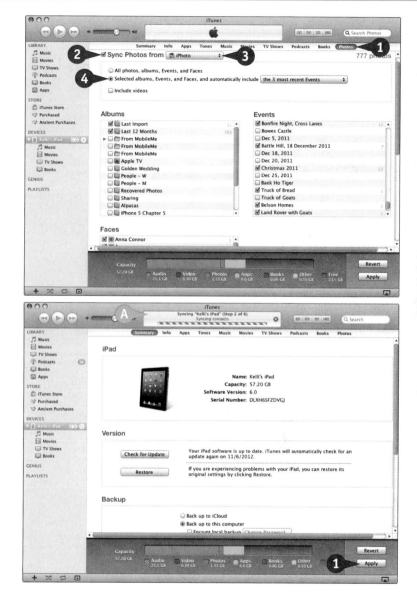

TIP

How do I sync TV shows, podcasts, iTunes U courses, and books?

To sync TV shows, podcasts, and iTunes U courses, click the appropriate tab in iTunes, and then use the controls to specify which items you want. For example, for TV shows, you can click **Sync TV Shows** (☐ changes to ☑) and then choose a setting such as **Automatically include the 3 newest unwatched episodes of all shows**.

Sync Your iPad with iTunes via Wi-Fi

The normal way to sync your iPad with iTunes is by using the USB-to-Lightning cable to connect the iPad to your computer. But if you connect both your computer and your iPad to the same network, you can sync the iPad with iTunes wirelessly. This is called syncing "over the air."

To use wireless sync, you must first enable it in iTunes. You can then have the iPad sync automatically when it is connected to a power source and to the same wireless network as the computer. You can also start a sync manually from the iPad even if it is not connected to a power source.

Sync Your iPad with iTunes via Wi-Fi

Set Your iPad to Sync with iTunes via Wi-Fi

1 Connect your iPad to your computer with the USB cable.

The iTunes window appears.

2 Click your iPad.

Note: Your iPad appears in iTunes with the name you gave it.

The iPad's control screens appear.

3 Click **Summary**.

The Summary screen appears.

4 Click **Sync with this iPad over Wi-Fi** (☐ changes to ☑).

5 Click **Apply**.

iTunes applies the change.

6 Disconnect your iPad from your computer.

Perform a Manual Sync via Wi-Fi

1 Press the Home button.

The Home screen appears.

2 Tap **Settings**.

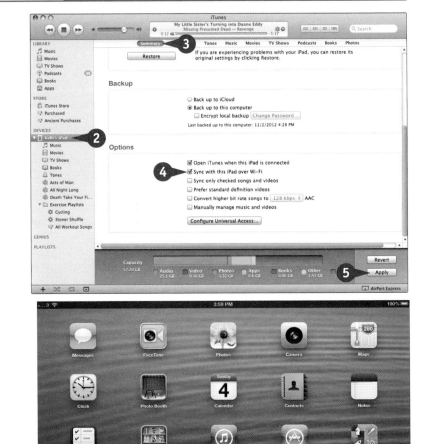

The Settings screen appears.

 Tap **General**.

The General screen appears.

④ Tap **iTunes Wi-Fi Sync**.

The iTunes Wi-Fi Sync screen appears.

⑤ Tap **Sync Now**.

The sync runs.

The Sync symbol (◎) appears in the status bar.

The readout shows which part of the sync is currently running.

TIP

Can I sync my iPad automatically via Wi-Fi?

To sync your iPad automatically via Wi-Fi, connect your iPad to a power source — for example, the USB Power Adapter. Make sure your computer is on and connected to your network, and that iTunes is running. Your iPad automatically connects to your computer across the wireless network. iTunes syncs the latest songs, videos, and data once a day if these conditions are met, but not at a set time. You can run a sync manually any time you want.

Transfer Files to Your iPad Using iTunes File Sharing

When you need to transfer files to the iPad, you can use the File Sharing feature built in to iTunes. This feature enables you to transfer files to the iPad's storage area devoted to a particular app. For example, when you need to use a file with the DocsToGo app on the iPad, you transfer it to the DocsToGo area using File Sharing.

Only some apps can transfer files, and you must install an app capable of transferring files via File Sharing before you can use File Sharing, as described on these pages.

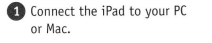

Transfer Files to Your iPad Using iTunes File Sharing

 Connect the iPad to your PC or Mac.

iTunes launches or becomes active, and the iPad appears in the Devices category in the Source list.

2 Click your iPad.

The iPad's control screens appear, with the Summary screen at the front.

3 Click **Apps**.

The Apps screen appears.

4 Scroll down.

The File Sharing area appears.

5 Click the app to which you want to add the file.

6 Click **Add**.

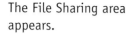

The Open dialog appears.

7 Click the file you want to copy to the iPad.

Note: You can copy multiple files at once by selecting them. For example, click the first file, and then **Shift**+click the last file to select a range of files.

8 Click **Open**.

iTunes copies the file or files to the iPad.

TIP

How do I copy a file from the iPad to my computer?

1 Open File Sharing as discussed in this task.

2 In the Apps box, click the app that contains the file.

3 In the Documents box, click the file.

4 Click **Save to**. The Open dialog appears.

5 Click the folder to save the file in.

6 Click **Open**. iTunes copies the file.

Set Up Your iPad Using iCloud

Instead of using iTunes and your computer to set up and sync your iPad, you can set it up and sync it without a computer using Apple's iCloud online service. To do this, you need an Apple ID. You can create an Apple ID using either your existing e-mail address or a new iCloud account that you create during setup.

Set Up Your iPad Using iCloud

1 Follow steps **1** to **4** of the task "Set Up Your iPad Using iTunes" to begin setting up your iPad.

2 On the Wi-Fi Networks screen, tap your wireless network.

The Enter Password screen appears.

3 Type the password.

4 Tap **Join**.

The Wi-Fi Networks screen appears again.

5 Tap **Next**.

The Location Services screen appears.

6 Tap **Enable Location Services** or **Disable Location Services**, as appropriate.

7 Tap **Next**.

The Set Up iPad screen appears.

8 Tap **Set Up as New iPad**.

9 Tap **Next**.

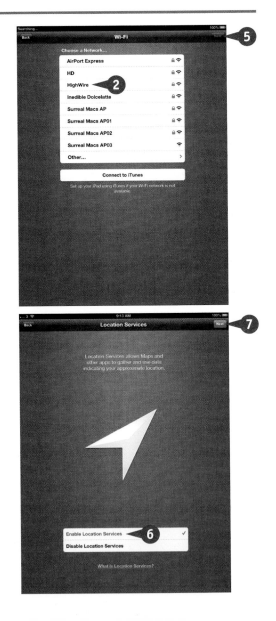

The Apple ID screen appears.

10 Tap **Create a Free Apple ID**.

The Birthday screen appears.

11 Move the spin wheels to your birthday or the date you want to claim is your birthday.

12 Tap **Next**.

The Name screen appears.

13 Tap the First Name box and type your first name.

14 Tap the Last Name box and type your last name.

15 Tap **Next**.

The Create Apple ID screen appears.

16 Tap **Get a free iCloud email address**.

17 Tap **Next**.

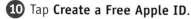

Should I sync my iPad with iCloud rather than with my computer?

If you have a main computer that you use most of the time, you will probably be better off syncing your iPad with the computer than with iCloud. You can keep all your music and videos on your computer, organize them with iTunes, and then sync the items you want with your iPad, as discussed earlier in this chapter.

If you do not have a computer you use regularly, sync with iCloud. For example, if you use an iPad as your main computer, you must sync your iPad with iCloud because you cannot sync the iPad directly with the iPad. The disadvantages to syncing with iCloud are that you get only 5GB of storage unless you pay for more, and syncing is slower than syncing with a computer.

continued ▶ **27**

By using iCloud, you can synchronize your songs, videos, apps, and documents with other devices running Apple's iOS operating system. For example, if you have an iPhone or an iPod touch, you can use iCloud sync to keep that device's contents synced with your iPad's contents, and vice versa.

If you have a Mac or PC, you can also use iCloud to sync various items to the computer. In Windows, you must install iCloud Control Panel, which you can download for free from the Apple website (www.apple.com/icloud/setup/pc.html).

Set Up Your iPad Using iCloud (continued)

The iCloud Email screen appears.

18 Type the address you want to use.

19 Tap **Next**.

The Apple ID Password screen appears.

20 Type your password twice.

21 Tap **Next**.

The Security Info screen appears.

22 Tap the question you want to use. You can use a custom question for added security.

23 Tap the Answer box and type the answer to your question.

24 Tap **Next**.

The Email Updates screen appears.

25 Tap the **Email Updates** switch and move it to Off if you do not want to receive e-mail updates from Apple.

26 Tap **Next**.

The Terms and Conditions screen appears.

27 Read the terms and conditions, and then tap **Agree** if you want to proceed.

28 In the Terms and Conditions dialog, tap **Agree**.

29 On the Set Up iCloud screen, tap **Use iCloud**.

30 Tap **Next**.

31 On the iCloud Backup screen, tap **Back Up to iCloud**.

32 Tap **Next**.

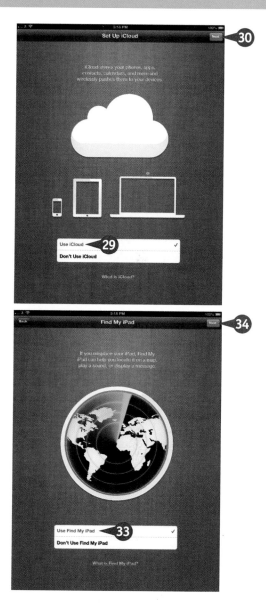

33 On the Find My iPad screen, tap **Use Find My iPad**.

34 Tap **Next**.

35 On the Siri screen, tap **Use Siri** or **Don't Use Siri**, as needed.

36 On the Diagnostics screen, tap the **Send Diagnostics** switch, tap **Automatically Send** or **Don't Send**, as appropriate.

37 Tap **Next**.

38 On the Thank You screen, tap **Start Using iPad**.

The Home screen appears, and you can start using the iPad, as discussed in the following task.

TIP

Should I use the Find My iPad feature, or is it a threat to my privacy?
The Find My iPad feature can help you locate your iPad if you have mislaid it or if someone has removed it.

To use Find My iPad, you log in to iCloud using your Apple ID. You can then give the command to locate your iPad.

Unless you share your Apple ID with others, no one but you can use Find My iPad to locate your iPad, so it is not a privacy threat worth worrying about.

Explore the iPad's User Interface and Launch Apps

After you sync the iPad with your computer or set it up with iCloud, you are ready to start using the iPad. When you press the Sleep/Wake button or open the Smart Cover, the iPad displays the lock screen. You then unlock the iPad to reach the Home screen, which contains icons for running the apps installed on the iPad.

You can quickly launch an app by tapping its icon on the Home screen. From the app, you can return to the Home screen by pressing the Home button. You can then launch another app as needed.

Explore the iPad's User Interface and Launch Apps

1 Press the Sleep/Wake button.

The iPad's screen lights up and shows the lock screen.

2 Tap the slider and drag it to the right.

The iPad unlocks, and the Home screen appears.

A The iPad has two or more Home screens, depending on how many apps are installed. The gray dots at the bottom of the Home screen show how many Home screens there are. The white dot shows the current Home screen. The leftmost item in the row of dots is a magnifying glass representing Spotlight, the search feature.

3 Tap **Notes**.

The Notes app opens.

Note: If you chose to sync notes with your iPad, the synced notes appear in the Notes app. Otherwise, the list is empty until you create a note.

4 Tap **New** (⊞).

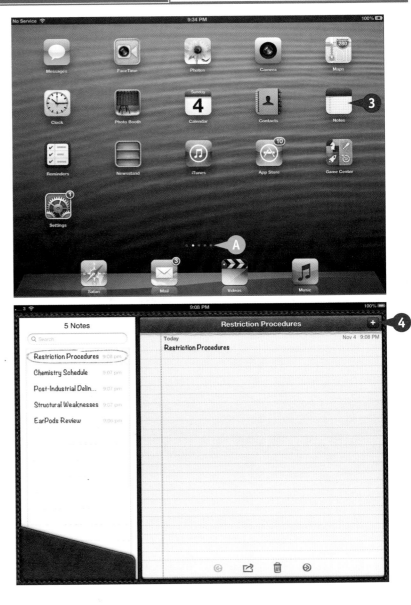

30

A new note opens, and the on-screen keyboard appears.

5 Type a short note by tapping the keys.

B The note appears in the Notes list on the left. The first line of the note becomes the title.

C If a pop-up bubble suggests a correction, tap **space** to accept it. Tap × on the bubble to reject it.

D If you need to hide the keyboard, tap ⌨.

The on-screen keyboard closes.

6 Press the Home button.

The Home screen appears.

7 Tap and drag to the left to display the second Home screen.

You can now launch another app by tapping its icon.

8 Press the Sleep/Wake button or close the Smart Cover.

Your iPad goes to sleep.

TIP

Where do I get more apps to perform other tasks?
You can find an amazingly wide selection of apps — both free and ones you must pay for — on Apple's App Store. See Chapter 6 for instructions on finding and downloading the apps you need.

Use Notification Center

As your communications hub, your iPad handles many types of alerts for you: e-mail messages, text messages, reminders, meetings, and so on.

To help you keep on top of all these alerts, your iPad integrates them into Notification Center. You can quickly access Notification Center from the Home screen or any other screen. After you display Notification Center, you can respond to an alert, start a tweet, or start a Facebook post.

Use Notification Center

Open Notification Center and Switch to an App

1 When an alert appears at the top of the screen you are using, tap the alert bar and drag it downward.

Notification Center appears.

Note: To clear all the notifications from a particular category in Notification Center, tap × at the right end of the category head, and then tap **Clear**, the button that appears in place of ×.

2 Tap the notification you want to see.

Notification Center displays the notification in its app.

3 You can now work with the notification as needed. For example, you can reply to an instant message.

Take Other Actions from Notification Center

1 Tap the status bar and drag it downward.

Notification Center opens.

2 Take other actions as needed:

Ⓐ Tap **Tap to Tweet** to start a tweet in the Twitter app.

Ⓑ Tap **Tap to Post** to start a post in the Facebook app.

Ⓒ Tap an event to open Calendar and display that event.

Ⓓ If Mail appears in Notification Center, tap a message to open it in Mail.

Ⓔ Tap the handle and drag up to close Notification Center.

TIP

What happens if I receive a notification when my iPad is locked?

What happens when you receive a notification while the screen is locked depends on the type of notification. For most types of notifications, your iPad displays an alert on the lock screen to alert you to the notification. Unlocking your iPad while the alert is displayed takes you directly to the notification in whatever app it belongs to — for example, to an instant message in the Messages app. If there are multiple alerts, drag across the one you want to open.

CHAPTER 2

Making Your iPad Work Your Way

In this chapter, you learn how to control notifications, audio preferences, screen brightness, and other key iPad behaviors.

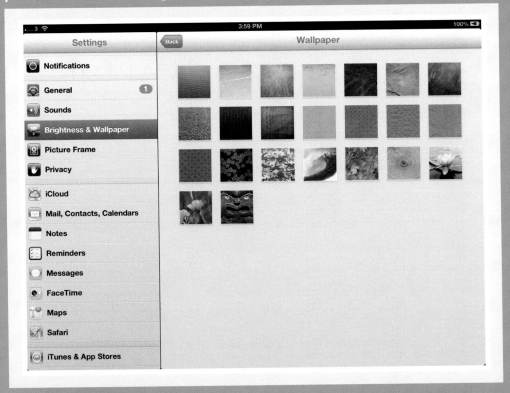

Find the Settings You Need

To configure the iPad, you work with its settings using the Settings app. This app contains settings for the iPad's system software, the apps the iPad includes, and third-party apps you have added. To reach the settings, you first display the Settings screen, and then display the category of settings you want to configure. Some apps provide access to settings through the apps themselves. So if you cannot find the settings for an app on the Settings screen, look within the app. In this task, you learn how to open the Settings screen and see the main categories of settings it contains.

Find the Settings You Need

Display the Settings Screen

1 Press the Home button.

The Home screen appears.

2 Tap **Settings**.

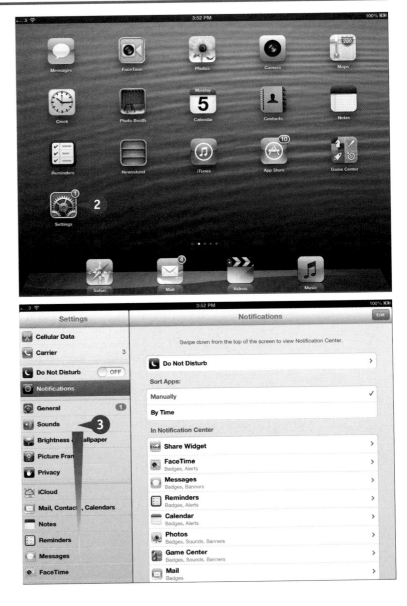

The Settings screen appears.

3 Tap and drag up to scroll down the screen.

Display a Settings Screen

1 On the Settings screen, tap the button for the settings you want to display. For example, tap **General** to display the General screen.

Display the Settings for an App

1 On the Settings screen, scroll down toward the bottom.

2 Tap the button for the app whose settings you want to display. For example, tap **DEVONthink** to display the DEVONthink settings.

3 When you finish using the Settings app, press the Home button.

The Home screen appears again.

Why do only some apps have a Settings entry?
The Settings screen contains entries for only those apps that have settings you can configure. For example, the iBooks app's settings include setting the justification, controlling whether the app syncs your bookmarks and collections, and choosing whether to play online audio and video. Other apps have no settings you can configure and so have no entry on the Settings screen.

Set Up iCloud

Apple's iCloud service adds powerful online sync features to your iPad. With iCloud, you can sync your e-mail, contacts, calendars and reminders, Safari bookmarks, Photo Stream photos, and iWork documents and data. You can also use the Find My iPad feature to locate your iPad when it goes missing.

To use iCloud, you set your iPad to use your Apple ID, and then choose which features to use. If you set up your iPad using iCloud, your account is already active, but you may want to choose different settings for iCloud.

Set Up iCloud

① Press the Home button.

The Home screen appears.

② Tap **Settings**.

The Settings screen appears.

③ Tap **iCloud**.

The iCloud screen appears.

④ Type your Apple ID.

Ⓐ If you do not yet have an Apple ID, tap **Get a Free Apple ID**, and then follow the prompts.

⑤ Type your password.

⑥ Tap **Sign In**.

Your iPad signs in to iCloud.

The iCloud controls appear.

⑦ In the Allow iCloud to Use the Location of Your iPad? dialog, tap **OK** if you want to use the Find My iPad feature. This is normally helpful.

8 Set **Mail** to On to use e-mail.

9 Set **Contacts** to On to use contacts.

10 Set **Calendars** to On to use calendars.

11 Set **Reminders** to On to use reminders.

12 Set **Safari** to On to sync Safari bookmarks.

13 Set **Notes** to On to sync notes.

14 Tap **Photo Stream**.

15 On the Photo Stream screen, set **My Photo Stream** to On to use Photo Stream.

16 Set **Shared Photo Streams** to On to use shared photo streams.

17 Tap **iCloud**.

18 Tap **Documents & Data**.

19 On the Documents & Data screen, set **Documents & Data** to On to store documents and data in iCloud.

20 Tap **iCloud**.

21 Set **Find My iPad** to On if you want to use the Find My iPad Feature.

TIP

How much space does iCloud provide?
iCloud provides 5GB of space for a free account; content and apps you acquire from Apple do not count against this space. You can buy more space by tapping **Storage & Backup**, and then tapping **Change Storage Plan** on the Storage & Backup screen.

Choose Which Apps Can Give Notifications

Some iPad apps can notify you when you have received messages or when updates are available. You can choose which apps give which notifications, or prevent apps from showing notifications altogether. You can also choose the order in which the notifications appear in Notification Center and control which notifications appear on the lock screen.

iPad apps use three types of notifications. See the tip for details.

Choose Which Apps Can Give Notifications

Display the Notifications Screen

1 Press the Home button.

The Home screen appears.

A A badge notification shows how many new items an app has.

2 Tap **Settings**.

The Settings screen appears.

3 Tap **Notifications**.

The Notifications screen appears.

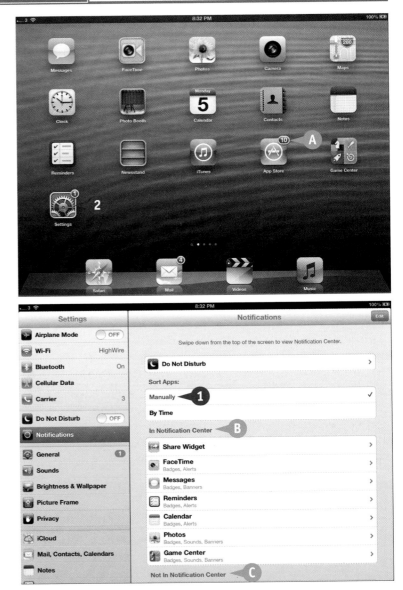

Choose How to Sort Apps That Give Notifications

1 Tap **Manually** to use manual sorting for apps that give notifications. Tap **By Time** to have Notification Center sort the apps by the times of their notifications.

B The In Notification Center list shows the apps currently set to appear in Notification Center.

C The Not In Notification Center list shows the apps that do not appear in Notification Center.

Choose Which Notifications Each App Can Give

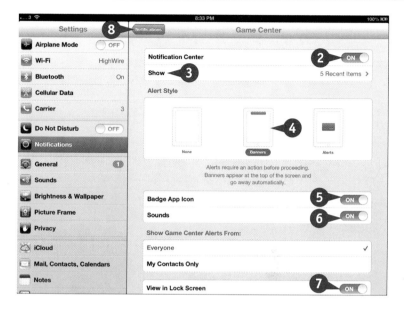

1 On the Notifications screen, tap the app's name.

The Notifications screen for the app appears.

2 Move the **Notification Center** switch to On to have the app's notifications appear in Notification Center. Move the switch to Off if you do not want the notifications in Notification Center.

3 Tap **Show**, tap the number of recent items to display, and then tap the app's name button to return.

4 In the Alert Style box, tap **Alerts** to display alerts, **Banners** to display banners, or **None** to suppress alerts.

5 Move the **Badge App Icon** switch to On to show badges or Off to hide them.

6 Move the **Sounds** switch to On or Off.

7 Move the **View in Lock Screen** switch to On or Off.

8 Tap **Notifications** to return to the Notifications screen.

TIP

What are the three kinds of notifications?

A *badge* (Ⓐ) is a red circle or rounded rectangle that appears on the app's icon on the Home screen and shows a white number indicating how many notifications there are. An *alert* (Ⓑ) is a text message that appears in front of the running app; you can also display an alert as a banner across the top of the screen. A *sound* notification plays a sound to get your attention.

Choose Sounds Settings

To control how the iPad gives you audio feedback, choose settings on the Sounds screen. Here, you can set the volume for the ringer and for alerts, choose your default ringtone for FaceTime and text tone for Messages, and choose whether to receive alerts for calendar items and reminders.

Playing lock sounds helps confirm that you have locked or unlocked the iPad as you intended. Playing keyboard clicks confirms each key press on the iPad's keyboard.

Choose Sounds Settings

1 Press the Home button.

The Home screen appears.

2 Tap **Settings**.

The Settings screen appears.

3 Tap **Sounds**.

The Sounds screen appears.

4 Tap and drag the **Ringer and Alerts** slider to set the volume.

Ⓐ When **Change with Buttons** is On, you can change the Ringer and Alerts volume by pressing the volume buttons on the side of the iPad.

5 Tap **Ringtone**.

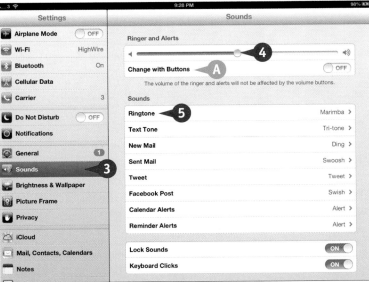

The Ringtone screen appears.

6 Tap the ringtone you want to hear for FaceTime calls.

Your iPad plays the ringtone so you can decide whether to use it.

B You can tap **Store** to buy extra ringtones or alert tones.

Note: Scroll down the Ringtone screen to display the list of alert tones.

7 Tap **Sounds**.

The Sounds screen appears again.

8 Repeat steps **5** to **7** to set other tones.

9 Tap the **Lock Sounds** switch and move it to On or Off, as needed.

10 Tap the **Keyboard Clicks** switch and move it to On or Off, as needed.

TIP

How do I use different ringtones for different callers?

The ringtone you set in the Ringtone area of the Sounds screen is your default tone for FaceTime calls; the text tone is the default for messaging calls. To set different tones to identify a contact, press the Home button and tap **Contacts**. In the Contacts app, tap the contact, tap **Edit**, and then tap **ringtone**. In the Ringtone dialog, tap the ringtone, and then tap **Save**. You can also change the text tone for the contact. Tap **Done** when you finish.

Set Screen Brightness and Wallpaper Backgrounds

To make the screen easy to see, you can change its brightness. You can also have the iPad's Auto-Brightness feature automatically set the screen's brightness to a level suitable for the ambient brightness that the iPad's light sensor detects.

To make the screen attractive to your eye, you can choose which picture to use as the wallpaper that appears in the background. You can set different wallpaper for the lock screen — the screen you see when the iPad is locked — and for the Home screen.

Set Screen Brightness and Wallpaper Backgrounds

1 Press the Home button.

The Home screen appears.

2 Tap **Settings**.

The Settings screen appears.

3 Tap **Brightness & Wallpaper**.

The Brightness & Wallpaper screen appears.

4 Tap the **Brightness** slider and drag it left or right to set brightness.

5 Tap the **Auto-Brightness** switch and move it to On or Off, as needed.

6 Tap **Wallpaper**.

Note: The Wallpaper button is a single button, even though it looks like two buttons.

The Wallpaper screen appears, showing the list of picture categories.

7 Tap **Wallpaper**.

Ⓐ To choose a picture from a different picture category, tap that category. For example, tap **Camera Roll** to display pictures you have taken with the iPad's camera, saved from e-mail or multimedia messages, or web pages.

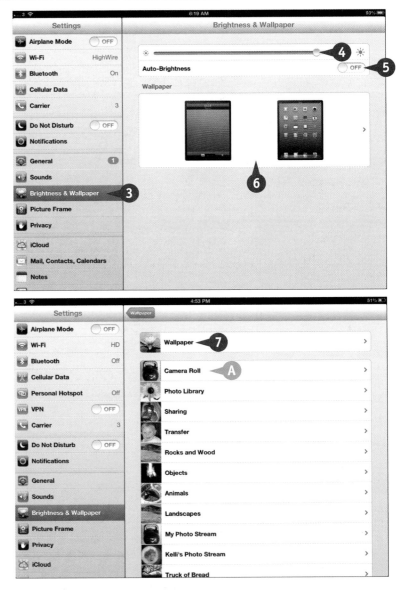

The Wallpaper category screen appears.

8 Tap the wallpaper you want.

The Wallpaper preview screen appears.

9 Tap **Set Lock Screen**, **Set Home Screen**, or **Set Both**.

10 Tap **Back**.

11 Tap **Wallpaper**.

The Brightness & Wallpaper screen appears.

TIP

How do I use only part of a picture as the wallpaper?
The iPad wallpapers are the right size for the screen, so you do not need to resize them. But when you use a photo for the wallpaper, you usually need to choose which part of it to display. When you choose a photo as wallpaper, the iPad displays the screen for moving and scaling the photo. Pinch in or out to zoom the photo out or in, and tap and drag to move the picture around. When you have chosen the part you want, tap **Set**.

Choose Privacy and Location Settings

Your iPad contains a huge amount of information about you, the people you communicate with, what you do, and where you go. To keep this information safe, you need to choose suitable privacy and location settings.

Privacy settings enable you to control which apps may access your contacts, calendars, reminders, and photos. You can also choose which apps can use your iPad's location services, which track the iPad's location using known wireless networks and the Global Positioning System, or GPS, on cellular iPads.

Choose Privacy and Location Settings

1 Press the Home button.

The Home screen appears.

2 Tap **Settings**.

The Settings screen appears.

3 Tap **Privacy**.

The Privacy screen appears.

4 Tap **Location Services**.

The Location Services screen appears.

5 If you need to turn location services off completely, tap the **Location Services** switch and move it to Off.

6 Tap the switch for an app, and move it to On or Off, as needed. For example, tap the **Siri** switch and move it to On.

7 Tap **Find My iPad**.

The Find My iPad screen appears.

⑧ Tap the **Find My iPad** switch and move it to On if you want to be able to locate your iPad should it go missing.

⑨ Tap the **Status Bar Icon** switch and move it to On if you want to see an arrow in the status bar when the iPad is being tracked.

⑩ Tap **Location Services**.

⑪ Tap **System Services**.

The System Services screen appears.

⑫ Tap the switch for a system service, and move it to On or Off, as needed.

⑬ Tap the **Status Bar Icon** switch and move it to On or Off.

⑭ Tap **Location Services**.

⑮ On the Location Services screen, tap **Privacy**.

⑯ On the Privacy screen, tap **Contacts**.

⑰ Set the switches to choose which apps can access your contacts.

⑱ Tap **Privacy**, and then repeat steps **15** and **16** for Calendars, Reminders, and Photos.

TIP

Why do some apps need to use location services?

Some apps and system services need to use location services to determine where you are. For example, the Maps app needs to use location services so that it can display your location, and the Compass service needs to learn your position in order to display accurate compass information.

If you allow the Camera app to use location services, it stores location data in your photos. You can then sort the photos by location in applications such as iPhoto on OS X. Other apps use location services to provide context-specific information, such as information about nearby restaurants. For security, review which apps are using location services and turn off any that do not have a compelling reason for doing so.

Configure Spotlight Search to Find What You Need

Your iPad can put a huge amount of data in your hand, and you may often need to search to find what you need.

To make your search results more accurate and helpful, you can configure your iPad's Spotlight Search feature. You can turn off searching for items you do not want to see in your search results, and you can change the order in which Spotlight displays the items it finds.

Configure Spotlight Search to Find What You Need

1 Press the Home button.

The Home screen appears.

2 Tap **Settings**.

The Settings screen appears.

3 Tap **General**.

The General screen appears.

4 Tap **Spotlight Search**.

The Spotlight Search screen appears.

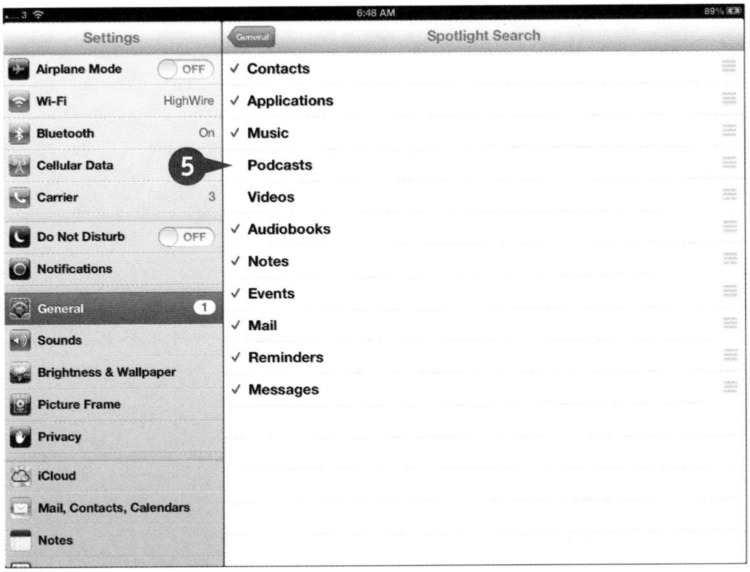

5 Tap to remove the check mark from each item you do not want to search.

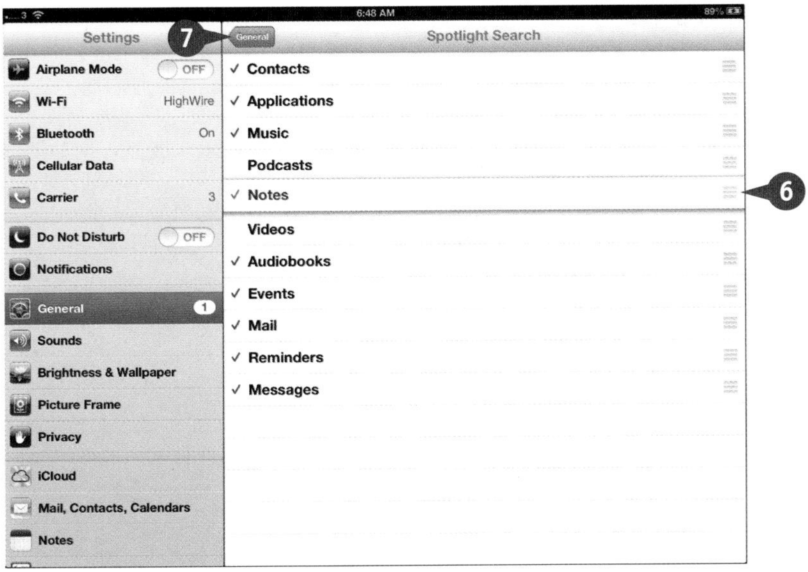

6 Tap a movement handle and drag an item up or down the search order.

Note: Spotlight displays the search results in descending order, starting with the first item on the list.

7 Tap **General**.

The General screen appears.

TIP

Which items should I make Spotlight search?
This depends on what you need to be able to search for. For example, if you do not need to search for music, videos, or podcasts, remove the check marks for the Music, Podcasts, and Videos items on the Spotlight Search screen to exclude them from Spotlight searches. For normal use, you may want to leave all the check marks in place but move the items most important to you to the top of the Spotlight Search list.

Choose Locking and Sleep Settings

To avoid unintentional taps on the screen, your iPad automatically locks itself after a period of inactivity. After locking itself, your iPad turns off its screen and goes to sleep to save battery power.

You can choose how long your iPad waits before locking itself. Setting your iPad to lock quickly helps preserve battery power, but you may prefer to leave your iPad on longer so that you can continue work. You can then lock your iPad manually.

Choose Locking and Sleep Settings

1 Press the Home button.

The Home screen appears.

2 Tap **Settings**.

The Settings screen appears.

3 Tap **General**.

The General screen appears.

④ Tap **Auto-Lock**.

The Auto-Lock screen appears.

⑤ Tap the interval — for example, **5 Minutes**.

⑥ Tap **General**.

The General screen appears.

TIPS

How do I put the iPad to sleep manually?

You can put the iPad to sleep at any point by pressing the Sleep/Wake button for a moment. If your iPad has a Smart Cover or Smart Case, close the cover or case.

Putting the iPad to sleep as soon as you stop using it helps to prolong battery life. If you apply a passcode, as discussed later in this chapter, putting the iPad to sleep also starts protecting your data sooner.

When should I use the Never setting for Auto-Lock?

Choose the Never setting for Auto-Lock if you need to make sure the iPad never goes to sleep. For example, if you are playing music with the lyrics displayed, turning off auto-locking like this may be helpful.

Set Up and Use Do Not Disturb Mode

When you do not want your iPad to disturb you, turn on Do Not Disturb mode. You can configure Do Not Disturb mode to turn on and off automatically at set times each day. For example, you can set Do Not Disturb mode to turn on at 10 PM and off at 7 AM. You can turn Do Not Disturb mode on and off manually, as needed.

Optionally, you can allow particular groups of contacts to bypass Do Not Disturb mode so they can contact you even when Do Not Disturb is on.

Set Up and Use Do Not Disturb Mode

Configure Do Not Disturb Mode

1 Press the Home button.

The Home screen appears.

2 Tap **Settings**.

The Settings screen appears.

3 Tap **Notifications**.

The Notifications screen appears.

4 Tap **Do Not Disturb**.

The Do Not Disturb screen appears.

5 If you want to schedule your quiet hours, tap the **Scheduled** switch and move it to the On position.

The From, To button appears.

6 Tap **From, To**.

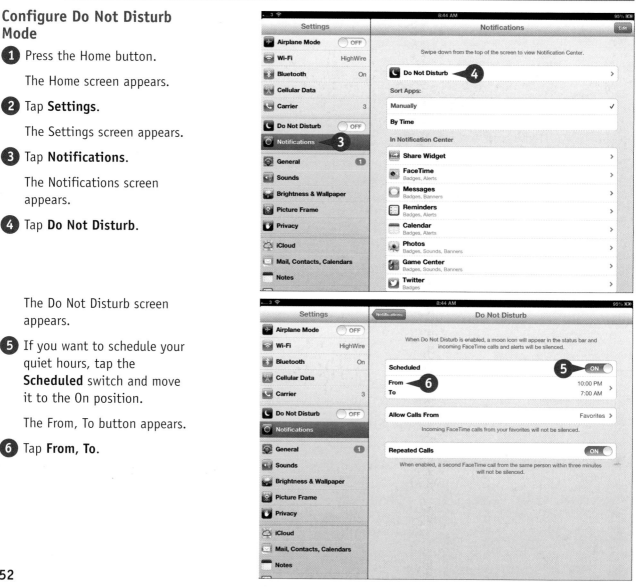

7 In the Quiet Hours dialog, tap **From**.

8 Use the spin wheels to set the From time.

9 Tap **To**.

10 Set the To time.

11 Tap **Allow Calls From**.

12 On the Allow Calls From screen, tap the group you will allow to call you via FaceTime during quiet hours.

13 Tap **Do Not Disturb**.

14 Tap the **Repeated Calls** switch and set it to On or Off, as needed. Setting Repeated Calls to On allows a second call from the same caller within three minutes to ring.

15 Tap **Notifications**.

Turn Do Not Disturb Mode On or Off Manually

1 Press the Home button.

2 On the Home screen, tap **Settings**.

3 On the Settings screen, tap the **Do Not Disturb** switch and move it to the On position or the Off position, as needed.

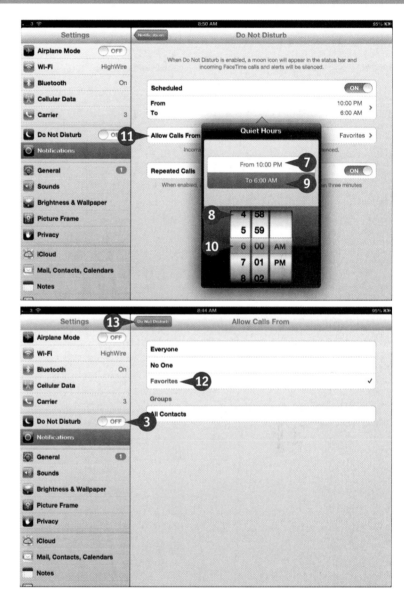

TIP

How can I tell whether Do Not Disturb is on?
When Do Not Disturb is on, a crescent moon symbol (Ⓐ) appears in the status bar to the left of the time.

Secure Your iPad with a Passcode Lock

To prevent anyone who picks up your iPad from accessing your data, you can lock the iPad with a passcode. This is a code that takes effect when you lock your iPad or it locks itself. When you unlock the iPad, you must provide the passcode.

For added security, you can set the iPad to automatically erase its data after ten failed attempts to enter the passcode. You can also choose between a standard, four-digit passcode and a longer password in which you can use numbers, letters, and other characters.

Secure Your iPad with a Passcode Lock

1 Press the Home button.

The Home screen appears.

2 Tap **Settings**.

The Settings screen appears.

3 Tap **General**.

The General screen appears.

4 Scroll down, and then tap **Passcode Lock**.

The Passcode Lock screen appears.

5 To follow this example, make sure the **Simple Passcode** switch is On. If not, tap and move it to On.

6 Tap **Turn Passcode On**.

The Set Passcode dialog appears.

7 Type your passcode.

The iPad displays the Set Passcode dialog again, this time with the message "Re-enter your passcode."

8 Type the passcode again.

The Passcode Lock screen appears.

9 Tap **Require Passcode**.

The Require Passcode screen appears.

10 Tap the button for the length of time you want — for example, **Immediately** or **After 1 minute**.

11 Tap **Passcode Lock**.

The Passcode Lock screen appears.

12 In the Allow Access When Locked box, set the **Siri** switch and the **Picture Frame** switch to Off or On, as needed.

13 If you want the iPad to erase all its data after ten failed passcode attempts, tap the **Erase Data** switch and move it to On.

The iPad displays a confirmation dialog.

14 Tap **Enable**.

TIPS

How can I make my passcode even more secure?
If you feel a four-digit passcode is not secure enough, tap the **Simple Passcode** switch on the Passcode Lock screen and move it to Off. When you tap **Turn Passcode On**, the Set Passcode screen lets you set a passcode of any length.

What Require Passcode setting should I choose?
Choose **Immediately** for greatest security. Choose **After 1 minute** for good security but greater convenience.

Configure Restrictions and Parental Controls

Like any other computer than can access the Internet, the iPad can reach vast amounts of content not suitable for children or business contexts.

You can restrict the iPad from accessing particular kinds of content. You can use the restrictions to implement parental controls — for example, preventing the iPad's user from buying content in apps or watching adult-rated movies.

Configure Restrictions and Parental Controls

1 Press the Home button.

The Home screen appears.

2 Tap **Settings**.

The Settings screen appears.

3 Tap **General**.

The General screen appears.

4 Tap **Restrictions**.

The Restrictions screen appears.

5 Tap **Enable Restrictions**.

The Set Passcode dialog appears.

Note: The passcode you set to protect restrictions is separate from the passcode you use to lock the iPad. Do not use the same code.

6 Type the passcode.

Note: The iPad shows dots instead of your passcode digits in case someone is watching.

The iPad displays the Set Passcode dialog again, this time with the message "Re-enter your Restrictions Passcode."

7 Type the passcode again.

The Restrictions screen appears with the controls in the Allow box now available.

8 In the Allow box, move each switch to On or Off, as needed.

9 If you need to change the country used for rating content, tap **Ratings For**. On the Ratings For screen, tap the country, and then tap **Restrictions**.

10 Choose settings for Music & Podcasts, Movies, TV Shows, and Apps. For example, tap **Movies**.

11 On the Movies screen, tap the highest rating you will permit.

12 Tap **Restrictions**.

13 Move the **In-App Purchases** switch to Off to prevent the user buying items from within apps.

14 Choose other settings in the Privacy box.

15 Choose Accounts settings and Volume Limit settings.

16 Move the **Multiplayer Games** switch and the **Adding Friends** switch to On or Off, as needed.

TIPS

What are in-app purchases?
In-app purchases are items that you can buy from within apps without needing to use the App Store app. These are a popular and easy way for developers to sell extra features for apps, especially low-cost apps or free apps. They are also an easy way for the iPad's user to spend money.

What do the Privacy settings in Restrictions do?
The Privacy settings in Restrictions enable you to control which apps can access the iPad's location information, contacts, calendars, reminders, and photos.

Choose Date, Time, and International Settings

To keep yourself on time and your data accurate, you need to make sure the iPad is using the correct date and time.

To make dates, times, and other data appear in the formats you prefer, you may need to change the iPad's International settings.

Choose Date, Time, and International Settings

Choose Date and Time Settings

1 Press the Home button.

The Home screen appears.

2 Tap **Settings**.

The Settings screen appears.

3 Tap **General**.

The General screen appears.

4 Scroll down to the bottom.

5 Tap **Date & Time**.

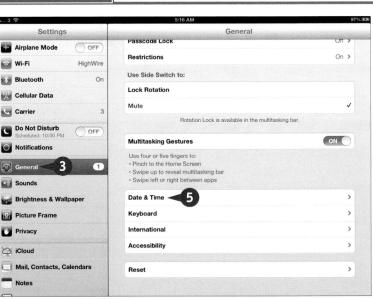

The Date & Time screen appears.

6 Tap the **24-Hour Time** switch and move it to On if you want to use 24-hour times.

7 To set the date and time manually, tap the **Set Automatically** switch and move it to Off.

8 Tap **Set Date & Time**.

The Date & Time dialog appears.

9 Set the date and time.

10 Tap **General**.

The General screen appears.

Choose International Settings

1 From the General screen, tap **International**.

The International screen appears.

2 Tap **Region Format**.

The Region Format screen appears.

3 Tap the region you want, placing a check mark next to it.

4 Tap **International**.

The International screen appears.

Note: From the International screen, you can also change the language used for the iPad's user interface.

How does the iPad set the date and time automatically?

The iPad sets the date and time automatically by using time servers, computers on the Internet that provide date and time information to computers that request them. The iPad automatically determines its geographical location so that it can request the right time zone from the time server.

Set Up Your Facebook and Twitter Accounts

Your iPad has built-in support for posting updates to your Facebook and Twitter accounts. For example, you can quickly create a post or a tweet from Notification Center, or you can share a photo from the Photos app or the Camera app.

Before you can use Facebook or Twitter, you must enter the details of your account as described in this task.

Set Up Your Facebook and Twitter Accounts

1 Press the Home button.

Note: If you try to post an update to Facebook or Twitter before you set up your account, your iPad automatically prompts you for the account details.

The Home screen appears.

2 Tap **Settings**.

The Settings screen appears.

3 Scroll down until you see the box containing the Twitter button and the Facebook button.

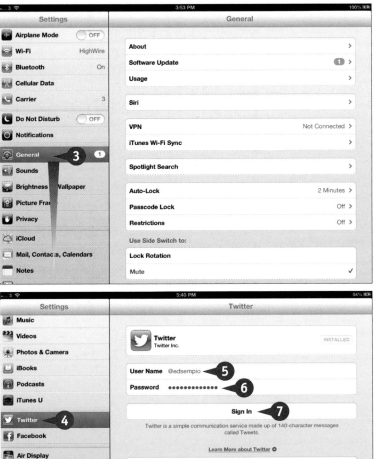

4 Tap **Twitter**.

The Twitter screen appears.

5 Type your username.

Note: If you do not have a Twitter account, tap **Create New Account** and follow the resulting screens to create an account.

6 Type your password.

7 Tap **Sign In**.

Twitter verifies your username and password, and then sets up your account on the iPad. If the Twitter app is not yet installed, your iPad installs it.

8 Tap **Facebook**.

The first Facebook screen appears.

9 Type your username.

10 Type your password.

11 Tap **Sign In**.

Another Facebook screen appears.

12 Tap **Sign In**.

Facebook verifies your username and password.

13 Tap **Settings**.

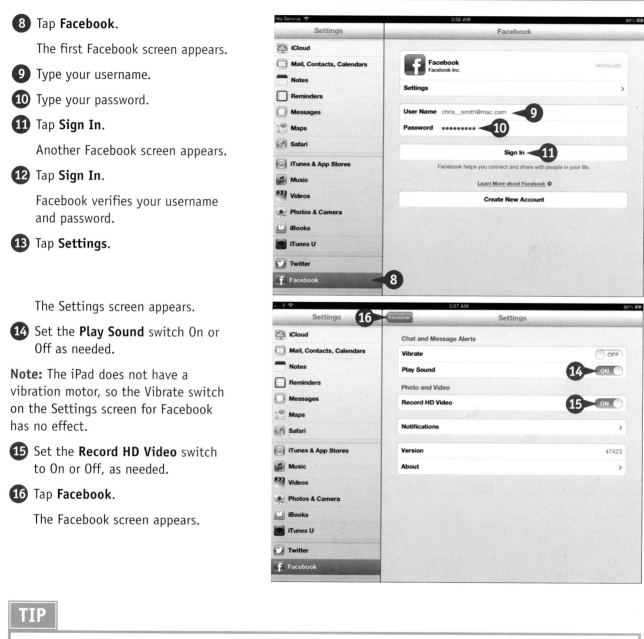

The Settings screen appears.

14 Set the **Play Sound** switch On or Off as needed.

Note: The iPad does not have a vibration motor, so the Vibrate switch on the Settings screen for Facebook has no effect.

15 Set the **Record HD Video** switch to On or Off, as needed.

16 Tap **Facebook**.

The Facebook screen appears.

TIP

How do I start a Facebook post or a tweet?
You can start a Facebook post or a Twitter tweet in various ways. Perhaps the easiest way is to open Notification Center and then tap the **Tap to Tweet** button for Twitter or the **Tap to Post** button for Facebook.

Install a Configuration Profile

Instead of choosing settings in the Settings app, you can also configure the iPad by installing one or more configuration profiles provided by an administrator. The most common way of providing a configuration profile is via e-mail.

Usually, you will need to install configuration profiles only when your iPad is managed by an administrator rather than by yourself. For example, a configuration profile can contain the settings needed for your iPad to connect to a corporate network or a campus network.

Install a Configuration Profile

1 Press the Home button.

The Home screen appears.

2 Tap **Mail**.

The Mailboxes screen appears.

3 Tap the mailbox that contains the message with the configuration profile.

The mailbox opens.

4 Tap the message that contains the configuration profile.

The message opens.

5 Tap the button for the configuration profile.

The Settings app opens and displays the Install Profile dialog.

6 In the Install Profile dialog, look for the Verified badge.

Note: Never install a configuration profile that does not have the Verified badge. The configuration profile may not be from the source claimed and may damage your iPad, compromise your data, or both.

7 Review the configuration profile.

8 To see more information about the profile, tap **More Details**.

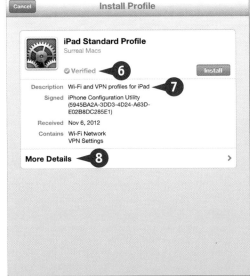

The configuration profile's details appear.

 You can tap an item in the Details dialog to see further details.

9 Tap **Install Profile**.

10 In the Install Profile dialog, tap **Install**.

The Install Profile dialog opens.

11 Tap **Install Now**.

Your iPad installs the configuration profile.

Note: If the configuration profile requires you to enter information, the appropriate dialogs appear. For example, if the configuration profile requires you to set a passcode, the Set Passcode dialog appears.

The Profile Installed dialog appears.

12 Tap **Done**.

The Mail app appears again.

9 Install Profile   iPad Standard Profile

Signing Certificate

iPhone Configuration Utility (5945BA2A-3D...
Issued by: iPhone Configuration Utility (5945BA2A-3DD3-4D2...
Expires: July 17, 2012   >

VPN

VPN (Surreal Macs VPN) **A**

Wi-Fi Network

Wi-Fi (HD)
Network: HD
Encryption: WPA

Profile Installed   Done **12**

iPad Standard Profile
Surreal Macs

✓ Verified

Description   Wi-Fi and VPN profiles for iPad
Signed   iPhone Configuration Utility
(5945BA2A-3DD3-4D24-A63D-
E02B8DC285E1)
Received   Nov 6, 2012
Contains   Wi-Fi Network
VPN Settings

More Details   >

TIP

Is there a way of installing a configuration profile other than using e-mail?
Yes. An administrator can place a configuration profile on a web page. You download the configuration profile using Safari, and then install it using installation dialogs similar to those shown in this task.

Use VoiceOver to Identify Items On-Screen

If you have trouble identifying the iPad's controls on-screen, you can use the VoiceOver feature to read them to you. VoiceOver changes your iPad's standard finger gestures so that you tap to select the item whose name you want it to speak, double-tap to activate an item, and flick three fingers to scroll.

VoiceOver can make your iPad easier to use. Your iPad also includes other accessibility features, which you can learn about in the next task.

Use VoiceOver to Identify Items On-Screen

1 Press the Home button.

2 On the Home screen, tap **Settings**.

3 Tap **General**.

4 On the General screen, tap and drag up to scroll all the way down.

5 Tap **Accessibility**.

6 On the Accessibility screen, tap **VoiceOver**.

7 On the VoiceOver screen, tap the **VoiceOver** switch and move it to On.

Note: You cannot use VoiceOver and Zoom at the same time. If Zoom is on when you try to switch VoiceOver on, your iPad prompts you to choose which of the two to use.

8 Tap **VoiceOver Practice**.

Ⓐ A selection border appears around the button, and VoiceOver speaks its name.

9 Double-tap **VoiceOver Practice**.

10 Practice tapping, double-tapping, triple-tapping, and swiping. VoiceOver identifies each gesture and displays an explanation.

11 Tap **Done** to select the button, and then double-tap **Done**.

Swipe up with three fingers.

The screen scrolls down.

 Move the **Speak Hints** switch to On if you want VoiceOver to speak hints about using VoiceOver.

14 Tap **Speaking Rate** to select it, and then swipe up or down to adjust the rate.

15 Tap **Typing Feedback** to select it, and then double-tap.

The Typing Feedback screen appears.

16 In the Software Keyboards box, tap and then double-tap the feedback type you want: **Nothing**, **Characters**, **Words**, or **Characters and Words**.

17 In the Hardware Keyboards box, tap and then double-tap the feedback type you want: **Nothing**, **Characters**, **Words**, or **Characters and Words**.

18 Tap and then double-tap **VoiceOver**.

The VoiceOver screen appears again.

TIP

Is there an easy way to turn VoiceOver on and off?
Yes. You can set your iPad to toggle VoiceOver on or off when you press the Home button three times in rapid sequence. From the Accessibility screen, tap **Triple-click the Home Button for** to display the Triple-Click screen. Tap **VoiceOver** (Ⓐ), placing a check mark next to it, and then tap **Accessibility** (Ⓑ).

Use Other Accessibility Features

VoiceOver can be helpful, but you will probably also want to explore the other accessibility features that your iPad offers. These include zooming in the screen, displaying text at a larger size, changing the screen to reverse video, playing audio in mono, and speaking automatic corrections made while you type.

Use Other Accessibility Features

1 Press the Home button.

The Home screen appears.

2 Tap **Settings**.

The Settings screen appears.

3 Tap **General**.

The General screen appears.

4 Tap and drag up to scroll all the way down.

The bottom of the screen appears.

5 Tap **Accessibility**.

The Accessibility screen appears.

6 Tap **Zoom**.

The Zoom screen appears.

7 Tap the **Zoom** switch and move it to On.

8 Double-tap the screen with three fingers to zoom in.

9 Double-tap again with three fingers to zoom out.

10 Tap **Accessibility**.

The Accessibility screen appears again.

11 Tap **Large Text**.

The Large Text screen appears.

12 Tap the text size you want.

13 Tap **Accessibility**.

The Accessibility screen appears again.

14 Tap the **Invert Colors** switch and move it to On.

The screen changes to reverse video.

15 Tap the **Speak Auto-text** switch and move it to On if you want your iPad to speak text corrections.

16 Tap the **Mono Audio** switch and move it to On if you want to use mono audio. Drag the slider to the left or the right as needed.

Note: Mono audio combines both audio channels into a single channel that it plays in both earphones or speakers. You can adjust the balance as needed.

17 Tap **General**.

The General screen appears.

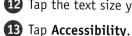

TIP

Is there an easy way to turn the Zoom feature on and off?
Yes. You can set your iPad to toggle Zoom on or off when you press the Home button three times in rapid sequence. From the Accessibility screen, tap **Triple-click the Home Button for** to display the Triple-Click screen. Tap **Zoom** (Ⓐ), placing a check mark next to it. You can also use the Home triple-press to toggle the Invert Colors feature.

Accessorize Your iPad

Consider a Smart Cover

A Smart Cover enables you to protect your iPad's screen from dust and scratches, while still maintaining the iPad's sleek appearance. The Smart Cover attaches to the iPad via magnets and covers only the screen. You can fold the Smart Cover to position your iPad upright, tilt it into a typing position, or prop it up for viewing movies. Smart Covers come in various colors.

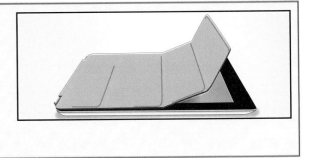

Protect Your iPad with an iPad Case

When you need more protection than the Smart Cover offers, put your iPad in a case that will prevent its body and screen from becoming scratched or collecting dust. Many cases are available, made of various materials and offering different features such as the ability to prop your iPad up in different positions for work or play. You can get Smart Cases that automatically wake and sleep the iPad. You can even get waterproof cases.

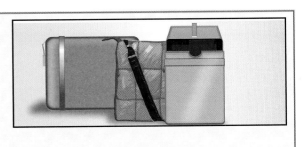

Charge Your iPad with an iPad Dock

If you need to be able to park your iPad neatly on your desk and easily charge it, consider getting an iPad dock. Some docks also provide an audio line-out port for connecting the iPad to powered speakers or your stereo so you can play music. You may also be able to use other accessories with the dock, such as the Apple Digital AV Adapter and the iPad Camera Connection Kit.

Type Fast with a Wireless Keyboard

If you need to enter a lot of text on your iPad, buy a Bluetooth keyboard. For example, the Apple Wireless Keyboard gives you the added convenience of actually typing with a physical keyboard while using the iPad. Some other wireless keyboards come built in to iPad cases that enable you to prop up the iPad at a helpful angle as you type on the keyboard.

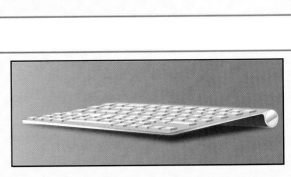

Learn about the Lightning Digital AV Adapter

The Lightning Digital Apple TV Adapter enables you to mirror your iPad out to a larger HDTV or a projector, so a larger audience can view your content. This is great for presentations you create in Keynote on your iPad, or for teaching a class lesson from an app. One end of the adapter fits into the iPad's Lightning port; the other has an HDMI port you connect to the HDMI port of the HDTV using a third-party HDMI cable.

Discover How to Connect Your Camera to the iPad

If you want to connect your camera to your iPad, you need an extra piece of hardware. If your camera has a removable SD card, get the Lightning to SD Card Camera Reader. If your camera has only a USB connection, get the Lightning to USB Camera Adapter.

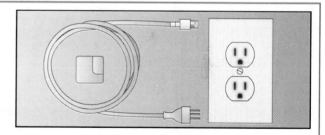

Get an Extra USB Power Adapter

If you regularly use your iPad both at home and at work, you may decide to get an extra USB power adapter so you can have one at home and one at work and keep your iPad well charged.

If you need to charge your iPad in the car, look for a power adapter with a 12-volt adapter.

If you travel with your iPad, look for a travel adapter that will work in all the countries you visit.

Consider an AirPrint-Enabled Printer

Add an AirPrint-enabled printer to the mix and you can print your e-mails, web pages, photos, and documents wirelessly from your iPad. An AirPrint-enabled printer uses Wi-Fi to print your images, so you have no cables to connect, and also no software to download and no drivers. All you need is a working Wi-Fi network. Visit http://store.apple.com for a list of AirPrint-enabled printers.

CHAPTER 3

Working with Siri and Text

To enable you to give voice commands and dictate text, your iPad includes the powerful personal assistant called Siri. You can also work with text manually, cutting, copying, and pasting it, and applying bold, italics, and underline.

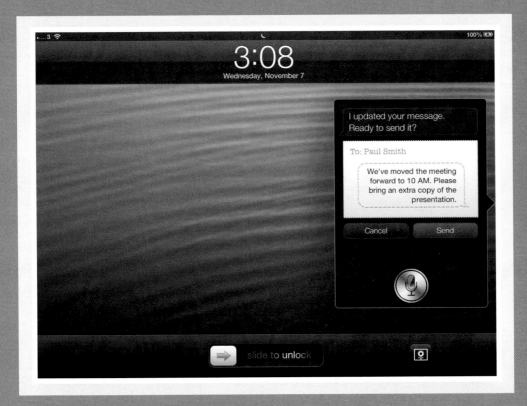

Give Commands with Siri

The iPad's powerful Siri feature enables you to take essential actions by using your voice to tell your iPad what you want. Siri requires an Internet connection, because the speech recognition runs on servers in Apple's data center.

You can use Siri either with the iPad's built-in microphone or with a microphone on a headset. Unless you are in a quiet environment, you are free to speak loudly and clearly, or you speak as close to the built-in microphone as possible, a headset microphone gives better results than the built-in microphone.

Open Siri

From the Home screen or any app, press the Home button or the headset clicker button for several seconds. The Siri screen appears. A tone indicates that Siri is ready to take your commands.

Send an E-Mail Message

Say "E-mail" and the contact's name, followed by the message. Siri creates an e-mail message to the contact and enters the text. Review the message, and then tap **Send** to send it.

Send a Text Message

Say "Tell" and the contact's name. When Siri responds, say the message you want to send. For example, say "Tell Chris Smith" and then "I'm stuck in traffic but I'll be there in an hour." Siri creates a text message to the contact, enters the text, and sends the message.

You can also say "tell" and the contact's name followed immediately by the message. For example, "Tell Bill Sykes the package will arrive at 10 a.m."

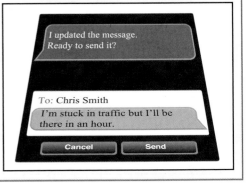

Set a Reminder for Yourself

Say "Remind me" and the details of what you want Siri to remind you of. For example, say "Remind me to take my iPad to Acme Industries tomorrow morning." Siri listens to what you say and creates a reminder. Check what Siri has written, and then tap **Confirm** if it is correct.

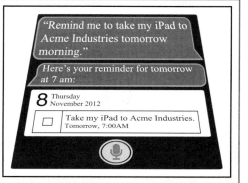

Set an Alarm

Say "Set an alarm for 5 a.m." and check the alarm that Siri displays.

Set Up a Meeting

Say "Meet with" and the contact's name, followed by brief details of the appointment. For example, say "Meet with Don Williamson for lunch at noon on Friday." Siri listens, sends a meeting invitation to the contact if it finds an e-mail address, and adds the meeting to your calendar.

Dictate Text Using Siri

One of Siri's strongest features is the capability to transcribe your speech quickly and accurately into correctly spelled and punctuated text. Using your iPad, you can dictate into any app whose keyboard displays the microphone icon (🎤), so you can dictate e-mail messages, notes, documents, and more. To dictate, simply tap the microphone icon (🎤), speak after Siri beeps, and then tap **Done** or 🎤.

To get the most out of dictation, it is helpful to know the standard terms for dictating punctuation, capitalization, symbols, layout, and formatting.

Insert Punctuation

To insert punctuation, use standard terms: "comma," "period" (or "full stop"), "semicolon," "colon," "exclamation point" (or "exclamation mark"), "question mark," "hyphen," "dash" (for a short dash, –), or "em dash" (for a long dash, —).

You can also say "asterisk" (*), "ampersand" (&), "open parenthesis" and "close parenthesis," "open bracket" and "close bracket," and "underscore" (_).

Insert Standard Symbols

To insert symbols, use these terms: "at sign" (@), "percent sign" (%), "greater-than sign" (>) and "less-than sign" (<), "forward slash" (/) and "backslash" (\), "registered sign" (®), and "copyright sign" (©).

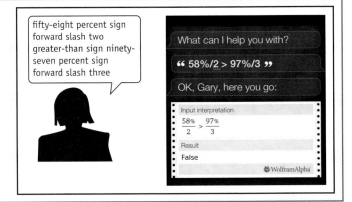

Insert Currency Symbols

To insert currency symbols, say the currency name and "sign." For example, say "dollar sign" to insert $, "cent sign" to insert ¢, "euro sign" to insert €, "pound sterling sign" to insert £, and "yen sign" to insert ¥.

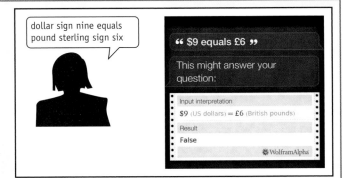

Control Layout

You can control layout by creating new lines and new paragraphs as needed. A new paragraph enters two blank lines, creating a blank line between paragraphs.

To create a new line, say "new line." To create a new paragraph, say "new paragraph."

> dear Anna comma new paragraph thank you for the parrot period new paragraph it's the most amazing gift I've ever had period

New Message

To:

Cc/Bcc:

Subject:

Dear Anna,

Thank you for the parrot.

It's the most amazing gift I've ever had.

Control Capitalization

You can apply capitalization to the first letter of a word or to a whole word. You can also switch capitalization off temporarily to force lowercase:

> give the cap head cap dining cap table a no caps French polish period

Household Tasks

Today

Household Tasks

Give the Head Dining Table a french polish.

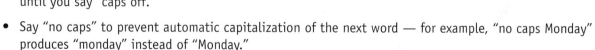

- Say "cap" to capitalize the first letter of the next word.

- Say "caps on" to capitalize all the words until you say "caps off."

- Say "no caps" to prevent automatic capitalization of the next word — for example, "no caps Monday" produces "monday" instead of "Monday."

- Say "no caps on" to force lowercase of all words until you say "no caps off."

Insert Quotes and Emoticons

To insert double quotes, say "open quotes" and "close quotes." To insert single quotes, say "open single quotes" and "close single quotes."

To enter standard emoticons, say "smiley face," "frown face," and "wink face."

> she said open quotes I want to go to Paris next summer exclamation point close quotes

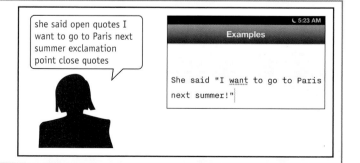

Examples

She said "I want to go to Paris next summer!"

Gather and Share Information with Siri

You can use Siri to research a wide variety of information online — everything from sports and movies to restaurants worth visiting or worth avoiding. You can also use Siri to perform hands-free calculations.

When you need to share information quickly and easily, you can turn to Siri. By giving the right commands, you can quickly change your Facebook status or post on your wall. Similarly, you can send tweets using your Twitter account.

Find Information about Sports

Launch Siri and ask a question about sports. For example:

- "Siri, when's the next Patriots game?"

- "Did the Lakers win their last game?"

- "When's the end of the NBA season?"

> ❝ Siri when's the next patriots game ❞
>
> The Patriots - Bills game is Sunday at 1 pm:
>
> **NFL SCHEDULE**
> **SUN, NOV 11, 2012**
> **BILLS** 3-5, 2-3 Away — 1:00 PM EST
> **PATRIOTS** 5-3, 2-1 Home — TV: CBS

Find Information about Movies

Launch Siri and ask a question about movies. For example:

- "Siri, where is the movie *Skyfall* playing in Chicago?"

- "What's the name of Blake Lively's latest movie?"

- "Who's the star of *The Amazing Spider-Man*?"

> ❝ Siri where is the movie Skyfall playing in Chicago today ❞
>
> Here's 'Skyfall' playing in Chicago, IL, US today:
>
> **SKYFALL**
> 3 Theaters - Tomorrow
>
> **NAVY PIER IMAX THEATRE** 3,796.3 MI
> 12:07 IMAX
>
> **AMC RIVER EAST 21** 3,796.7 MI

Find a Restaurant

Launch Siri, and then tell Siri what type of restaurant you want. For example:

- "Where's the best Cambodian food in Oakland, California?"

- "Where can I get sushi in Albuquerque?"

- "Is there a brew-pub in Minneapolis?"

> ❝ Where is the best Cambodian restaurant in Oakland California ❞
>
> I found five Cambodian restaurants... four of them are in Oakland, CA, US. I've sorted them by rating:
>
> **PHNOM PENH HOUSE**
> CAMBODIAN .... $$$$
> 251 8TH ST
> ★★★★☆ 376 REVIEWS

Address a Query to the Wolfram Alpha Computational Knowledge Engine

Launch Siri, and then say "Wolfram" and your question. For example, say "Wolfram, what is the cube of 27?"

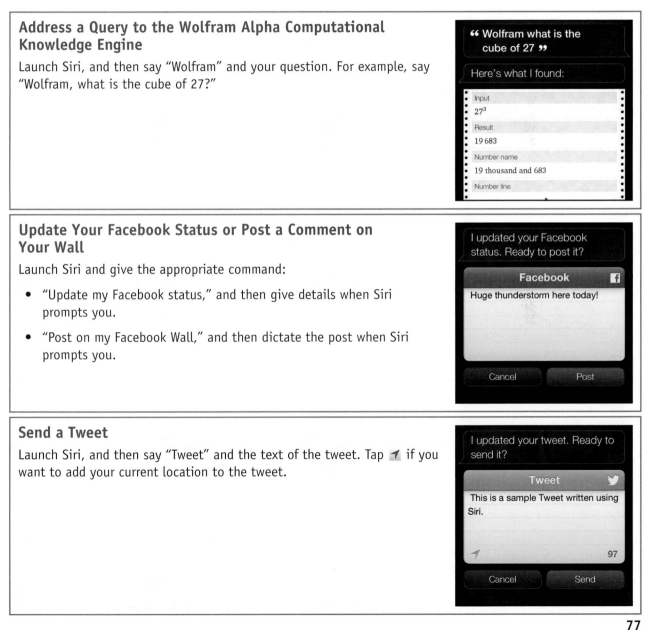

66 Wolfram what is the cube of 27 99

Here's what I found:

Input
27^3
Result
19 683
Number name
19 thousand and 683
Number line

Update Your Facebook Status or Post a Comment on Your Wall

Launch Siri and give the appropriate command:

- "Update my Facebook status," and then give details when Siri prompts you.

- "Post on my Facebook Wall," and then dictate the post when Siri prompts you.

I updated your Facebook status. Ready to post it?

Facebook

Huge thunderstorm here today!

Cancel   Post

Send a Tweet

Launch Siri, and then say "Tweet" and the text of the tweet. Tap ◢ if you want to add your current location to the tweet.

I updated your tweet. Ready to send it?

Tweet

This is a sample Tweet written using Siri.

97

Cancel   Send

Configure Siri to Work Your Way

To get the most out of Siri, spend a few minutes configuring Siri. You can set the language Siri uses, choose when Siri should give you voice feedback, or temporarily turn Siri off.

Most importantly, you can tell Siri which contact record contains your information, so that Siri knows your name, address, phone numbers, e-mail address, and other essential information.

Configure Siri to Work Your Way

1 Press the Home button.

The Home screen appears.

2 Tap **Settings**.

The Settings screen appears.

3 Tap **General**.

The General screen appears.

4 Tap **Siri**.

The Siri screen appears.

5 Make sure the **Siri** switch is in the On position if you want to use Siri.

6 Tap **Language**.

The Language screen appears.

7 Tap the language you want to use, placing a check mark next to it.

8 Tap **Siri**.

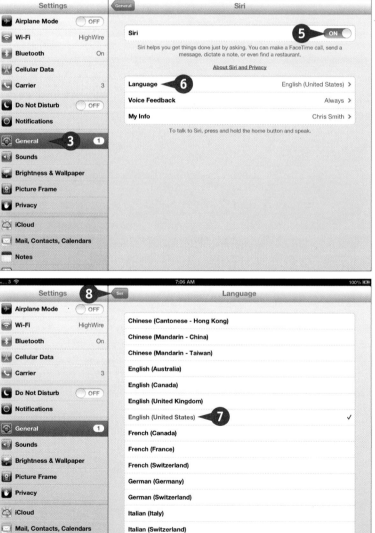

The Siri screen appears.

9 Tap **Voice Feedback**.

The Voice Feedback screen appears.

10 Tap **Handsfree Only** or **Always**, as needed, to choose when to receive voice feedback.

11 Tap **Siri**.

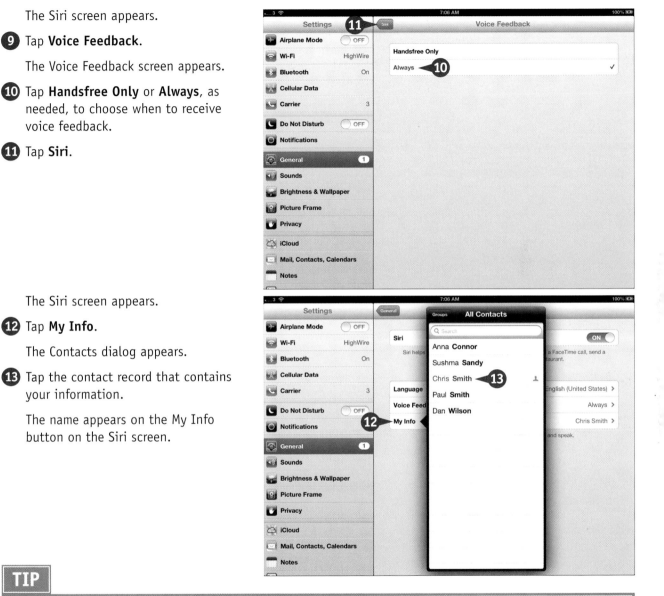

The Siri screen appears.

12 Tap **My Info**.

The Contacts dialog appears.

13 Tap the contact record that contains your information.

The name appears on the My Info button on the Siri screen.

TIP

Does Apple store the details of what I ask Siri?

Yes, but not in a way that will come back to haunt you. When you use Siri, your iPad passes your input to servers in Apple's data center in North Carolina, USA for processing. The servers analyze your request and tell Siri how to respond to it. Apple's data center stores the details of your request and may analyze them to determine what people use Siri for and work out ways of making Siri more effective. Apple does not associate your Siri data with other data Apple holds about you — for example, the identity and credit card data you used to pay for iTunes Match.

Cut, Copy, and Paste Text

Your iPad makes it easy for you to transfer data such as editable and noneditable text by copying or cutting it and pasting it in a new location. Editable text includes text found in e-mails or in an editable document such as Pages. An example of noneditable text would be text found on a website.

Cut, copy, and paste come in handy when you need to reuse or share a block of text. You can copy the text and then paste it into its destination, such as a note or an e-mail message. The procedure differs depending on if the text is editable or noneditable.

Cut, Copy, and Paste Text

Select and Copy Noneditable Text

Note: An example of noneditable text would be text found on a website.

1. Tap and hold in the section of the noneditable text that you want to copy.

   A selection highlight with handles appears around the text. The Copy button appears above the selection.

2. Drag the handles of the selection highlight around the text that you want.

3. Tap **Copy**.

   The text is placed on the Clipboard, which you do not see, but it is there.

Select and Copy Editable Text

Note: An example of editable text would be a URL for a website or the body of an e-mail message you are writing.

1. Tap and hold until you see the magnifying glass and then release.

   A bar appears containing the Select button and Select All button.

2. Tap **Select**.

Note: Tap **Select All** to select all the text.

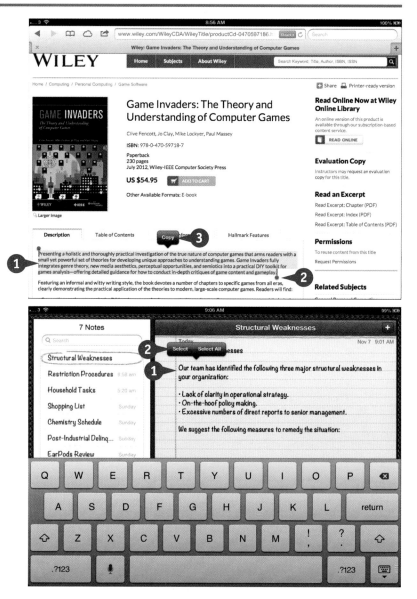

Blue selection handles appear
around the current word, and
further options appear on the
selection bar.

 Tap and drag the selection
handles around the text that
you want.

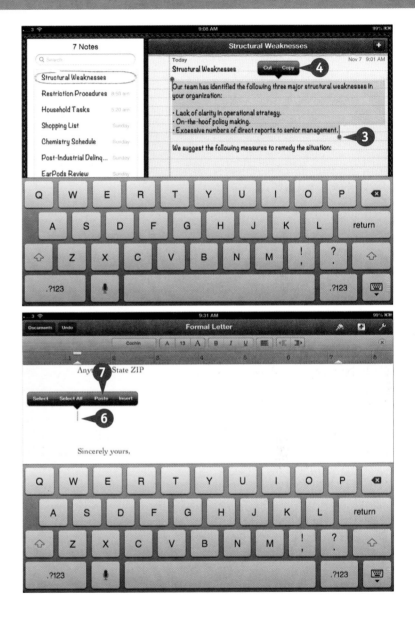

4 Tap the option you want.

Note: Copy is chosen for this
example.

5 Open the app in which you
want to paste the text.

Note: In this example, text is
pasted into a new e-mail message.

6 Tap where you want to paste
the text.

7 Tap **Paste**.

iPad adds the copied text to
the e-mail.

TIP

What does the Replace option do?
When you highlight a word in editable text, the option to replace the word with another appears in the
pop-up menu. Tap **Replace** to be given suggestions for replacing the word.

Bold, Italicize, and Underline Text

You can add some text formatting to your e-mails such as boldface fonts, italics, and underlining to distinguish certain words from others. The process is similar to cutting or copying text, but you can format only editable text. After you select the text, the pop-up bar displays options for selecting the formatting you want to apply.

Bold, Italicize, and Underline Text

1 Tap and hold the editable text that you want to bold, italicize, or underline.

A pop-up bar of text options appears.

2 Tap **Select**.

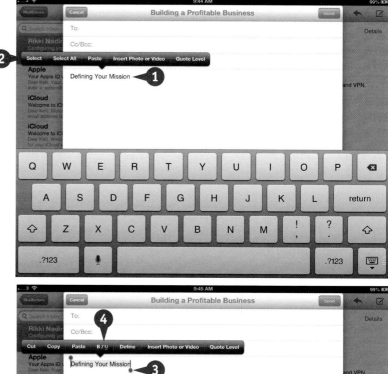

Part of the text is highlighted and handles appear.

3 Drag the handles to select the text that you want to bold, italicize, or underline.

4 Tap the **B**_I_U button in the pop-up bar.

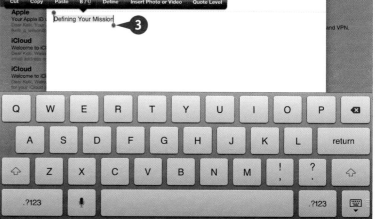

The pop-up bar displays formatting options.

5 Tap **Bold**, **Italics**, or **Underline**, as needed.

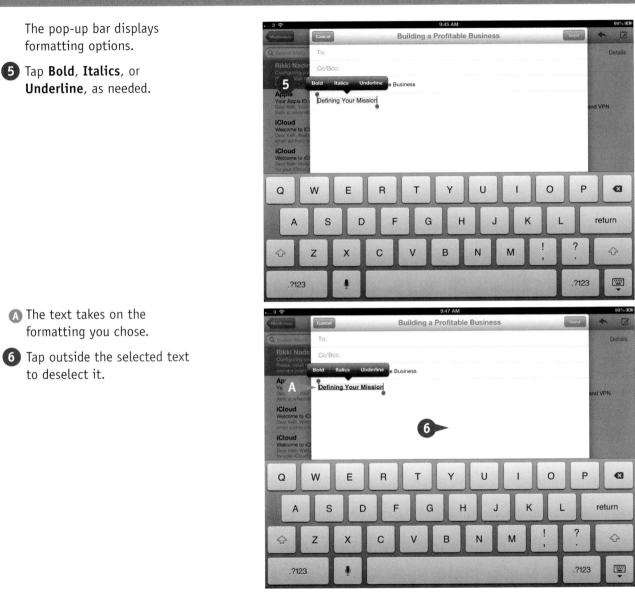

A The text takes on the formatting you chose.

6 Tap outside the selected text to deselect it.

TIP

Why do I not see the Select option in the pop-up menu when I select the text?
The options that appear in the pop-up menu differ depending on if the text is editable or noneditable. For example, an e-mail message you receive is noneditable, but an e-mail message you compose is editable. The Bold, Italics, and Underline options appear only when you select editable text.

CHAPTER 4

Setting Up Mail, Contacts, and Calendar

In this chapter, you learn how to add your e-mail accounts to the Mail app, and choose options for your contacts, calendars, and notes.

Set Up Your E-Mail Accounts

The easiest way to set up an e-mail account on your iPad is to synchronize the details from your PC or Mac, as discussed in Chapter 1. But if the e-mail account is not set up on the computer with which you synchronize the iPad, you can set the account up directly on the iPad as explained in this task.

To set up an e-mail account, you need to know the e-mail address and password, as well as the e-mail provider. You may also need to know the addresses of the mail servers the account uses. For Microsoft Exchange, you must know the domain name as well; see the next task.

Set Up Your E-Mail Accounts

1 Press the Home button.

The Home screen appears.

2 Tap **Settings**.

The Settings screen appears.

Note: If you have not yet set up an e-mail account on the iPad, you can also open the Add Account screen by tapping **Mail** on the iPad's Home screen.

3 Tap **Mail, Contacts, Calendars**.

The Mail, Contacts, Calendars screen appears.

4 Tap **Add Account**.

Note: This example uses a Gmail account. Setting up a Yahoo! account or an AOL account uses the same fields of information. For an iCloud account, you enter only the e-mail address and password. For details on setting up an iCloud account, see the tip.

The Add Account screen appears.

5 Tap the kind of account you want to set up.

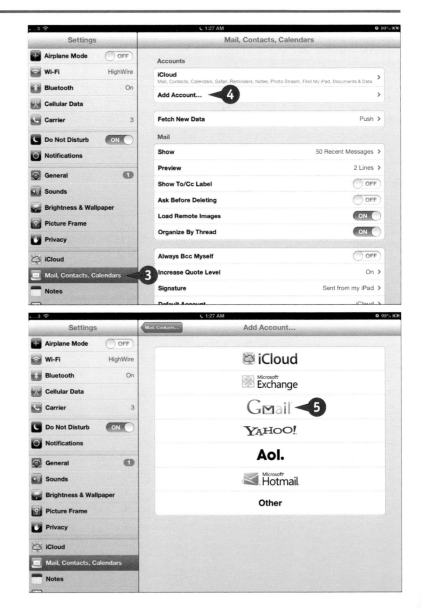

The screen for setting up that type of account appears.

6 Tap **Name** and type your name as you want it to appear in messages you send.

7 Tap **Email** and type the e-mail address.

8 Tap **Password** and type the password.

9 Tap **Description** and type a descriptive name.

10 Tap **Next**.

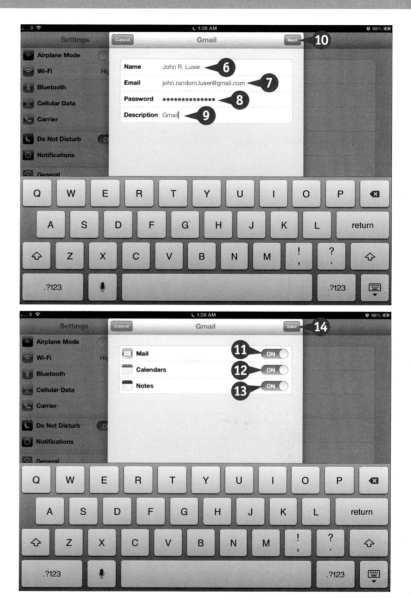

The configuration screen for the account appears.

11 Make sure the **Mail** switch is set to On.

12 Tap the **Calendars** switch and move it to On or Off.

13 Tap the **Notes** switch and move it to On or Off.

14 Tap **Save**.

The account appears on the Mail, Contacts, Calendars screen.

TIP

How do I change the name for an iCloud account?

When you set up an iCloud account, the iCloud screen prompts you for only your Apple ID (which is your e-mail address) and password. The account appears under the name iCloud in the Accounts list on the Mail, Contacts, Calendars screen. To change the name, press the Home button, tap **Settings**, and then tap **Mail, Contacts, Calendars**. Tap the iCloud account and then tap **Account**. Tap **Description** and type the name to identify the account. Tap **Done** and then tap **Mail, Contacts, Calendars**.

Connect Your iPad to Exchange Server

If your company or organization uses Microsoft Exchange Server, you can set up your iPad to connect to Exchange for e-mail, contacts, calendaring, and reminders.

Before setting up your Exchange account, ask an administrator for the details you need. These are your e-mail address, your password, the server name, and the domain name.

Connect Your iPad to Exchange Server

1 Press the Home button.

The Home screen appears.

2 Tap **Settings**.

The Settings screen appears.

3 Tap **Mail, Contacts, Calendars**.

The Mail, Contacts, Calendars screen appears.

4 Tap **Add Account**.

The Add Account screen appears.

5 Tap **Microsoft Exchange**.

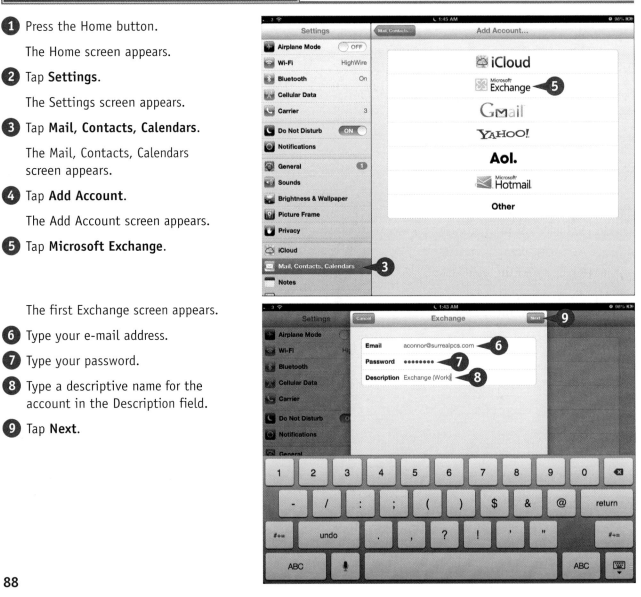

The first Exchange screen appears.

6 Type your e-mail address.

7 Type your password.

8 Type a descriptive name for the account in the Description field.

9 Tap **Next**.

The second Exchange screen appears.

10 Type the server's address.

11 Type the domain if needed.

12 Type your username.

13 Tap **Next**.

The configuration screen for the Exchange account appears.

14 Tap the **Mail** switch and move it to On or Off, as needed.

15 Tap the **Contacts** switch, and move it to On or Off, as needed.

16 Tap the **Calendars** switch, and move it to On or Off, as needed.

17 Tap the **Reminders** switch, and move it to On or Off, as needed.

18 Tap **Save**.

TIPS

Is there an alternative way to set up an Exchange account?

Yes. An administrator can provide the Exchange details in a file called a configuration profile, either via another e-mail account or via a web page. Either way, open the configuration profile and follow the prompts to install it.

How do I know whether to enter a domain name when setting up my Exchange account?

You need to ask an administrator because some Exchange implementations require you to enter a domain, whereas others do not.

Set Your Default E-Mail Account and Create Signatures

If you set up two or more e-mail accounts on your iPad, take a minute to make sure that you set the right e-mail account to be the default account — the account from which the Mail app sends messages unless you choose another account.

However many accounts you have, you can save time by creating e-mail signatures for them. A signature is text that the Mail app automatically adds to each message you compose — for example, your name and contact information. The iPad's default signature is "Sent from my iPad."

Set Your Default E-Mail Account and Create Signatures

1 Press the Home button.

The Home screen appears.

2 Tap **Settings**.

The Settings screen appears.

3 Tap **Mail, Contacts, Calendars**.

The Mail, Contacts, Calendars screen appears.

4 Tap and drag up to scroll down until the Mail box is at the top of the screen.

5 Tap **Default Account**.

The Default Account screen appears.

6 Tap the account you want to make the default.

A A check mark appears next to the account you tapped.

7 Tap **Mail, Contacts, Calendars**.

The Mail, Contacts, Calendars screen appears again.

8 Tap **Signature**.

The Signature screen appears.

9 Tap **All Accounts** if you want to use the same signature for each e-mail account. Tap **Per Account** to use different signatures.

Note: If you do not want to use a signature, simply delete the default signature.

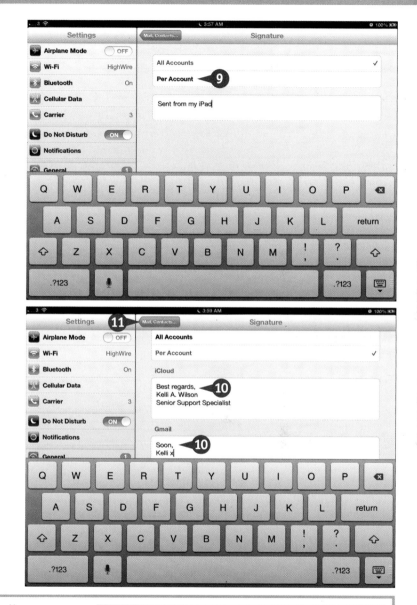

If you tap **Per Account** in step **9**, a box appears for each account.

10 Type the text of the signature or signatures.

Note: To make your signatures easy to read, keep them to four lines or fewer and use plain text without formatting.

11 Tap **Mail, Contacts, Calendars**.

The Mail, Contacts, Calendars screen appears.

TIP

How do I send a message from an e-mail account other than the default account?

After starting to compose a message, tap **Cc/Bcc, From** to display the Cc, Bcc, and From lines. Tap **From** (Ⓐ) to display the pop-up menu of e-mail addresses, and then tap the address (Ⓑ) you want to use.

Choose When and How Your iPad Gets Your E-Mail

Your iPad can get your e-mail messages by using two different technologies, Push and Fetch. If you choose Push, the e-mail server "pushes" your new messages to your iPad as soon as the server receives them. If you choose Fetch, your iPad checks in periodically with the server and downloads the new messages it discovers.

Push is normally more convenient than Fetch, but some e-mail providers do not support Push. In this case, you must use Fetch instead. You can configure the interval at which Fetch retrieves your e-mail. You can also check manually for e-mail at any point.

Choose When and How Your iPad Gets Your E-Mail

1 Press the Home button.

The Home screen appears.

2 Tap **Settings**.

The Settings screen appears.

3 Tap **Mail, Contacts, Calendars**.

The Mail, Contacts, Calendars screen appears.

Ⓐ The Fetch New Data button shows whether Mail is using Push or Fetch.

4 Tap **Fetch New Data**.

The Fetch New Data screen appears.

5 To use Push, set the **Push** switch to On.

6 To control how frequently Fetch runs, tap **Every 15 Minutes**, **Every 30 Minutes**, **Hourly**, or **Manually**.

7 If you need to use different settings for different accounts, tap **Advanced**.

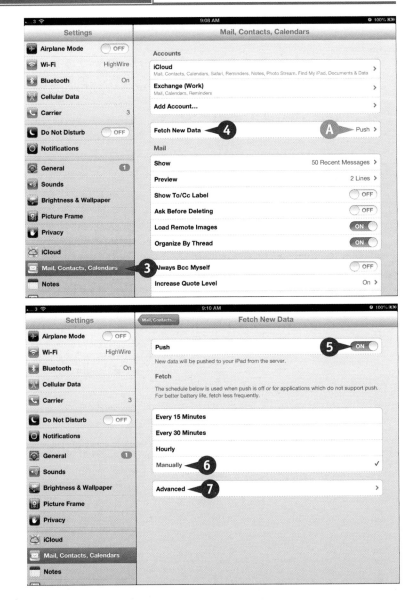

The Advanced screen appears, showing a list of your e-mail accounts.

8 Tap the account you want to configure.

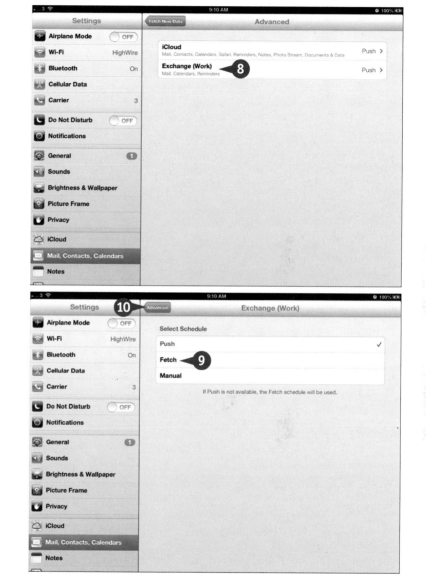

The account's screen appears.

9 Tap **Push**, **Fetch**, or **Manual**, as needed.

Note: Push uses more battery power, especially if you receive many messages or large attachments.

10 Tap **Advanced**.

The Advanced screen appears.

11 Tap **Fetch New Data**.

The Fetch New Data screen appears.

12 Tap **Mail, Contacts, Calendars**.

The Mail, Contacts, Calendars screen appears.

TIP

How do I check manually for new e-mail messages?
In a mailbox, tap the list of messages and drag down. A refresh icon (⟳) appears, and then stretches (Ⓐ) as you continue to drag down. Drag until the icon explodes to make Mail check for new messages.

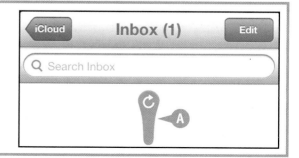

Control How the iPad Displays Your E-Mail

To make your iPad's Mail app easy to use, you can choose settings that suit the way you work.

You can choose how many messages to show in each mailbox and how many lines to include in the preview. To make messages easy to read, you can change the minimum font size. You can also choose whether to load remote images in messages.

Control How the iPad Displays Your E-Mail

1 Press the Home button.

The Home screen appears.

2 Tap **Settings**.

The Settings screen appears.

3 Tap **Mail, Contacts, Calendars**.

The Mail, Contacts, Calendars screen appears.

4 Tap **Show**.

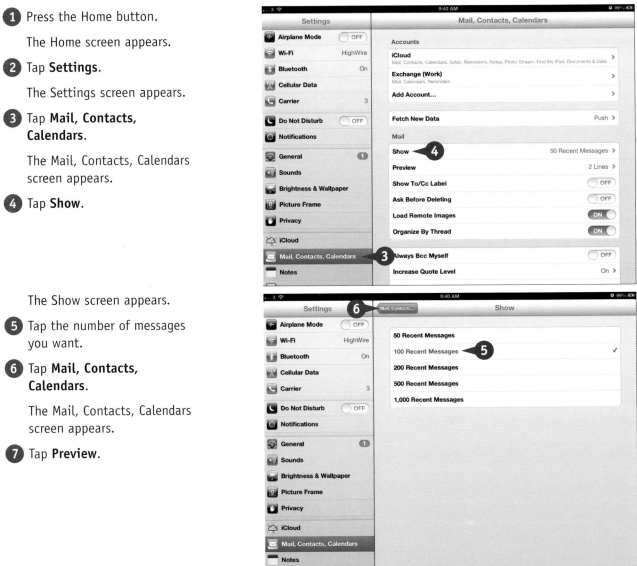

The Show screen appears.

5 Tap the number of messages you want.

6 Tap **Mail, Contacts, Calendars**.

The Mail, Contacts, Calendars screen appears.

7 Tap **Preview**.

The Preview screen appears.

8 Tap the number of lines you want to see in previews.

9 Tap **Mail, Contacts, Calendars**.

The Mail, Contacts, Calendars screen appears.

10 Tap the **Show To/Cc Label** switch and move it to On or Off.

11 Tap the **Load Remote Images** switch and move it to On or Off.

Why would I turn off the Load Remote Images feature?

Loading a remote image enables the sender to learn that you have opened the message. When Mail requests the remote image, the server that provides the image can log the date and time and tie it to the message sent to you. The server can also learn your Internet connection's IP address and determine your approximate location.

What is the Always Bcc Myself setting useful for?

Most e-mail services automatically put a copy of each message you send or forward into a folder with a name such as Sent, so that you can easily review the messages you have sent. If your e-mail service does not use a Sent folder, move the **Always Bcc Myself** switch to On to send a bcc copy of each message to yourself. You can then file these messages in a folder of your choosing — for example, a folder named Sent — to keep a record of your sent messages.

Organize Your E-Mail Messages by Threads

The Mail app gives you two ways to view e-mail messages. You can view the messages as a simple list, or you can view them with related messages organized into *threads* that are sometimes called *conversations*.

Having Mail display your messages as threads can help you navigate your Inbox quickly and find related messages easily. You may find threading useful if you tend to have long e-mail conversations, because threading reduces the number of messages you see at once.

Organize Your E-Mail Messages by Threads

Set Mail to Organize Your Messages by Thread

1 Press the Home button.

The Home screen appears.

2 Tap **Settings**.

The Settings screen appears.

3 Tap **Mail, Contacts, Calendars**.

The Mail, Contacts, Calendars screen appears.

4 Tap the **Organize By Thread** switch and move it to the On position.

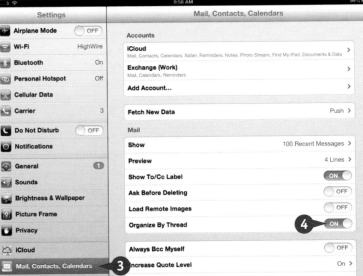

Read Messages Organized into Threads

 1 Press the Home button.

The Home screen appears.

2 Tap **Mail**.

The Mailboxes screen appears.

3 Tap the mailbox.

The Inbox for the account appears.

(A) A number on the right indicates a threaded message.

4 Tap the threaded message.

(B) The left pane shows the list of threaded messages.

5 Tap the message you want to display.

(C) The message appears.

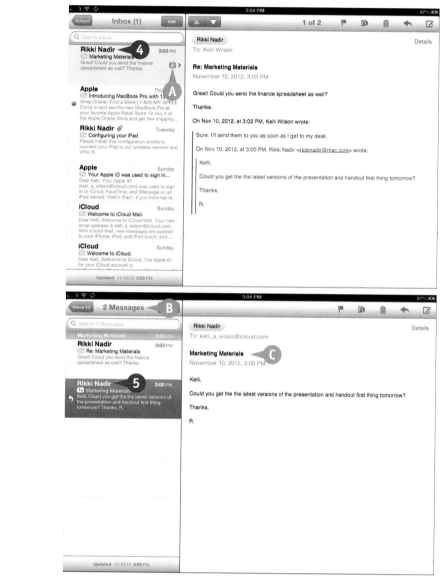

TIP

What does the Ask Before Deleting switch do?

This switch lets you control whether your iPad displays the Delete Message dialog to confirm deletion of a message by tapping 🗑. Turn Ask Before Deleting on if you find you tap 🗑 by accident sometimes — for example, when using your iPad on public transit.

Configure and Use the VIP Inbox

The Mail app includes an inbox named VIP for collecting your most important messages so that you do not miss any. Mail automatically monitors your incoming messages and adds those from your designated VIPs to the VIP inbox.

To start using your VIP inbox, you must add people to the VIP list. You can add people either from your Contacts list or from e-mail messages you receive. After designating your VIPs, you can tap the VIP inbox to display its contents.

Configure and Use the VIP Inbox

1 Press the Home button.

The Home screen appears.

2 Tap **Mail**.

The Mailboxes screen appears.

3 Tap the **VIP** mailbox.

The VIP List appears.

4 Tap **Add VIP**.

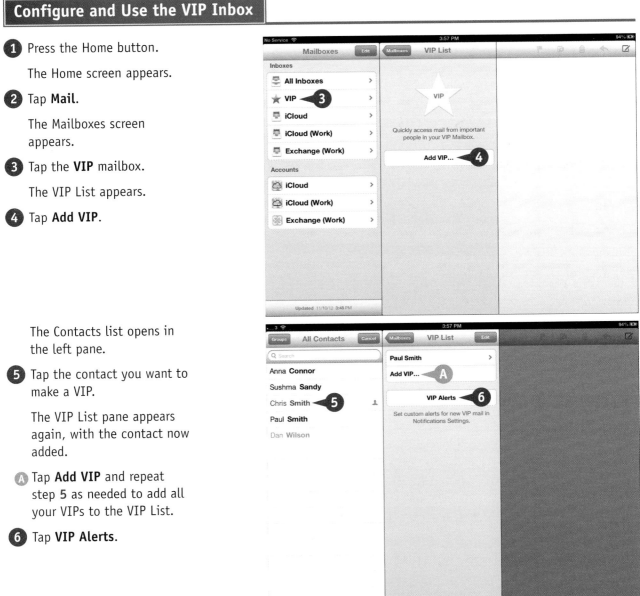

The Contacts list opens in the left pane.

5 Tap the contact you want to make a VIP.

The VIP List pane appears again, with the contact now added.

Ⓐ Tap **Add VIP** and repeat step **5** as needed to add all your VIPs to the VIP List.

6 Tap **VIP Alerts**.

The VIP screen on the Notifications screen in the Settings app appears.

7 Choose the notifications you want to use for your VIPs. For example, tap **New Mail Sound** and then tap the sound you want to use to identify the arrival of messages from VIPs.

B If you want to be able to parse your VIP messages easily, tap **Alerts** in the Alert Style box, set the **Show Preview** switch to On, and set the **View in Lock Screen** switch to On.

8 Tap **Mail**.

The VIP List screen in the Mail app appears, showing the e-mail messages from your VIPs.

9 Tap a message.

The message's contents appear.

Is there any other way to add someone to my VIP list?

Yes. Open a message you have received, and then press and hold **From** (A) until the Sender dialog appears. Tap **Add to VIP** (B) to add the sender to your VIP list. From here, you can also tap **Create New Contact** to create a new contact from the sender or tap **Add to Existing Contact** to add the sender's e-mail address to an existing contact.

Choose How Your iPad Displays Your Contacts

To find the contacts you need swiftly and easily, you can set your iPad to sort and display the contacts in your preferred order.

Your iPad can sort contacts either by first name or by last name. Whichever way you sort the contacts, your iPad can display them in alphabetical order either by first name or by last name. By entering data only in the Company field for a business, you can make business names sort correctly whether you sort people's names by first name or last name.

Choose How Your iPad Displays Your Contacts

1 Press the Home button.

The Home screen appears.

2 Tap **Settings**.

The Settings screen appears.

3 Tap **Mail, Contacts, Calendars**.

The Mail, Contacts, Calendars screen appears.

4 Tap and drag up to display the Contacts box.

5 Tap **Sort Order**.

The Sort Order screen appears.

6 Tap **First, Last** to sort by first name and then last name, or tap **Last, First** to sort by last name and then first name.

7 Tap **Mail, Contacts, Calendars**.

The Mail, Contacts, Calendars screen appears.

⑧ Tap **Display Order**.

The Display Order screen appears.

⑨ Tap **First, Last** to display the first name and then the last name, or tap **Last, First** to display the last name and then the first name.

⑩ Tap **Mail, Contacts, Calendars**.

The Mail, Contacts, Calendars screen appears.

Which sort order and display order should I use?
This is entirely up to you. If you tend to think of people by first name, try using the First, Last sort order and see if you find it helpful. Otherwise, use the Last, First sort order with the First, Last display order for a more conventional presentation of your contacts.

Choose Alert Options for Calendar Events

B y synchronizing your calendars from your PC or Mac with your iPad, you can keep details of your events in the palm of your hand.

To keep yourself on schedule, you can set the iPad to alert you to new invitations you receive. You can also set default alert times to give you the warning you need before a regular event, an all-day event, or a birthday.

Choose Alert Options for Calendar Events

1 Press the Home button.

The Home screen appears.

2 Tap **Settings**.

The Settings screen appears.

3 Tap **Mail, Contacts, Calendars**.

The Mail, Contacts, Calendars screen appears.

4 Tap and drag up to display the bottom of the screen.

5 Tap the **New Invitation Alerts** switch and move it to On or Off.

6 Tap the **Shared Calendar Alerts** switch and move it to On or Off.

7 Tap **Default Alert Times**.

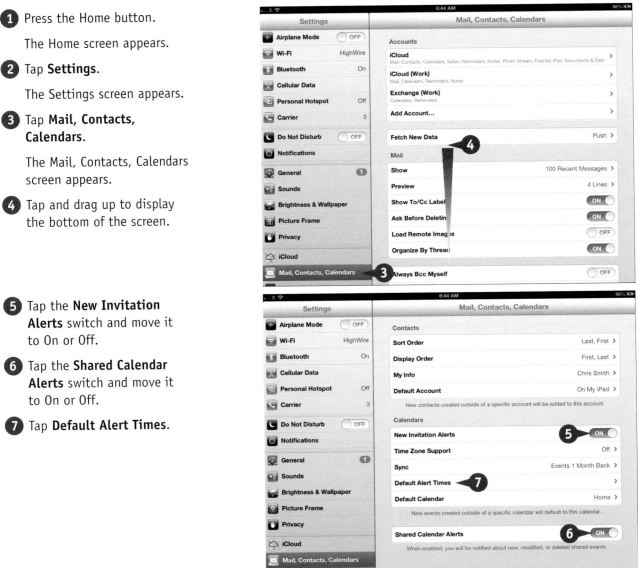

The Default Alert Times screen appears.

8 Tap the event type to set the default alert time for. For example, tap **Events**.

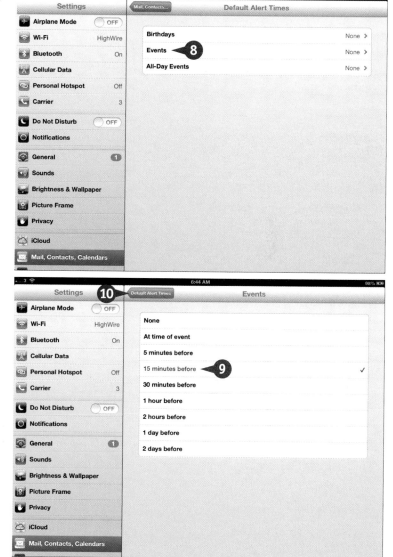

The corresponding screen appears — the Events screen, the Birthdays screen, or the All-Day Events screen.

9 Tap the amount of time for the warning. For example, for an event, tap **15 minutes before**.

10 Tap **Default Alert Times**.

The Default Alert Times screen appears.

11 Set default alert times for other event types by repeating steps **8** to **10**.

12 Tap **Mail, Contacts, Calendars**.

TIP

How can I make the most of the Default Alert Times feature?

To make the most of the Default Alert Times feature, you will probably want to set a different length of time for the three categories of events — Birthdays, Events, and All-Day Events. For example, set **One week before** for Birthdays so you can buy and send a card; set **10 minutes before** for Events so that you can arrive on time; and set **1 day before** for All-Day Events.

Choose Your Default Calendar and Time Zone

When you use multiple calendars on your iPad, you need to set your default calendar. This is the calendar that receives events you create outside any specific calendar. For example, if you have a Work calendar and a Home calendar, you can set the Home calendar as the default calendar.

If you travel to different time zones, you may need to specify which time zone to show event dates and times in. Otherwise, Calendar uses the time zone for your current location.

Choose Your Default Calendar and Time Zone

1 Press the Home button.

The Home screen appears.

2 Tap **Settings**.

The Settings screen appears.

3 Tap **Mail, Contacts, Calendars**.

The Mail, Contacts, Calendars screen appears.

4 Tap and drag up to scroll down all the way to the bottom of the screen.

The bottom part of the Mail, Contacts, Calendars screen appears.

5 Tap **Time Zone Support**.

The Time Zone Support screen appears.

6 Tap the **Time Zone Support** switch and move it to On.

7 Tap **Time Zone**.

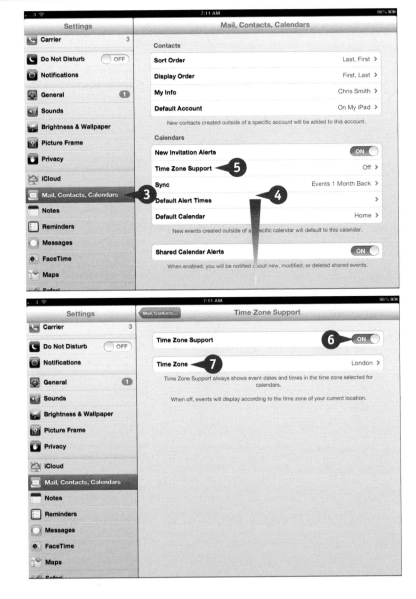

The Time Zone screen appears.

8 Type the first letters of a city in the time zone.

9 Tap the search result you want.

10 Tap **Time Zone Support**.

11 Tap **Mail, Contacts, Calendars**.

12 Tap **Default Calendar**.

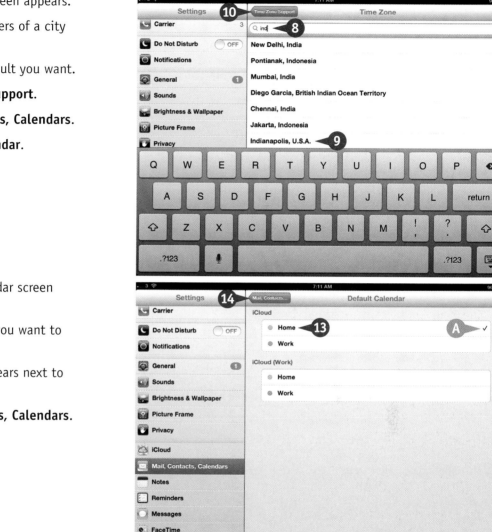

The Default Calendar screen appears.

13 Tap the calendar you want to make the default.

A A check mark appears next to the calendar.

14 Tap **Mail, Contacts, Calendars**.

TIP

How do I choose which calendars to display in the Calendar app?
You choose the calendars in the Calendar app. Press the Home button to display the Home screen, tap **Calendar**, and then tap **Calendars**. On the Calendars screen, tap to place a check mark on each calendar you want to display. Tap to remove a check mark from a calendar you want to hide. Then tap **Done**.

Set Your Default Account for Notes

As described earlier in this chapter, you can set up multiple e-mail accounts on your iPad. Each e-mail account can synchronize notes if the e-mail provider supports them.

You can set the default account for notes to tell the iPad which e-mail account it should store new notes in unless you specify storing them elsewhere.

Set Your Default Account for Notes

1 Press the Home button.

The Home screen appears.

2 Tap **Settings**.

The Settings screen appears.

3 Scroll down to display the third group of buttons.

④ Tap **Notes**.

The Notes screen appears.

⑤ Tap **Default Account**.

Note: To change the font used for notes, tap **Noteworthy**, **Helvetica**, or **Marker Felt** in the Font area on the Notes screen.

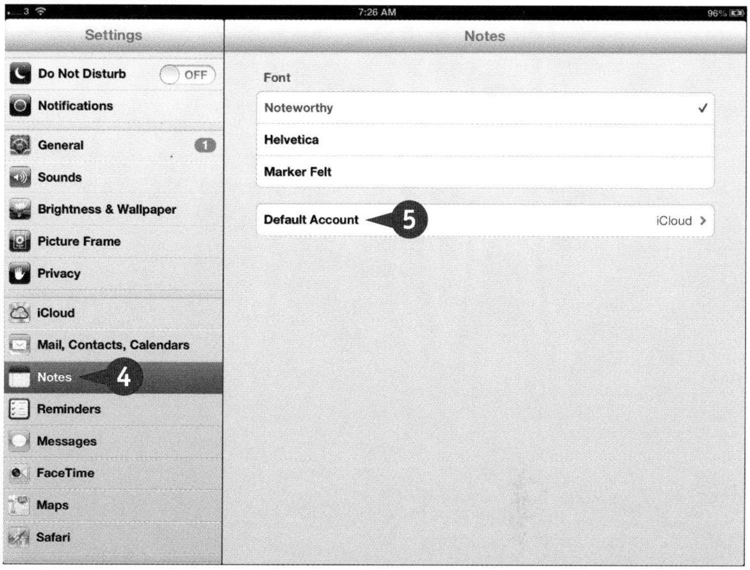

The Default Account screen appears.

⑥ Tap the account you want to make the default.

Ⓐ A check mark appears next to the account you tapped.

⑦ Tap **Notes**.

The Notes screen appears.

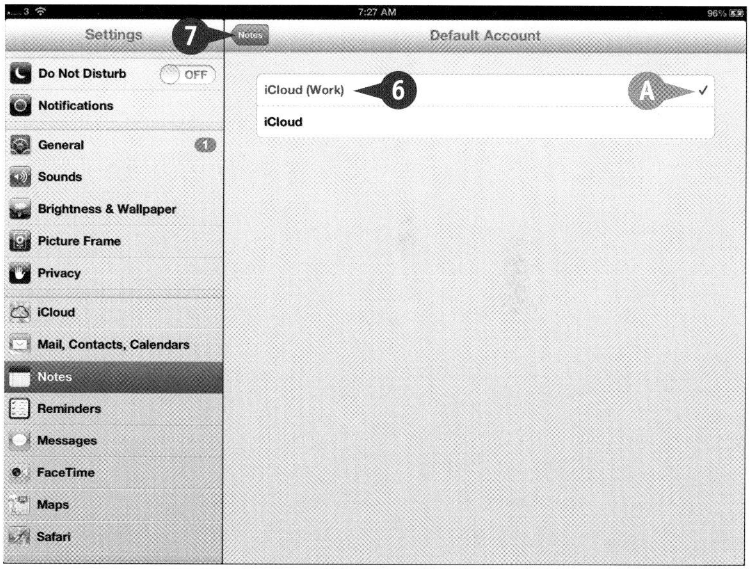

Why does the Default Account setting not appear on the Notes screen on my iPad?
The Default Account setting appears on the Notes screen in the Settings app when you have set up two or more e-mail accounts to synchronize notes. If you add multiple e-mail accounts to the iPad, but set up only one account to synchronize notes, the Default Account setting does not appear because the only Notes account is the default account.

CHAPTER 5

Networking Your iPad

Your iPad connects to the Internet through wireless networks and Wi-Fi hotspots; if it has cellular capability, it can connect through the cellular network as well. The iPad also has Bluetooth connectivity for connecting headsets and other devices.

Turn Wi-Fi, Bluetooth, and Cellular Access On and Off

Normally, you will want to keep your iPad connected to the Internet so that you can send and receive messages and browse the web. But when you do not need or may not use the cellular network or Wi-Fi, you can turn on the iPad's Airplane Mode feature to cut off all connections.

Turning on Airplane Mode turns off Wi-Fi and Bluetooth connections as well. But you can also turn Wi-Fi and Bluetooth on and off separately when you need to.

Turn Wi-Fi, Bluetooth, and Cellular Access On and Off

1 Press the Home button.

The Home screen appears.

2 Tap **Settings**.

The Settings screen appears.

3 To turn Airplane Mode on, tap the **Airplane Mode** switch and move it to the On position.

Note: When your iPad has a wireless network connection, it uses that connection instead of the cellular connection. This helps keep down your cellular network usage and often gives a faster connection.

A The iPad turns off all cellular, Wi-Fi, and Bluetooth connections. An airplane icon appears in the status bar.

4 To turn on Wi-Fi, tap **Wi-Fi** if it is not already selected.

The Wi-Fi screen appears.

5 Tap the **Wi-Fi** switch and move it to the On position.

Ⓑ The list of available networks appears. If your iPad detects a known network, it connects automatically. If not, you can connect to a network manually as described later in this chapter.

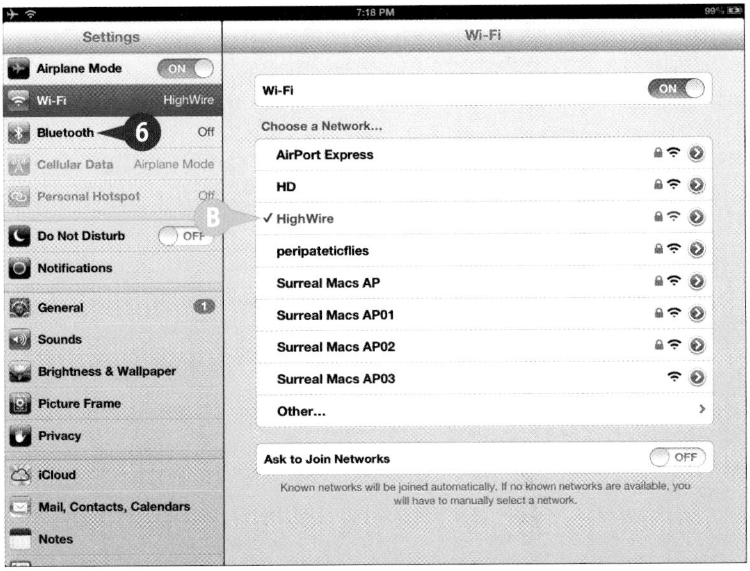

⑥ Tap **Bluetooth**.

The Bluetooth screen appears.

⑦ Tap the **Bluetooth** switch and move it to On if you need to use Bluetooth devices while Airplane Mode is on.

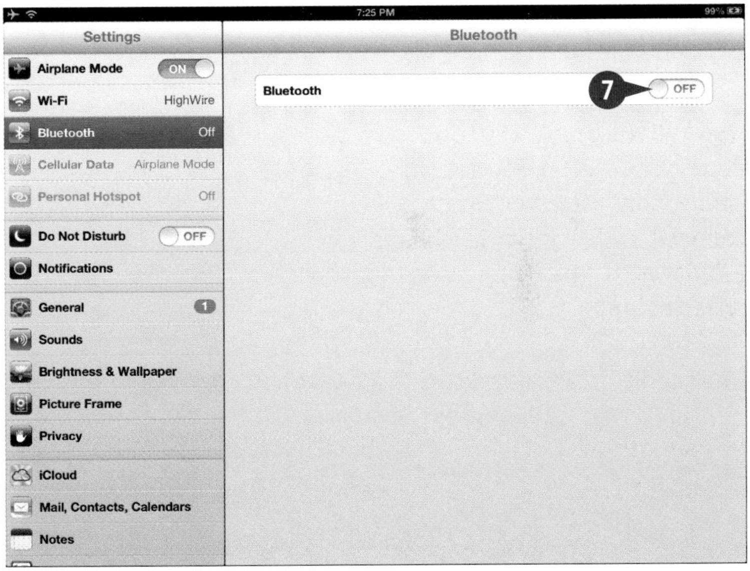

TIP

If I turn on Wi-Fi and Bluetooth on a non-cellular iPad, what effect does Airplane Mode have?
Even if you turn on both Wi-Fi and Bluetooth, Airplane Mode keeps your iPad's Location Services feature disabled. If your iPad has cellular connectivity, turning on Airplane Mode also keeps the GPS disabled.

Connect Bluetooth Devices to Your iPad

To extend your iPad's functionality, you can connect devices to it that communicate using the wireless Bluetooth technology.

For example, you can connect a Bluetooth keyboard so that you can quickly type e-mail messages, notes, or documents. Or you can connect a Bluetooth headset so that you can listen to music and make and take FaceTime calls. If you connect a Bluetooth headset or headphones, you need to tell the iPad which audio device to use.

Connect Bluetooth Devices to Your iPad

Set Up a Bluetooth Device

1 Press the Home button.

The Home screen appears.

2 Tap **Settings**.

The Settings screen appears.

3 Tap **Bluetooth**.

The Bluetooth screen appears.

4 Tap the **Bluetooth** switch and move it to On.

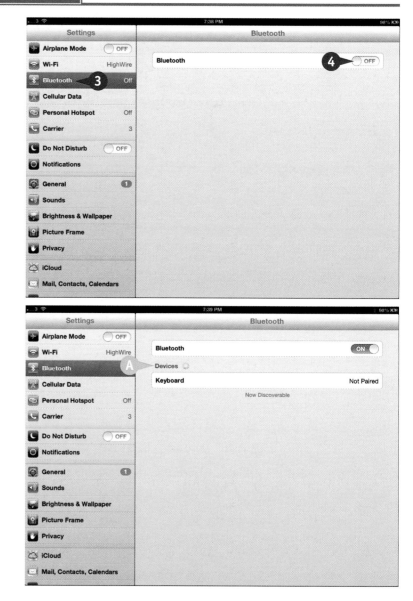

Ⓐ The Devices list appears, and the iPad scans for Bluetooth devices.

5 Turn on the Bluetooth device and make it discoverable.

Note: Read the Bluetooth device's instructions to find out how to make the device discoverable via Bluetooth.

The Bluetooth device appears in the Devices list, marked Not Paired.

6 Tap the device's button.

B The iPad pairs with the device, and then connects to it.

C For a keyboard, you may need to type a code to confirm the pairing request.

The Devices list shows the device as Connected. You can start using the device.

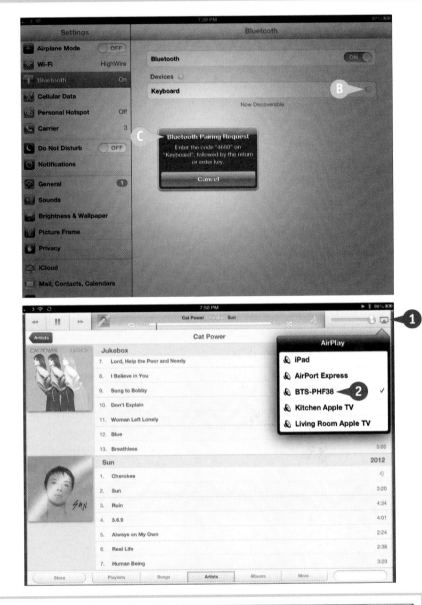

Choose the Device for Playing Audio

1 To select the audio playback device, tap ⬜.

The AirPlay dialog appears.

2 Tap the AirPlay device you want to use.

How do I stop using a Bluetooth device?

When you no longer need to use a particular Bluetooth device, tell your iPad to forget it. Press the Home button, tap **Settings**, and then tap **General**. On the General screen, tap **Bluetooth**, and then tap the device's ⊙ button. On the device's screen, tap **Forget this Device**, and then tap **Forget Device** in the confirmation dialog.

Control Data Roaming and Cellular Usage

When you need to use your cellular iPad in a location where your carrier does not provide Internet service, you can turn on the iPad's Data Roaming feature. Data roaming enables you to access the Internet using other carriers' networks. Data roaming often involves extra charges, so you will normally want to use data roaming only when no wireless network connection is available.

If you have a cellular iPad, you will normally have either a monthly plan with data allowances or a pay-as-you-go deal. Either way, if you use your iPad extensively, you may need to monitor your usage of the cellular network to avoid incurring extra charges.

Control Data Roaming and Cellular Usage

1 Press the Home button.

The Home screen appears.

2 Tap **Settings**.

The Settings screen appears.

3 Tap **Cellular Data**.

The Cellular Data screen appears.

A You can turn off cellular data altogether by tapping the **Cellular Data** switch and moving it to Off.

4 Tap the **Data Roaming** switch and move it to On.

5 Set the **iCloud Documents** switch to On or Off, as needed.

6 Set the **iTunes** switch to On or Off, as needed.

7 Set the **FaceTime** switch to On or Off, as needed.

8 Set the **Reading List** switch to On or Off, as needed.

Note: Syncing Reading List involves transferring only small amounts of data, so it is unlikely to cause problems with your data allowance. By contrast, iCloud Documents, iTunes, and FaceTime can involve huge amounts of data.

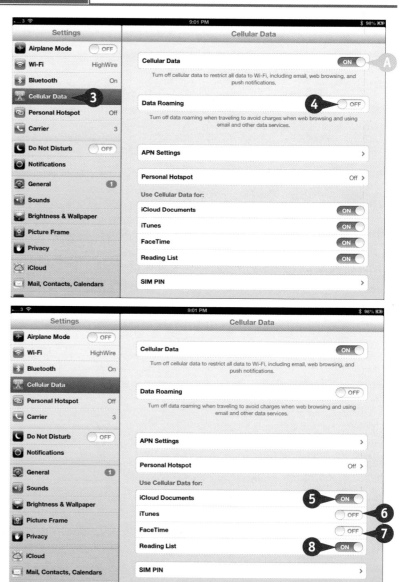

114

Monitor Your Cellular Network Usage

1 Still in the Settings app, tap **General**.

The General screen appears.

2 Tap **Usage**.

The Usage screen appears.

3 Scroll down to the bottom of the screen.

4 Tap **Cellular Usage**.

The Cellular Usage screen appears.

B The Sent button shows how much data your iPad has sent over the cellular connection.

C The Received button shows how much data your iPad has received over the cellular connection.

Note: To reset your usage statistics, tap **Reset Statistics** at the bottom of the Cellular Usage screen.

5 Tap **Usage**.

The Usage screen appears.

6 Tap **General**.

The General screen appears.

TIP

What can I do from the APN Settings screen?

APN, short for *Access Point Name*, is the name of a particular gateway between a cellular network and the Internet. Tapping **APN Settings** on the Cellular Data screen in Settings displays the APN Settings screen. Here, you can set your cellular iPad to access a specific cellular network by name, providing a username and password to make the connection. Normally, you do not need to do this, because your iPad's SIM card provides the data necessary to make a cellular connection.

Share Your iPad's Internet Access Using Personal Hotspot

Your cellular iPad can not only access the Internet itself from anywhere it has a suitable connection to the cell network, but it can also share that Internet access with your computer. This feature is called Personal Hotspot.

For you to use Personal Hotspot, your iPad's carrier must permit you to use it. Some carriers simply charge the Personal Hotspot data as part of the iPad's allowance, but others charge an extra fee per month for using the feature.

Share Your iPad's Internet Access Using Personal Hotspot

Set Up Personal Hotspot

1 Press the Home button.

The Home screen appears.

2 Tap **Settings**.

The Settings screen appears.

3 Tap **Personal Hotspot**.

The Personal Hotspot screen appears.

4 Tap **Wi-Fi Password**.

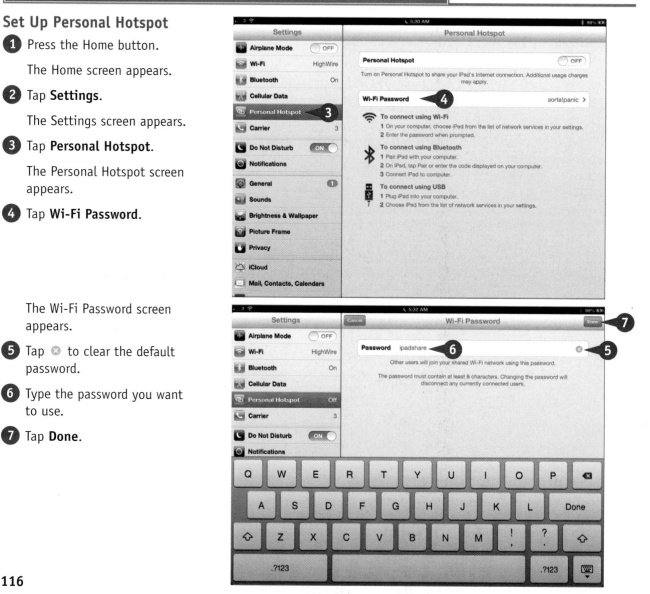

The Wi-Fi Password screen appears.

5 Tap ⊗ to clear the default password.

6 Type the password you want to use.

7 Tap **Done**.

The Personal Hotspot screen appears again.

8 Tap the **Personal Hotspot** switch and move it to On.

The Personal Hotspot screen shows the message Now Discoverable and displays information for connecting computers and devices to the hotspot.

Note: When Personal Hotspot is active — when a computer or device is using the connection — Personal Hotspot appears in a blue bar across the lock screen and the Home screen to remind you. The bar shows the number of connections.

You can now connect your PC or Mac to the iPad's Internet connection.

Connect a PC to Personal Hotspot via USB

1 Turn on Personal Hotspot on your iPad, as described earlier.

2 Connect the iPad to the PC via USB.

Windows detects the iPad's Internet connection as a new network connection and installs it.

The Driver Software Installation dialog box opens.

3 Click **Close**.

The Set Network Location dialog box opens.

4 Click **Home network** or **Public network**, as appropriate.

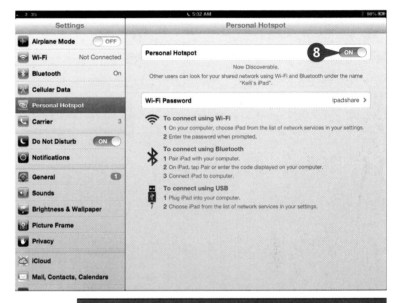

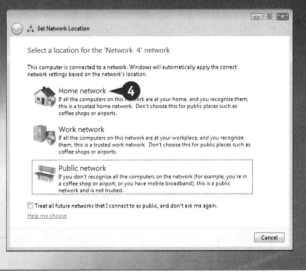

continued ▶

You can connect up to five computers or other devices, such as the iPod touch, to the Internet by using Personal Hotspot on your iPad. Because the devices share the connection, the more devices you use, the slower the connection speed will appear to be on each device. Connecting more devices will also typically increase the amount of data transferred across the iPad's Internet connection and so consume your data allowance faster.

Share Your iPad's Internet Access Using Personal Hotspot (continued)

The Set Network Location dialog box updates its contents.

 Click **Close**.

Your PC starts using the iPad's Internet connection.

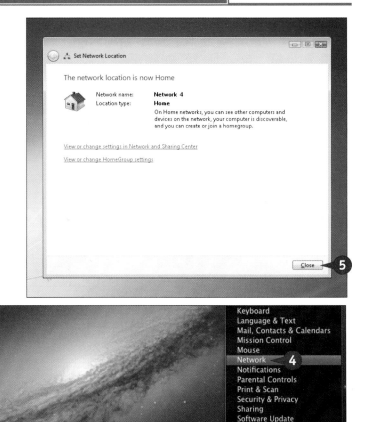

Connect a Mac via Personal Hotspot

 Turn on Personal Hotspot on your iPad, as described earlier.

❷ Connect the iPad to the Mac via USB.

Note: If your Mac displays the A New Network Interface Has Been Detected dialog, click **Network Preferences** to open Network Preferences.

❸ Control +click or right-click **System Preferences** (⚙) in the Dock.

The System Preferences context menu opens.

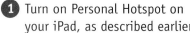

❹ Click **Network**.

The Network preferences pane of System Preferences opens.

5 Click **iPad USB**.

6 Click **Apply**.

Stop Using Personal Hotspot

1 Display the Personal Hotspot screen on your iPad by following steps **1** to **3** under the heading "Set Up Personal Hotspot" on the left page of the previous spread.

2 Tap the **Personal Hotspot** switch and move it to Off.

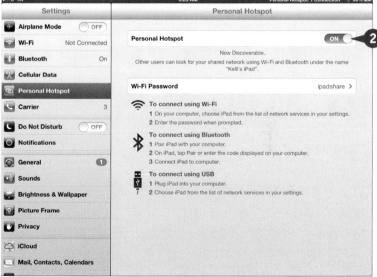

Can I use Personal Hotspot as my main Internet connection?

Yes. But make sure that your data plan provides enough data for your computer use as well as your iPad use. If it does not, you may incur extra charges, and you will do better to use Personal Hotspot only when your main Internet connection is not available.

The Internet connection speeds you get from a connection to your iPad's Personal Hotspot are usually slower than a broadband Internet connection such as a DSL or cable connection. But if your Internet use is light, you may find these speeds adequate.

Connect to Wi-Fi Networks

I f your iPad has cellular capability, it can connect to the Internet either via the cell phone network or via a Wi-Fi network. To conserve your data allowance, use a Wi-Fi network instead of the cell phone network whenever you can. If your iPad is Wi-Fi–only, you must always use Wi-Fi for connecting to the Internet.

The first time you connect to a Wi-Fi network, you must provide the network's password. After that, the iPad stores the password, so you can connect to the network without typing the password again.

Connect to Wi-Fi Networks

1 Press the Home button.

The Home screen appears.

2 Tap **Settings**.

The Settings screen appears.

3 Tap **Wi-Fi**.

The Wi-Fi screen appears.

4 If Wi-Fi is off, tap the **Wi-Fi** switch and move it to On.

The Choose a Network list appears. A lock icon (🔒) indicates the network has security such as a password.

5 Tap the network you want to connect to.

Note: If the network does not have a password, your iPad connects to it without prompting you for a password.

The Enter Password dialog appears.

6 Type the password.

7 Tap **Join**.

120

Your iPad connects to the wireless network.

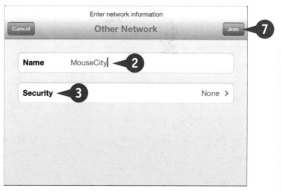

(A) The Wi-Fi screen shows a check mark next to the network the iPad has connected to.

(B) The Wi-Fi signal icon (🛜) in the status bar and on the Wi-Fi screen shows the strength of the Wi-Fi signal. The more bars that appear, the stronger the signal is.

Note: To stop your iPad from connecting to a particular wireless network, tap ⊘ to the right of the network's name on the Wi-Fi screen. On the network's screen, tap **Forget this Network**. In the dialog that opens, tap **Forget**.

TIP

How do I connect to a network not listed on the Wi-Fi screen?

If a wireless network is not broadcasting its network name, the network does not appear on the Wi-Fi screen. Follow these steps:

1 From the Wi-Fi screen, tap **Other**.

2 On the Other Network screen, type the network name.

3 Tap **Security**.

4 On the Security screen, tap the security type — for example, **WPA2**.

5 Tap **Other Network**.

6 Type the password in the Password box on the Other Network screen.

7 Tap **Join**.

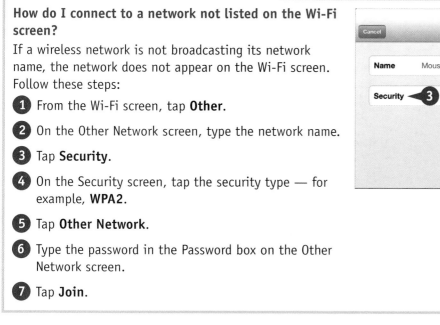

121

Log In to Wi-Fi Hotspots

When you are in town or on the road, you can log in to Wi-Fi hotspots to enjoy fast Internet access.

You can find Wi-Fi hotspots at many locations, including coffee shops and restaurants, hotels, and airports. Some municipal areas, and even some parks and highway rest stops, also provide public Wi-Fi. Some Wi-Fi hotspots charge for access, whereas others are free to use.

Log In to Wi-Fi Hotspots

1 Press the Home button.

The Home screen appears.

2 Tap **Settings**.

The Settings screen appears.

3 Tap **Wi-Fi**.

The Wi-Fi screen appears.

4 If Wi-Fi is off, tap the **Wi-Fi** switch and move it to On.

The list of wireless networks appears.

5 Tap the Wi-Fi hotspot you want to join.

Note: If the iPad prompts you to enter a username and password, type those the hotspot operator has given you. Many Wi-Fi hotspots use a login page instead of a username and password.

The iPad joins the hotspot. The Wi-Fi screen displays a check mark next to the hotspot.

⑥ If Safari opens and displays a login page, type the login information for the hotspot, and then tap the button for logging in.

After connecting to the hotspot, you can use the Internet. For example, you can browse the web using Safari or send and receive e-mail using the Mail app.

TIP

What precautions should I take when using Wi-Fi hotspots?

The main danger is that you may connect to a malevolent network.

To stay safe, connect only to hotspots provided by reputable establishments — for example, national hotel chains or restaurant chains — instead of hotspots run by unknown operators.

When you finish using a Wi-Fi hotspot that you do not plan to use again, tell the iPad to forget the network using the technique described in the previous task.

Forgetting the network avoids this problem: After you have connected the iPad to a wireless network, it will connect to another network that has the same name, security type, and password, even if that network is not the same network. This feature normally saves time, but it also enables an imposter to set up a fake hotspot that pretends to be a genuine hotspot you have previously used.

Connect to a Network via VPN

If you use your iPad for work, you may need to connect it to your work network. By using the settings, username, and password that the network's administrator provides, you can connect via virtual private networking, or VPN, across the Internet. You can also use VPN to connect to your home network if you set up a VPN server on it.

VPN uses encryption to create a secure connection across the Internet. By using VPN, you can connect securely from anywhere you have an Internet connection.

Connect to a Network via VPN

Set Up the VPN Connection on the iPad

1. Press the Home button.

   The Home screen appears.

2. Tap **Settings**.

   The Settings screen appears.

3. Tap **General**.

   The General screen appears.

4. Tap **VPN**.

The VPN screen appears.

5. Tap **Add VPN Configuration**.

Note: If your iPad already has a VPN you want to use, tap it, and then go to step **1** of the next section.

The Add Configuration screen appears.

6 Tap the tab for the VPN type: **L2TP**, **PPTP**, or **IPSec**.

7 Fill in the details of the VPN.

8 Tap **Save**.

The VPN configuration appears on the VPN screen.

Connect to the VPN

1 On the VPN screen, tap the **VPN** switch and move it to On.

The iPad connects to the VPN.

A The Status readout shows Connected and the duration.

B The VPN indicator appears in the status bar.

2 Work across the network connection as if you were connected directly to the network.

3 When you are ready to disconnect from the VPN, tap the **VPN** switch on the VPN screen and move it to Off.

TIP

Is there an easier way to set up a VPN connection?
Yes. An administrator can provide the VPN details in a file called a configuration profile, either via e-mail or via a web page. When you install the configuration profile, your iPad adds the VPN automatically. You can then connect to the VPN.

Send Instant Messages

When you need to communicate quickly with another person, but do not need to speak to him, you can send an instant message using the Messages app.

The Messages app runs on the iPad, the iPhone, the iPod touch, and the Mac. You can use Messages to send instant messages to other users of Messages on these devices. You can send either straightforward text messages or messages that include photos or videos.

Send Instant Messages

1. Press the Home button.

   The Home screen appears.

2. Tap **Messages**.

   The Messages screen appears.

3. Tap **New Message** (✏️).

   The New Message screen appears.

4. Tap ⊕.

   The Contacts dialog appears.

5. Tap the contact to whose phone you want to send the message.

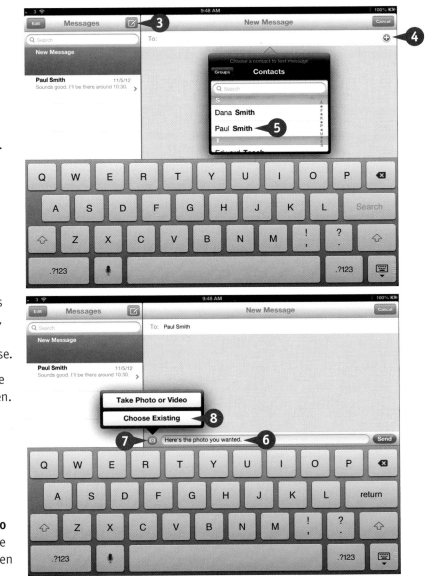

Note: If the contact's record contains multiple phone numbers or addresses, Messages displays the Info pane. Tap the number or address you want to use.

The contact's name appears in the To field of the New Message screen.

6. Tap in the text field, and then type your message.

7. To add a photo, tap 📷.

8. In the dialog that opens, tap **Choose Existing**. In this dialog, you can tap **Take Photo or Video** to take a photo or video with the camera (see Chapter 12), and then send it with the message.

The Photo Albums screen appears.

9 Tap the album that contains the photo.

The album opens.

10 Tap the photo.

The photo opens.

11 Tap **Use**.

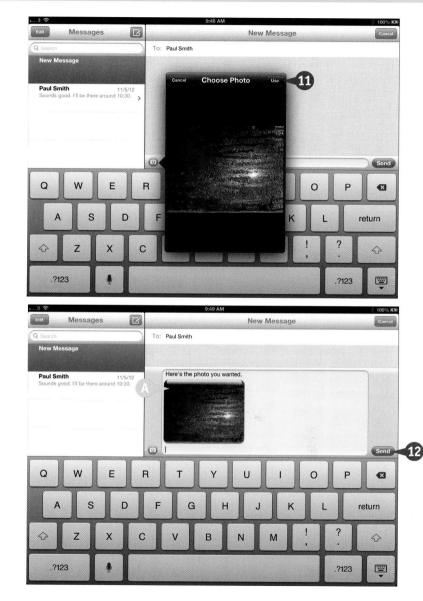

A The photo appears in the message.

Note: You can attach another photo or video by repeating steps **7** to **11**.

12 Tap **Send**.

Is there another way to send a photo or video?
Yes. You can start from the Camera app or the Photos app. This way of sending a photo or video is handy when you are taking photos or videos or when you are browsing your photos or videos. Tap the photo or video you want to share, and then tap 🔄. In the dialog that opens, tap **Message**. Your iPad starts a message containing the photo or video in Messages. You can then address and send the message.

Manage Your Instant Messages

essages is great for communicating quickly and frequently with your nearest, dearest, and your colleagues — so it may not take long before the interface is so full of messages that it becomes hard to navigate.

To keep your messages under control, you can forward messages to others and delete messages you do not need to keep. You can either delete messages from a conversation, leaving the conversation's other messages, or delete the entire conversation.

Manage Your Instant Messages

Forward or Delete One or More Messages from a Conversation

1 Press the Home button.

The Home screen appears.

2 Tap **Messages**.

The Messages screen appears.

3 In the Messages column, tap the conversation that contains the message or messages you will forward.

The conversation appears.

4 Tap ⬆.

A selection button (◯) appears to the left of each message.

5 Tap ◯ (◯ changes to ✅) for each message you want to affect.

6 Tap **Forward**.

Messages starts a new message containing the forwarded messages.

Note: Instead of forwarding the messages, you can tap **Delete** to delete them from the conversation.

7 Address the message and tap **Send** to send it.

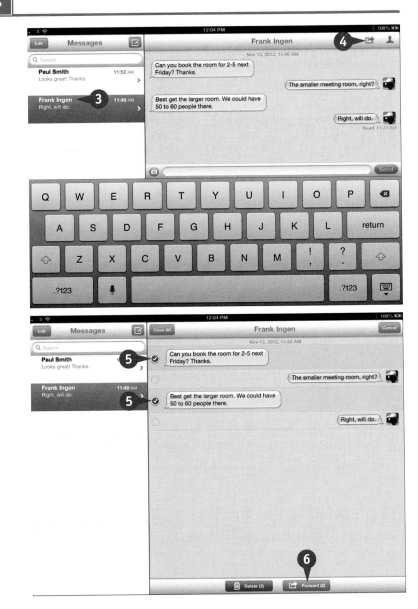

Delete a Conversation

1 Press the Home button.

The Home screen appears.

2 Tap **Messages**.

The Messages screen appears.

3 Tap **Edit**.

The Messages column switches to Edit mode.

4 Tap ⊖ for the conversation you want to delete
(⊖ changes to ⊙).

The Delete button appears.

5 Tap **Delete**.

Messages deletes the conversation.

6 When you finish deleting conversations, tap **Done**.

Messages turns off Edit mode.

TIP

Can I resend a message?

You can resend a message in either of these ways:

- If a red icon with an exclamation point appears next to the message, the message has not been sent. Tap the icon to try sending the message again.
- If the message has been sent, tap and hold the message text, and then tap **Copy** to copy it. Tap and hold in the message text box, and then tap **Paste** to paste in the text. Tap **Send** to send the message.

our iPad's apps are fully integrated with Twitter, the online microblogging service. If you need to send a short textual tweet, you can use the Twitter app. If you need to send a photo, you can start from the Photos app and create a tweet in moments.

Share Your Updates Using Twitter

Send a Text Tweet

1 Press the Home button.

The Home screen appears.

2 Tap **Twitter**.

Note: If Twitter does not appear on the Home screen, tap **Settings**, tap **Twitter**, and then tap **Install**.

The Twitter app opens.

3 Tap .

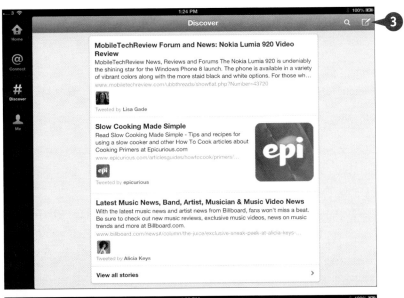

The New Tweet screen appears.

4 Type the text of the tweet.

Note: You can also tap the microphone icon (🎤) to activate Siri, and then dictate the text of the tweet.

5 Tap 📍 if you want to add your location to the tweet.

6 Tap **Tweet**.

Twitter posts the tweet to your Twitter account.

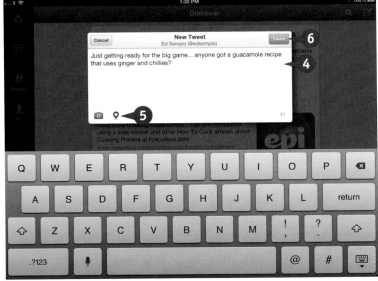

Send a Photo Tweet

1. From the Home screen, tap **Photos**.

   The Photos app opens.

2. Navigate to the photo you want to tweet. For example, tap **Albums** and then tap the album that contains the photo.

3. Tap the photo to display it.

4. Tap .

   The Share dialog appears.

5. Tap **Twitter**.

Ⓐ The Tweet dialog appears, showing the tweet with the photo attached.

6. Tap **Add Location** if you want to add the location to the tweet.

7. Type the tweet.

8. Tap **Send**.

TIP

How do I read other people's tweets?
To read other people's tweets, use the Twitter app. Press the Home button to display the Home screen, tap **Twitter**, and then tap **Home** to catch up on tweets from the Twitter accounts you are following.

Post Updates on Facebook

If you have an account on Facebook, the world's biggest social network, you can post updates directly from your iPad with a minimum of fuss.

The quick way to start a post is by using the Notification Center. You can also start from apps that contain content suitable for Facebook posts. For example, you can post a photo from the Photos app to Facebook.

Post Updates on Facebook

Post an Update from the Notifications

1. Tap the status bar and drag downward.

   Notification Center appears.

2. Tap **Tap to Post**.

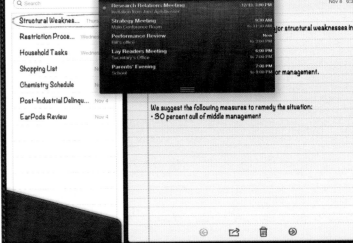

The Facebook dialog appears.

3. Type your update.

4. Optionally, tap **Add Location** to add your location to the post.

5. Tap **Post**.

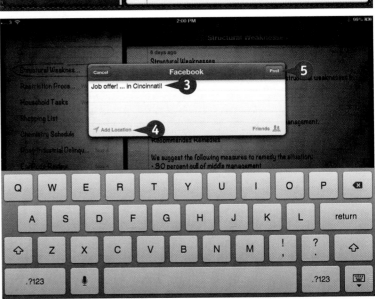

Post a Photo Update

1 Press the Home button.

The Home screen appears.

2 Tap **Photos**.

The Photos app opens.

3 Navigate to the photo you want to post. For example, tap **Albums** and then tap the album that contains the photo.

4 Tap the photo to display it.

5 Tap .

The Share dialog appears.

6 Tap **Facebook**.

A The Facebook dialog appears, with the photo ready for posting.

7 Type the text for the update.

8 Optionally, tap **Add Location** to add your location to the post.

9 Tap **Post**.

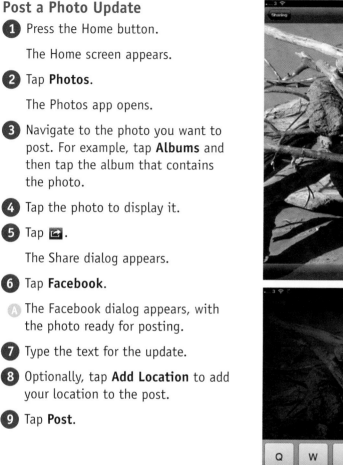

From what other apps can I post updates to Facebook?

You can post updates to Facebook from any app to which the developer has added Facebook integration. For example, you can post a location from the Maps app or a lecture from iTunes U to Facebook.

To see whether you can post updates to Facebook from an app, tap  from the app. If Facebook appears in the Share dialog, you can post an update to Facebook.

Chat Face to Face Using FaceTime

B y using your iPad's FaceTime feature, you can enjoy video chats with any of your contacts who have an iPhone 4 or later, an iPad 2 or later, an iPad mini, a fourth-generation or later iPod touch, or the FaceTime for Mac application.

To make a FaceTime call, you and your contact must both have Apple IDs or iPhones. Your iPad must be connected to either a wireless network or the cellular network. Using a wireless network is preferable because you typically get better performance and do not use up your cellular data allowance.

Chat Face to Face Using FaceTime

1 Press the Home button.

The Home screen appears.

2 Tap **FaceTime**.

The FaceTime app opens, showing the Contacts list.

3 Tap the contact you want to call with FaceTime.

The contact's record opens.

4 Tap **FaceTime** (⬛).

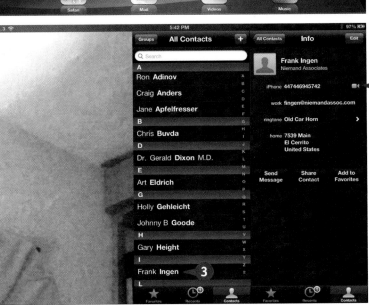

The iPad starts a FaceTime call, showing your video preview.

When your contact answers, smile and speak.

When the connection is established, your iPad displays the caller full screen, with your video inset.

5 If you need to mute your microphone, tap **Mute** (🎙). Tap **Mute** (🎙) when you want to turn muting off again.

6 If you need to show your contact something using the rear-facing camera, tap **Switch Cameras** (📷). Your inset video then shows the picture that is being sent to your contact. Tap **Switch Cameras** (📷) when you are ready to switch back.

7 When you are ready to end the call, tap **End**.

Note: When your iPad receives a FaceTime request, and the screen shows who is calling, aim the camera at your face, and then tap and drag the slider to answer.

TIP

Are there other ways of starting a FaceTime call?
Yes. Here are two other ways of starting a FaceTime call:

- In the Contacts app, tap the contact to display the contact record, and then tap **FaceTime**.
- In a Messages conversation, tap 👤 to display the Info pane, and then tap **FaceTime**.

CHAPTER 6

Working with Apps

In this chapter, you first learn to customize the Home screen, putting the icons you need most right to hand and organizing them into folders. You then grasp how to switch instantly among the apps you are running, how to find the apps you need on Apple's App Store, and how to update and remove apps. You also learn how to install apps provided by an administrator.

Customize the Home Screen

From the Home screen, you run the apps on your iPad. You can customize the Home screen to put the apps you use most frequently within easy reach. When the first Home screen fills up with icons, the iPad adds more Home screens automatically and populates them with apps you add. You can also create further Home screens — up to 11 screens total — and move the app icons among them. You can customize the Home screen by working on the iPad, as described here. If you synchronize your iPad with a computer, you can use iTunes instead. This is an easier way to make extensive changes.

Customize the Home Screen

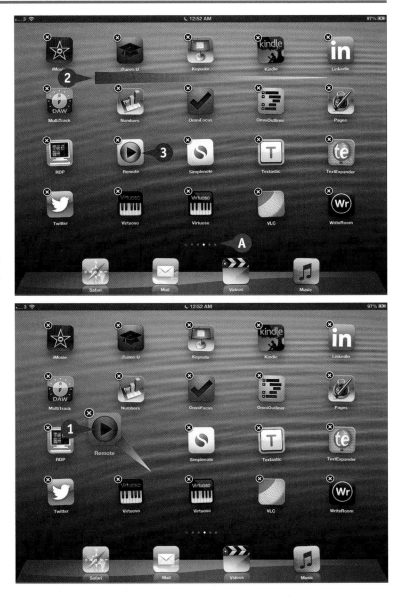

Unlock the Icons for Customization

1 Press the Home button.

The Home screen appears.

2 Tap and drag left or right to display the Home screen you want to customize.

Ⓐ You can also tap the dot for the Home screen you want to display.

3 Tap and hold the icon you want to move.

Note: You can tap and hold any icon until the apps start jiggling. Usually, it is easiest to tap and hold the icon you want to move, and then drag the icon.

The icons start to jiggle, indicating that you can move them.

Move an Icon within a Home Screen

1 After unlocking the icons, drag the icon to where you want it.

The other icons move out of the way.

2 When the icon is in the right place, drop it.

The icon stays in its new position.

Move an Icon to a Different Home Screen

1 After unlocking the icons, drag the icon to the left edge of the screen to display the previous Home screen or to the right edge to display the next Home screen.

The previous Home screen or next Home screen appears.

2 Drag the icon to where you want it.

The other icons move out of the way.

3 Drop the icon.

The icon stays in its new position.

Stop Customizing the Home Screen

1 Press the Home button.

The icons stop jiggling.

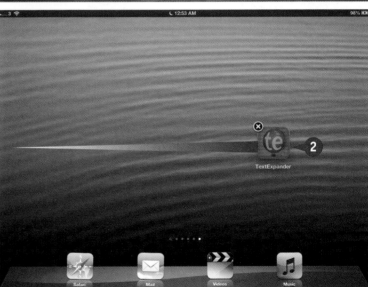

TIP

How can I put the default apps back on the Home screen?
Press the Home button, tap **Settings**, and then tap **General**. Tap and drag up to scroll down the screen, and then tap **Reset**. On the Reset screen, tap **Reset Home Screen Layout**, and then tap **Reset** in the dialog that opens. Press the Home button to return to the Home screen.

Organize Apps with Folders

To organize the Home screen, you can arrange the items into folders. The iPad's default Home screen layout does not include any folders, but you can create as many as you need.

You create a folder by dragging one icon onto another icon. Doing this creates a folder containing both items. You can then rename the folder.

Organize Apps with Folders

Create a Folder

1 Display the Home screen that contains the item you want to put into a folder.

2 Tap and hold the item until the icons start to jiggle.

Note: When creating a folder, you may find it easiest to first put both the items you will add to the folder on the same screen.

3 Drag the item to the other icon you want to place in the folder you create.

The iPad creates a folder, puts both icons in it, and assigns a default name based on the genre.

4 Tap ⊗ in the folder name box.

The keyboard appears.

5 Type the name for the folder.

6 Tap outside the folder.

The iPad applies the name to the folder.

Open an Item in a Folder

1 Display the Home screen that contains the folder.

2 Tap the folder's icon.

The folder's contents appear, and the items outside the folder fade.

3 Tap the item you want to open.

The item opens.

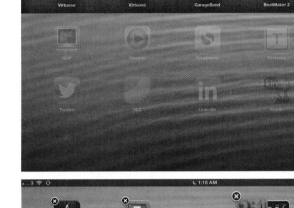

Add an Item to a Folder

1 Display the Home screen that contains the item.

2 Tap and hold the item until the icons start to jiggle.

3 Drag the icon on top of the folder and drop it there.

Note: If the folder is on a different Home screen from the icon, drag the icon to the left edge to display the previous Home screen or to the right edge to display the next Home screen.

The item goes into the folder.

4 Press the Home button to stop the icons jiggling.

TIP

How do I take an item out of a folder?

1 Tap the folder to display its contents.

2 Tap and hold the item until the icons start to jiggle.

3 Drag the item out of the folder. The folder closes and the Home screen appears.

4 Drag the item to where you want it, and then drop it.

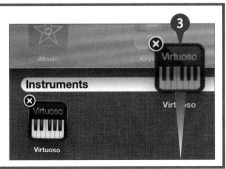

Switch Quickly from One App to Another

The most straightforward way of switching from one app to another is to press the Home button to display the Home screen, and then tap the icon for the app you want to start using. But the iPad also has an app-switching bar that enables you to switch quickly from one running app to another running app without needing to display the Home screen.

Switch Quickly from One App to Another

 Press the Home button.

The Home screen appears.

② Tap the app you want to launch.

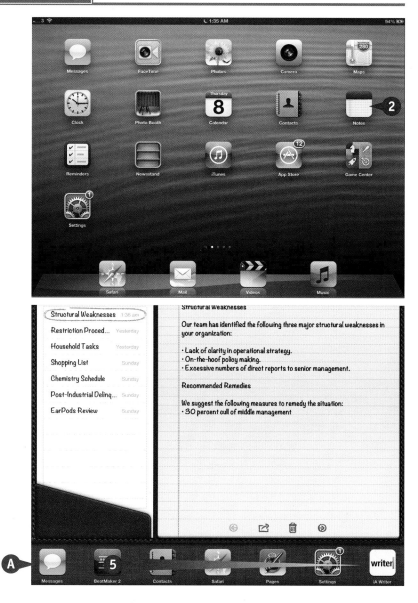

The app's screen appears.

③ Start using the app as usual.

④ Press the Home button twice in quick succession.

Ⓐ The app-switching bar appears.

⑤ Tap and drag left or right to scroll the app-switching bar until you see the app you want.

Note: If you have set the Multitasking Gestures switch on the General screen of the Settings app to On, you can also display the app-switching bar by dragging four fingers up from the bottom of the screen. You can also swipe left or right with four fingers to switch among the running apps.

6 Tap the app in the app-switching bar.

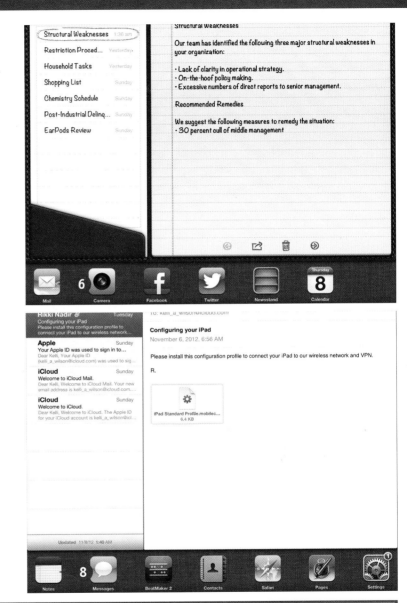

The app appears.

7 When you are ready to switch back, press the Home button twice in quick succession.

The app-switching bar appears.

8 Tap the app to which you want to return.

The app appears, ready to resume from where you stopped using it.

What else can I do with the app-switching bar?

Scroll as far left as possible to display the orientation lock, brightness, and playback controls. Tap ⟳ to lock the screen's orientation; tap ⟳ to unlock the orientation. Drag the **Brightness** slider (☀) to change the brightness, or drag the **Volume** slider (🔊) to change the volume. Tap **Music** (♫) to switch to the Music app.

Explore the App Store

Software developers from around the world have developed hundreds of thousands of apps for the iPad, iPhone, and iPod touch. You can add functionality or just fun to your iPad by installing other apps on it.

To get apps, you use the App Store on either your iPad or your computer. You can browse the App Store by category, such as Games, Entertainment, Utilities, Social Networking, Music, and Productivity. Alternatively, you can search for apps.

There are many free apps, as well as more advanced apps that you have to pay for, that you can download wirelessly to your iPad. To purchase apps in the App Store, you must have an iTunes Store account.

Access the App Store

You can access the App Store from your iPad by tapping the App Store icon or from your Mac or PC within the iTunes Store. Almost all the apps designed for the iPod touch and iPhone work with the iPad, so all you need to do is download them. You can also sync apps that you have previously downloaded for your iPhone or iPod touch to your iPad from your Mac or PC via the USB-to-Lightning cable or wirelessly.

Find Apps in the App Store

Searching and downloading apps in the App Store is very similar to browsing for songs and albums in the iTunes Store. Once you tap the App Store icon, you can sort through the apps in various ways, including Featured, Top Charts, and Search, or by using the Genius feature. Choosing Featured lists the hot new apps in the App Store, whereas Categories enables you to browse widely through collections such as Games, Social Networking, and Music. Top Charts lists the most popular apps, divided into Paid, Free, and Top Grossing groups. You can also perform a keyword search.

Download Video Games

Your iPad has strong graphics performance, so it is great for playing graphical games. The App Store has many games for you to download and play on your iPad. Some games are free; others you must pay for. Many of these games are specifically designed to take advantage of the iPad's motion-sensor technology, allowing you to tilt the iPad to control aspects of the game on-screen.

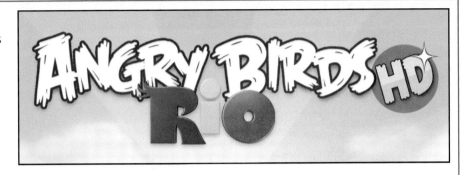

Read and Post Reviews for Apps

A half million apps are available for you to download to your iPad, so use your storage space carefully by reviewing apps before you download them. Reading descriptions and reviews is easy in the App Store. Tapping an app icon in the App Store immediately opens the app description, complete with screenshots from the app. The App Store uses a five-star rating system; tap in the rating fields to read customer reviews of the apps. You can post your own review for an app by tapping the Write a Review button on the overview screen for an app.

Update Your Apps

As software developers continue improving their apps, they often release updates to the software you may have already downloaded from the App Store. The App Store notifies you when developers have released an update for the software you have previously downloaded by placing a red badge on the App Store icon located on the Home screen. The badge signifies how many apps have updates by displaying a number. Tap **App Store** to open the App Store app, and then tap **Updates** to locate the updates. You can choose to update individual apps or update all of them automatically.

Find the Apps You Need on the App Store on Your iPad

The iPad comes with essential apps, such as Safari for surfing the web, Mail for e-mail, and Calendar for keeping your schedule. But to get the most out of your iPad, you will likely need to add other apps.

To get apps, you use the App Store, which provides apps that Apple has approved as correctly programmed, suitable for purpose, and not containing malevolent code. Before you can download any apps, including free apps, you must create an App Store account.

Find the Apps You Need on the App Store on Your iPad

① Press the Home button.

The Home screen appears.

② Tap **App Store**.

The App Store app opens, showing the All Categories screen at first.

③ Tap and drag up to scroll down.

Further lists on the All Categories screen appear.

④ Tap the category or group you want to see.

The category screen appears, showing its lists of apps.

 5 Tap and drag sideways to see further apps in a list, or tap and drag up to see other lists.

 6 Tap the app you want to view.

The app's dialog appears.

Note: To understand what an app does and how well it does it, look at the app's rating, read the description, and read the user reviews.

7 Tap the price button or the **Free** button.

The price button or Free button changes to an Install App button.

8 Tap **Install App**.

9 If the iPad prompts you to sign in, type your password and tap **OK**.

Note: If you have not created an App Store account already, the iPad prompts you to create one now.

The iPad downloads and installs the app.

10 Tap **Open** to launch the app.

 TIP

Why does the App Store not appear on the Home screen or when I search?
If the App Store does not appear on the Home screen, and if searching for it does not show a result, the iPad has restrictions applied that prevent you from installing apps. You can remove these restrictions if you know the restrictions passcode. Press the Home button, tap **Settings**, and then tap **General**. Scroll down, and then tap **Restrictions**. Type the passcode in the Enter Passcode dialog, and then tap the **Installing Apps** switch and move it to On.

Find the Apps You Need on the App Store with iTunes

I f you sync your iPad with your computer, you can find, buy, and download apps using iTunes on your computer instead of using the App Store app on your iPad.

Browsing apps with iTunes can be faster and easier than on the iPad, especially if your computer has a large screen. You have the choice of browsing within the main iTunes window or opening a separate window showing the iTunes Store.

Find the Apps You Need on the App Store with iTunes

1 In iTunes, click **iTunes Store** in the Store category of the Source list.

Note: Double-click **iTunes Store** if you want to open a separate iTunes window showing the iTunes Store.

The iTunes Store screen appears.

2 Click **App Store**.

The App Store screen appears.

3 Click **iPad**.

The iTunes Store displays iPad apps instead of iPhone apps.

4 Click the category of apps you want to view.

iTunes displays the category you clicked.

5 Click an app that interests you.

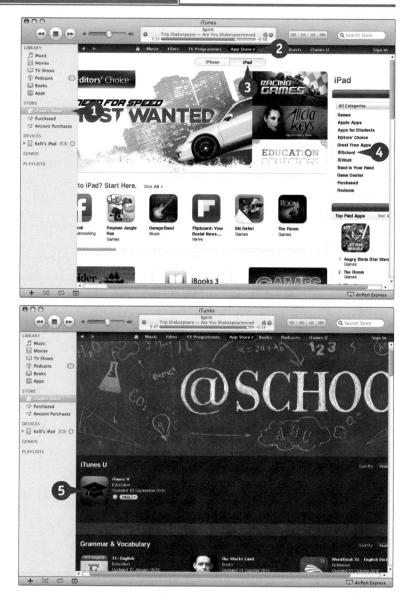

The app's screen appears.

6 Read the description of the app, view the screenshots, and read the reviews to help you decide whether to get the app.

7 Click the price button or **Free App** button.

The Sign In to download from the iTunes Store dialog appears.

8 Type your Apple ID if iTunes has not already entered it.

9 Type your password.

10 Click **Get** for a free app or **Buy** for a paid app.

iTunes downloads the app.

TIP

After I download an app using iTunes, how do I put it on my iPad?

After downloading an app using iTunes, sync your iPad to install the app. Connect your iPad to your computer using the USB-to-Lightning cable, and then click your iPad in the Source list. Click **Apps** at the top of the screen, and then click the app's check box (☐ changes to ☑) in the Apps list. Then click **Apply** to run the sync. If you click **Automatically sync new apps** (☐ changes to ☑) below the Apps list, iTunes installs each new app automatically on your iPad.

Update and Remove Apps

To keep your iPad's apps running well, you should install app updates when they become available. Most updates for paid apps are free, but you must usually pay to upgrade to a new version of the app. You can download and install updates using either iTunes or the iPad.

When you no longer need an app, you can remove it from the iPad and recover the space it was occupying.

Update and Remove Apps

Update an App

1 In iTunes, click **Apps**.

The Apps list appears.

2 Click **Check for Updates**.

iTunes displays the Sign In to Download from the iTunes Store dialog.

3 Type your Apple ID if iTunes has not already entered it.

4 Type your password.

5 Click **Sign In**.

The My App Updates screen appears.

6 Click **Download All Free Updates**.

iTunes downloads the updates.

7 Connect the iPad if it is not already connected.

8 If the iPad does not sync automatically, click **Sync** to start synchronization.

Remove an App from the iPad

1 Press the Home button.

The Home screen appears.

2 Display the Home screen that contains the app you want to delete.

3 Tap and hold the item until the icons start to jiggle.

4 Tap ⊗ on the icon.

The Delete dialog appears.

5 Tap **Delete**.

The iPad deletes the app, and the app's icon disappears.

TIP

Can I update an app on the iPad as well?

Yes. To update an app on the iPad, press the Home button. The badge on the App Store icon (**A**) shows the number of available updates. Tap **App Store**, tap **Updates**, and then tap **Update All**. Type your password in the Apple ID Password dialog, and then tap **OK**. The iPad then downloads and installs the updates. The icons on the Updates screen show the progress of the updates.

Install an App Provided by an Administrator

If you use an iPad administered by a company or organization, an administrator may provide apps for you to install using iTunes. You will usually copy the app's file from a network drive, but you may also receive it attached to an e-mail message.

To install the app, you add it to iTunes on your PC or Mac, and then sync the iPad with iTunes.

Install an App Provided by an Administrator

Add the App to iTunes

1 Click **File**.

The File menu opens.

2 Click **Add File to Library** in Windows or **Add to Library** on a Mac.

The Add To Library dialog opens.

Note: If you receive the app's file attached to an e-mail message, save it to a folder, and then use the Add To Library dialog to add it to iTunes. In Mail on a Mac, you can simply click an attached app's file to add it to iTunes.

3 Open the folder that contains the app's file.

4 Click the app's file.

5 Click **Open**.

A iTunes adds the app to the apps list.

Sync the App to Your iPad

1 Connect your iPad to the PC or Mac via the USB cable.

The iPad appears in the Source list.

Note: You can also install an app provided by an administrator by syncing wirelessly.

2 Click the iPad.

The iPad's control screens appear.

3 Click **Apps**.

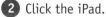

The Apps screen appears.

4 Click **Sync Apps** (☐ changes to ☑).

5 Click the app's check box (☐ changes to ☑).

Note: You can also click **Automatically sync new apps** (☐ changes to ☑) to make iTunes automatically sync all new apps.

6 Click **Apply**. If you have not made changes, this button is named Sync.

iTunes installs the app on your iPad.

TIP

Is there another way to add an app's file to iTunes?

Yes. You can quickly add an app's file to iTunes by dragging the app's file from a Windows Explorer window or a Finder window to the Library area at the top of the Source list on the left side of the iTunes window. On a Mac, you can also add the app to iTunes by dragging the app's file to the iTunes icon on the Dock and dropping it there.

Choose Which Items to Download Automatically

Once you have set up your Apple ID on your iPad, the iTunes Store and App Store apps can automatically download music, apps, and books for you.

Downloading these items automatically can be convenient, but you can turn off this feature if you prefer to run your downloads manually. If your iPad has cellular capability, you can choose whether to allow the iPad to download items over the cellular network.

Choose Which Items to Download Automatically

1 Press the Home button.

The Home screen appears.

2 Tap **Settings**.

The Settings screen appears.

3 Tap and drag your finger up the left column to scroll down.

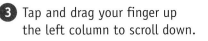

154

4 Tap **iTunes & App Stores**.

The iTunes & App Stores screen appears.

5 Tap the **Music** switch and move it to On or Off, as needed.

6 Tap the **Apps** switch and move it to On or Off, as needed.

7 Tap the **Books** switch and move it to On or Off, as needed.

8 If you have a cellular iPad, tap the **Use Cellular Data** switch and move it to On or Off, as needed.

TIP

Is it a good idea to download items automatically?

Whether to download items automatically is up to you, but having the items appear on your iPad without your intervention is often helpful.

If your iPad has cellular capability and you set the **Use Cellular Data** switch to On, be sure to monitor your data usage to avoid unpleasant surprises. Most e-book files are small and will put only a small dent in your cellular plan, but music files can go through your allowance quickly. Be especially careful about downloading apps automatically, because some of them are huge — more than 500MB in size in some cases.

CHAPTER 7

Browsing the Web and Sending E-Mail

Your iPad is fully equipped to browse the web and send e-mail via a Wi-Fi connection or cellular network.

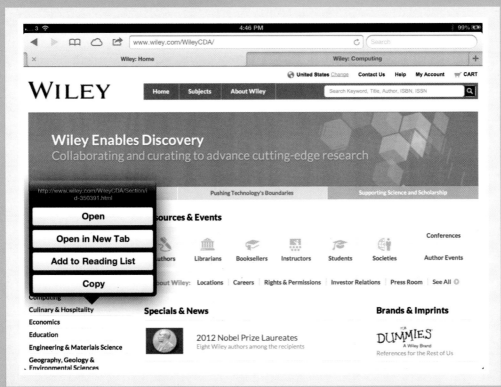

Browse the Web with Safari

Your iPad comes equipped with the Safari app, which you use for browsing the web. You can quickly go to a web page by typing its address in the Address box or by following a link.

Although you can browse quickly by opening a single web page at a time, you may prefer to open multiple pages in separate tabs and switch back and forth among them. Safari makes this easy to do.

Browse the Web with Safari

Open Safari and Navigate to Web Pages

1 Press the Home button.

The Home screen appears.

2 Tap **Safari**.

Safari opens and loads the last web page that was shown.

3 Tap the Address box.

The Address box expands, and the keyboard appears.

4 Tap ⊗ if you need to delete the contents of the Address box.

5 Type the address of the page you want to open.

6 Tap **Go**.

Safari displays the page.

7 Tap a link on the page.

Safari displays that page.

Ⓐ After going to a new page, tap ◀ to display the previous page. You can then tap ▶ to go forward again to the page you just went back from. Tap and hold ◀ or ▶ to display a list of pages you can go back or forward to.

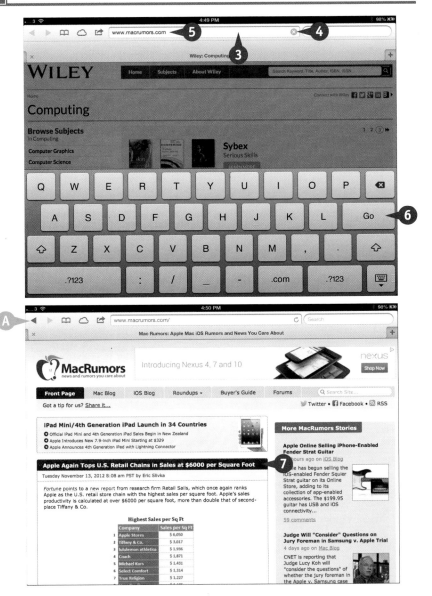

Open Multiple Pages and Navigate Among Them

1 Tap **New Tab** (➕).

Safari displays a new tab, puts the focus in the Address box, and shows the keyboard.

2 Type the address for the page you want to display.

Note: You can also go to a page by using a bookmark, as described in the next task.

3 Tap **Go**.

The page appears.

4 To switch to another page, tap its tab.

B You can tap the **Close** button (✖) to close a page.

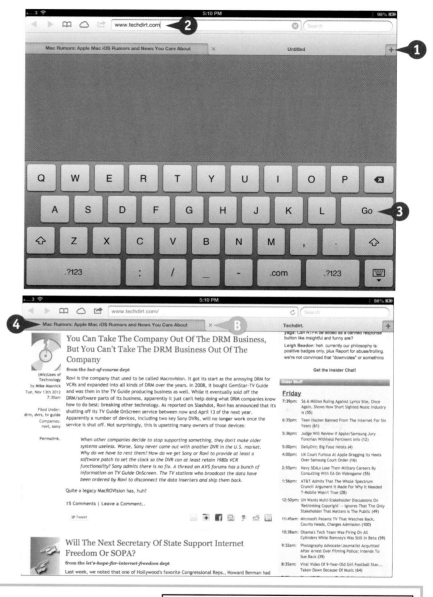

How do I search for information?

Tap the Search box to display the Search screen, and then type your search terms (**A**). Safari searches as you type; you can type further to narrow down the results, and stop as soon as you see suitable results. Tap the result you want to see (**B**), and then tap a link on the results page that Safari opens.

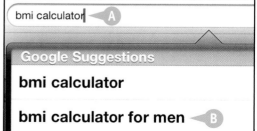

Access Websites Quickly with Your Bookmarks

Typing web addresses can be laborious, even with the help the iPad's on-screen keyboard or a hardware Bluetooth keyboard adds, so you will probably want to use bookmarks to access websites you value.

By syncing your existing bookmarks from your computer, as explained in Chapter 1, you can instantly provide your iPad with quick access to the web pages you want to visit most frequently. You can also use the iCloud Tabs feature to view open tabs in Safari on your computer or other iOS device or create bookmarks on your iPad, as discussed in the next task.

Access Websites Quickly with Your Bookmarks

Open the Bookmarks Screen

1 Press the Home button.

The Home screen appears.

2 Tap **Safari**.

Safari opens.

3 Tap **Bookmarks** (📖).

The Bookmarks dialog appears.

Explore Your History

1 In the Bookmarks dialog, tap **History** (🕐).

A scrollable list of the web pages you have recently visited appears.

Ⓐ Tap a day to display the list of web pages you visited on that day.

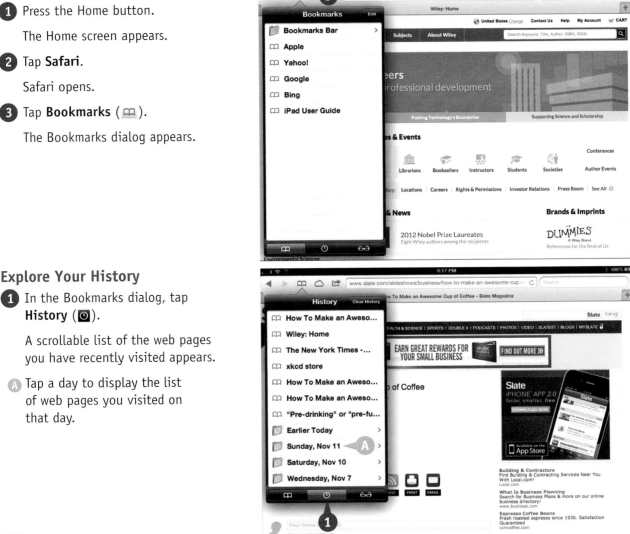

Explore a Bookmarks Category and Open a Bookmarked Page

1 In the Bookmarks dialog, tap the bookmarks folder or category you want to see. For example, tap **Bookmarks Bar**.

The contents of the folder or category appear. For example, the contents of the Bookmarks Bar folder appear.

2 Tap the page you want to view.

The Bookmarks dialog closes, and the web page opens.

B If you do not find a page to view, tap the button in the upper-left corner one or more times to go back. For example, tap **Bookmarks** to return to the Bookmarks screen.

Note: Tap ☁ to display the iCloud Tabs dialog, which shows a list of the tabs you have open in Safari on the other devices you sync with your iCloud account — for example, your computer and your iPhone.

TIP

How can I quickly access a website?

Creating a bookmark within Safari is good for sites you access now and then, but if you access a site frequently, create an icon for it on your Home screen. Tap **Share** (📤), tap **Add to Home Screen** (Ⓐ), type the name in the Add to Home dialog, and then tap **Add**. You can then go straight to the page by tapping its icon on the Home screen.

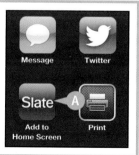

Create Bookmarks and Share Web Pages

When you find a page you want to access again, create a bookmark for it. If you have set your iPad to sync Safari information with iCloud, that bookmark becomes available to the other devices you sync with iCloud. Or if you have configured your iPad to sync bookmarks with your computer, the bookmark becomes available on your computer when you sync. You can also add a web page to your Reading List so that you can access it again quickly.

To share a web page with other people, you can quickly send the page's address via e-mail.

Create Bookmarks and Share Web Pages

Create a Bookmark on the iPad

1 Press the Home button.

The Home screen appears.

2 Tap **Safari**.

Safari opens and displays the last web page you were viewing.

3 Navigate to the web page you want to bookmark.

4 Tap **Share** ().

The Share dialog opens.

5 Tap **Bookmark**.

Note: To add the web page to your Reading List, tap **Add to Reading List** in the Share dialog.

The Add Bookmark dialog appears.

6 Edit the suggested name, or type a new name.

7 Tap the button at the bottom of the dialog.

Note: The button at the bottom of the dialog shows the last bookmarks folder you used. In this example, the button is named Bookmarks Bar.

The Bookmarks dialog appears.

8 Tap the folder you want to create the bookmark in.

The Add Bookmark dialog appears again.

9 Tap **Save**.

Safari creates the bookmark.

Share a Web Page's Address via E-Mail

1 In Safari, navigate to the web page whose address you want to share.

2 Tap **Share** (⤴).

The Share dialog appears.

3 Tap **Mail**.

The iPad starts a new message in the Mail app and adds the link to it.

4 Add the address by typing or by tapping ⊕ and choosing it in the Contacts dialog.

5 Edit the suggested subject line if necessary.

6 Type any explanatory text needed.

7 Tap **Send**.

TIPS

Can I change a bookmark I have created?
Yes. Tap 📖 to display the Bookmarks dialog, and then navigate to the bookmark you want to change. Tap **Edit** to display a button for opening a bookmark to change it and controls for deleting bookmarks and changing their order.

How do I access my Reading List?
Tap 📖 to display the Bookmarks dialog, and then tap 👓 to display the Reading List dialog. You can then tap the web page you want to view.

Configure Your Default Search Engine

To find information with Safari, you often need to search using a search engine. Safari's default search engine is Google, but you can change to another search engine. Your choices are Google, Yahoo!, and Bing.

Google, Yahoo!, and Bing compete directly with one another and return similar results to many searches. But if you experiment with the three search engines, you will gradually discover which one works best for you.

Configure Your Default Search Engine

1 Press the Home button.

The Home screen appears.

2 Tap **Settings**.

The Settings screen appears.

3 Tap in the left column and drag up to scroll down the screen until iCloud appears at the top.

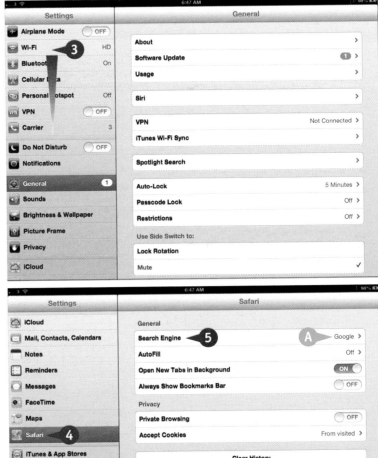

4 Tap **Safari**.

The Safari screen appears.

Ⓐ The Search Engine button shows your current search engine.

5 Tap **Search Engine**.

The Search Engine screen appears.

6 Tap the search engine you want — for example, **Yahoo!**.

A check mark appears next to the search engine you tapped.

7 Tap **Safari**.

The Safari screen appears again, now showing the search engine you chose.

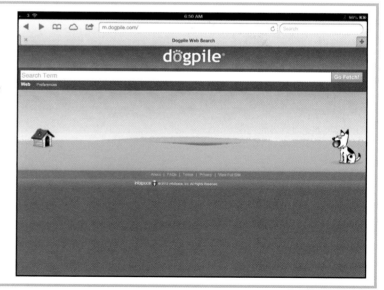

TIP

How can I search using a search engine other than Google, Yahoo!, or Bing?
You can search using any search engine you can find on the web. Open a web page to the search engine, and then perform the search using the tools on the page.

At this writing, you cannot set any search engine other than Google, Yahoo!, or Bing as the iPad's default search engine. Instead, either add the site to your Bookmarks bar or create a link on your Home screen to the site.

Fill in Forms Quickly with AutoFill

If you fill in forms using your iPad, you can save time by turning on the AutoFill feature. AutoFill can automatically fill in standard form fields, such as name and address fields, using the information from a contact card you specify.

AutoFill can also automatically store other data you enter in fields, and can store usernames and passwords to enter them for you automatically. For security, you may prefer not to store your usernames and passwords with AutoFill.

Fill in Forms Quickly with AutoFill

1 Press the Home button.

The Home screen appears.

2 Tap **Settings**.

The Settings screen appears.

3 Tap in the left column and drag up to scroll down the screen until iCloud appears at the top.

4 Tap **Safari**.

The Safari screen appears.

5 Tap **AutoFill**.

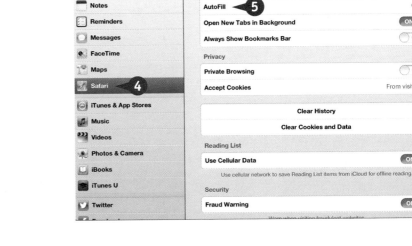

The AutoFill screen appears.

6 Tap the **Use Contact Info** switch and move it to On.

7 Tap the **Names and Passwords** switch and move it to On if you want to use AutoFill for names and passwords.

8 Tap **My Info**.

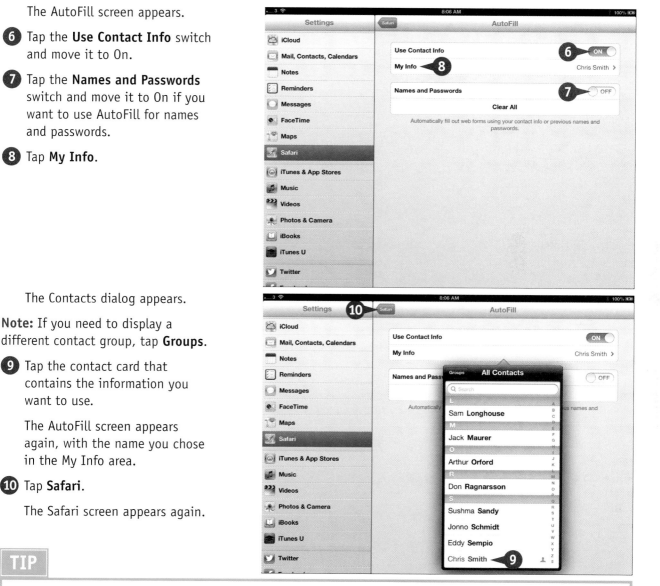

The Contacts dialog appears.

Note: If you need to display a different contact group, tap **Groups**.

9 Tap the contact card that contains the information you want to use.

The AutoFill screen appears again, with the name you chose in the My Info area.

10 Tap **Safari**.

The Safari screen appears again.

TIP

When should I clear my AutoFill information?
Clear your AutoFill information if you want to remove stored usernames and passwords from your iPad, or if AutoFill has stored incorrect information that you have entered in forms. To clear your AutoFill information, tap **Clear All** (Ⓐ) on the AutoFill screen, and then tap **Clear** (Ⓑ) in the Clear AutoFill Data dialog that opens.

Tighten Up Safari's Security

Along with its many and varied sites that provide useful information or services, the web contains sites that try to infect computers with malevolent software, or *malware*, or lure visitors into providing sensitive personal or financial information. Although Apple has built the iPad and Safari to be as secure as possible, it is wise to choose high-security settings. This task shows you how to turn on the Fraud Warning feature, block JavaScript and pop-ups, and choose which cookies to accept.

Tighten Up Safari's Security

1 Press the Home button.

The Home screen appears.

2 Tap **Settings**.

The Settings screen appears.

3 Tap in the left column and drag up to scroll down the screen until iCloud appears at the top.

4 Tap **Safari**.

The Safari screen appears.

5 Tap and drag up to scroll down the screen until the bottom of the screen appears.

6 Tap the **Fraud Warning** switch and move it to On.

7 Tap the **JavaScript** switch and move it to Off.

8 Tap the **Block Pop-ups** switch and move it to On.

9 Tap **Accept Cookies**.

Note: The Fraud Warning warns you when you try to open a site on a blacklist of offending sites. This feature misses many fraudulent sites but is rarely wrong when it raises warnings about a site.

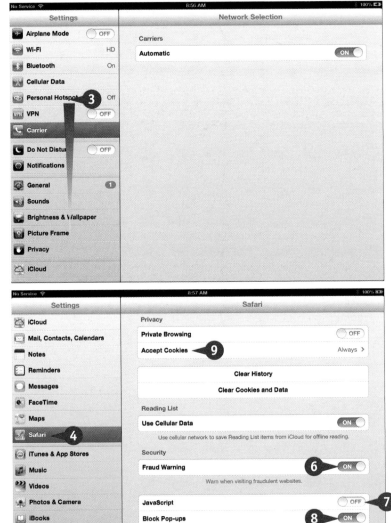

168

Note: JavaScript is used to provide extra features on web pages. Because JavaScript can be used to attack your iPad, disabling JavaScript is the safest option. The disadvantage is that disabling JavaScript may remove some or most functionality of harmless sites.

Note: A pop-up is an extra web page that opens automatically. Some pop-ups attempt to show information most visitors do not want to see.

The Accept Cookies screen appears. See the tip for an explanation of cookies.

⑩ Tap **From visited**.

⑪ Tap **Safari**.

The Safari screen appears again.

⑫ If you want to clear your browsing history, tap **Clear History**, and then tap **Clear** in the Clear History dialog.

⑬ If you want to clear your cookies and cached data, tap **Clear Cookies and Data**, and then tap **Clear** in the Clear Cookies and Data dialog.

TIP

What are cookies and what threat do they pose?
A *cookie* is a small text file that a website places on a computer to identify that computer in the future. This is helpful for many sites, such as shopping sites in which you add items to a shopping cart, but when used by malevolent sites, cookies can pose a threat to your privacy. You can set Safari to never accept cookies, but this prevents many legitimate websites from working properly. So accepting cookies only from sites you visit is normally the best compromise.

Read Your E-Mail Messages

After you have set up Mail by synchronizing accounts from your computer, as described in Chapter 1, or by configuring accounts manually on the iPad, as described in Chapter 4, you are ready to send and receive e-mail messages using your iPad.

This task shows you how to read your incoming e-mail messages. You learn to reply to messages and write messages from scratch later in this chapter.

Read Your E-Mail Messages

1 Press the Home button.

The Home screen appears.

2 Tap **Mail**.

The Mailboxes screen appears.

Note: If Mail does not show the Mailboxes screen, tap the button in the upper-left corner until the Mailboxes screen appears.

3 Tap the inbox you want to see.

Ⓐ To see all your incoming messages together, tap **All Inboxes**. Depending on how you use e-mail, you may find seeing all your messages at once helpful.

The inbox opens.

Ⓑ A blue dot to the left of a message indicates that you have not read the message yet.

Ⓒ A star to the left of a message indicates the message is from a VIP. See the second tip for information about VIPs.

4 Tap the message you want to display.

The message appears.

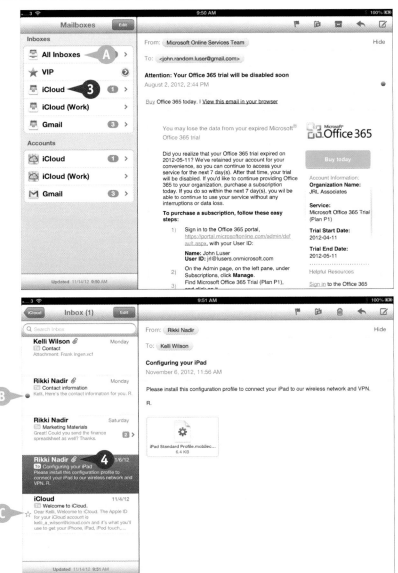

5 Tap another message to display its contents.

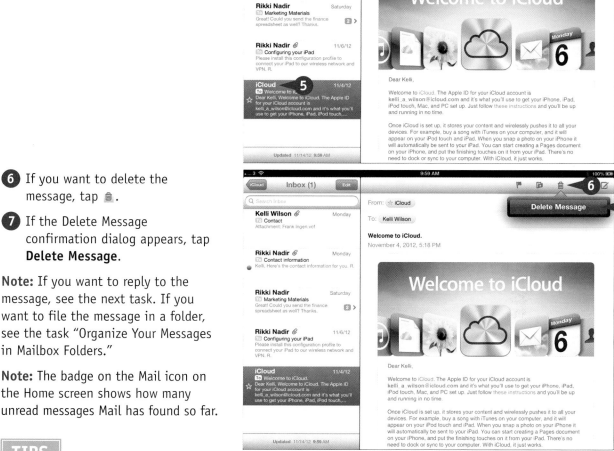

6 If you want to delete the message, tap 🗑.

7 If the Delete Message confirmation dialog appears, tap **Delete Message**.

Note: If you want to reply to the message, see the next task. If you want to file the message in a folder, see the task "Organize Your Messages in Mailbox Folders."

Note: The badge on the Mail icon on the Home screen shows how many unread messages Mail has found so far.

TIPS

How do I view the contents of another mailbox?

From an open message, tap **Inbox** or **All Inboxes** to return to the inbox or the screen for all the inboxes. Tap **Mailboxes** to go back to the Mailboxes screen. You can then tap the mailbox you want to view.

What is the VIP inbox on the Mailboxes screen?

The VIP inbox is a tool for identifying important messages, no matter which e-mail account they come to. You mark particular contacts as being very important people to you, and Mail then adds messages from these VIPs to the VIP inbox. See Chapter 4 for instructions on adding VIPs.

After receiving an e-mail message, you often need to reply to it. You can choose between replying only to the sender of the message and replying to the sender and all the other recipients in the To field and the Cc field, if there are any. Recipients in the message's Bcc field, whose names you cannot see, do not receive your reply.

Other times, you may need to forward a message you have received to one or more other people. The Mail app makes both replying and forwarding messages as easy as possible.

Reply To or Forward an E-Mail Message

1 Press the Home button.

The Home screen appears.

2 Tap **Mail**.

The Mailboxes screen appears.

Note: When you launch Mail, the app checks for new messages. This is why the number of new messages you see on the Mailboxes screen may differ from the number on the Mail badge on the Home screen.

3 Tap the inbox you want to see.

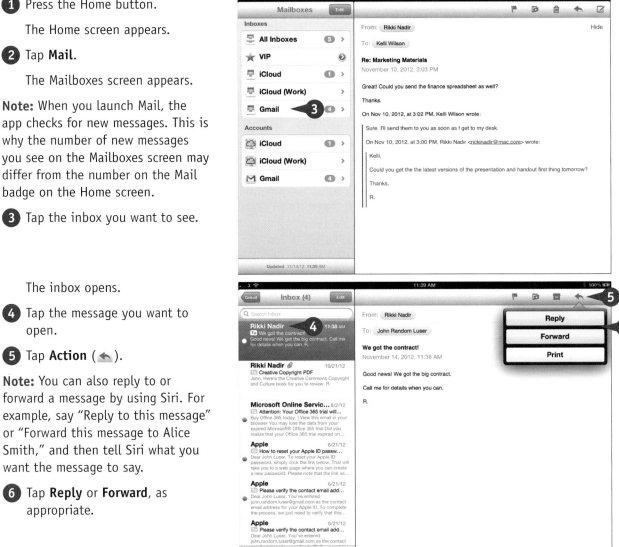

The inbox opens.

4 Tap the message you want to open.

5 Tap **Action** (↰).

Note: You can also reply to or forward a message by using Siri. For example, say "Reply to this message" or "Forward this message to Alice Smith," and then tell Siri what you want the message to say.

6 Tap **Reply** or **Forward**, as appropriate.

Reply to the Message

1️⃣ In the Action menu, tap **Reply**.

Note: To reply to all recipients, tap **Reply All**. Reply to all recipients only when you are sure that they need to receive your reply. Often, it is better to reply only to the sender.

The reply message appears.

2️⃣ Type your reply to the message.

3️⃣ Tap **Send**.

Mail sends the message.

Forward the Message

1️⃣ In the Action menu, tap **Forward**.

The forwarded message appears.

2️⃣ Type the recipient's name or address.

Alternatively, tap ⊕ and choose the recipient in your Contacts dialog.

3️⃣ Type a message if needed.

4️⃣ Tap **Send**.

Mail sends the message.

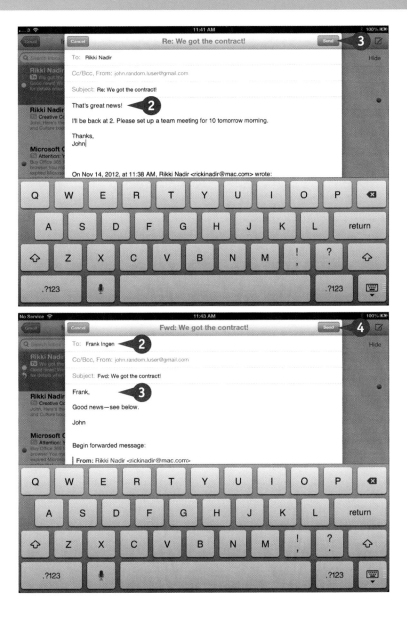

Can I reply to or forward only part of a message?
Yes. The quick way to do this is to select the part of the message you want to include before tapping **Action** (↩). Mail then includes only your selection. Alternatively, you can start the reply or forwarded message, and then delete the parts you do not want to include.

Organize Your Messages in Mailbox Folders

To keep your inbox or inboxes under control, you should organize your messages into mailbox folders.

You can quickly move a single message to a folder after reading it, or you can select multiple messages in your inbox and move them all to a folder in a single action.

Organize Your Messages in Mailbox Folders

Move a Single Message to a Folder

1. In your inbox, tap the message you want to read.

   The message opens.

2. Tap **Folders** ( ).

   The list of folders appears in the left pane.

3. Tap the folder you want to move the message to.

   Mail moves the message.

   The next message in the inbox appears, so that you can read it and file it if necessary.

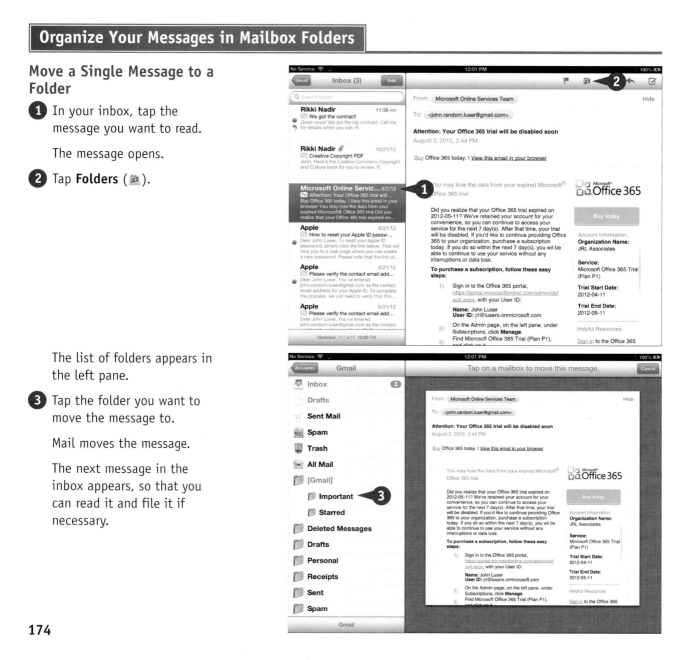

Move Multiple Messages to a Folder

1 In the inbox or another mail folder, tap **Edit**.

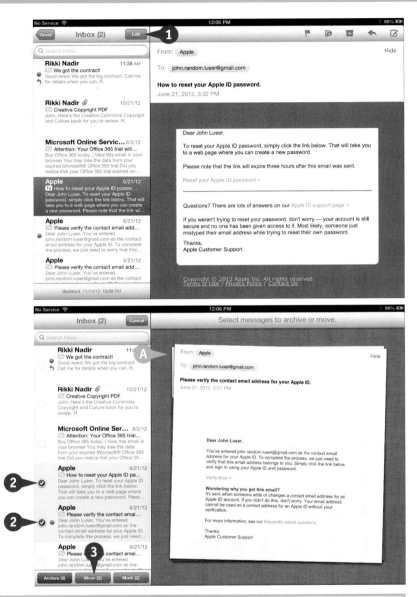

An empty selection button appears to the left of each message, and the Delete button and Move button appear.

2 Tap the selection button () next to each message you want to move.

A Mail displays the messages as a stack.

3 Tap **Move**.

The list of folders appears in the left pane.

4 Tap the folder you want to move the messages to.

Mail moves the messages.

Your inbox then appears again, so that you can work with other messages.

TIP

Can I move messages from an inbox in one account to a folder in another account?
Yes. In the inbox, tap **Edit**, and then tap the selection button (☑) for each message you want to affect. Tap **Move**, and then tap **Accounts**. In the Accounts screen, tap the account (Ⓐ) that contains the folder to which you want to move the messages, and then tap the folder.

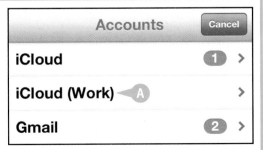

Write and Send E-Mail Messages

Your iPad is great for reading and replying to e-mail messages you receive, but you will likely also need to write new messages. When you do, you can use the data in the Contacts app to address your outgoing messages quickly and accurately. If the recipient's address is not one of your contacts, you can type the address manually.

You can attach one or more files to an e-mail message to send those files to the recipient. This works well for small files, but many mail servers reject files larger than several megabytes in size.

Write and Send E-Mail Messages

1 Press the Home button.

The Home screen appears.

2 Tap **Mail**.

The Mailboxes screen appears.

3 Tap **New Message** (✉).

The New Message dialog appears.

4 Tap ⊕.

The Contacts dialog appears.

Note: If necessary, change the Contacts list displayed by tapping **Groups**, making your choice on the Groups dialog, and then tapping **Done**.

Ⓐ If the person you are e-mailing is not a contact, type the address in the To area. You can also start typing here and then select a matching contact from the list that the Mail app displays.

5 Tap the contact you want to send the message to.

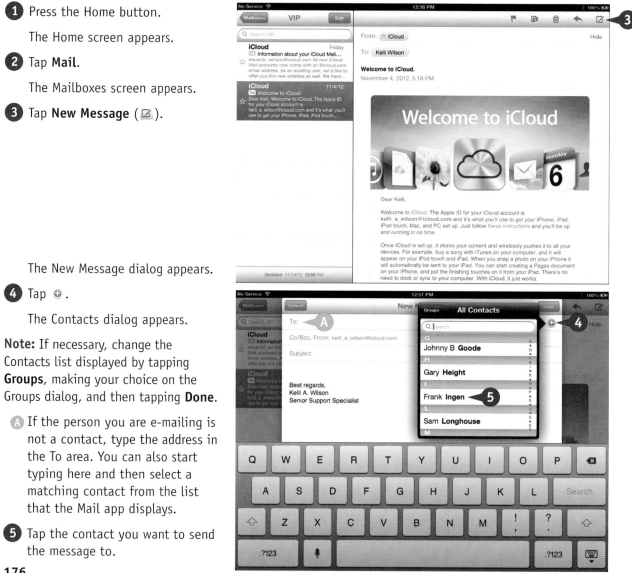

176

Ⓑ The contact's name appears as a button in the To area.

Note: You can add other contacts to the To area by repeating steps **4** and **5**.

⑥ If you need to add a Cc or Bcc recipient, tap **Cc/Bcc, From**.

The Cc, Bcc, and From fields expand.

⑦ Tap the Cc area or Bcc area, and then follow steps **4** and **5** to add a recipient.

Ⓒ To change the e-mail account you are sending the message from, tap **From**, and then tap the account to use.

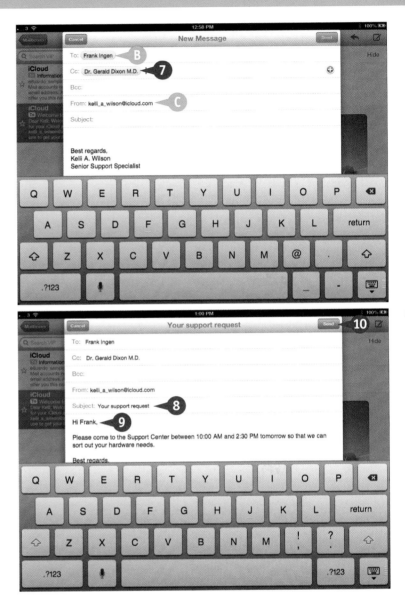

⑧ Tap **Subject**, and then type the message's subject.

⑨ Tap below the Subject line, and then type the body of the message.

⑩ Tap **Send**.

Mail sends the message.

TIP

How do I attach a file to a message?
To attach a file to the message, start the message from the app that contains the file. For example, to send a photo, open the Photos app. Select the photo, tap **Share** (▣), and then tap **Mail**. Mail starts a message with the photo attached. You then address the message and send it.

View Files Attached to Incoming E-Mail Messages

E-mail is not just a great way to communicate, but you can use it to transfer files quickly and easily. When you receive an e-mail message with a file attached to it, you can often quickly view the file from the Mail app.

When you receive an e-mail message that has a small file attached, the Mail app automatically downloads the whole file. If the attachment is a large file, the Mail app downloads part of it, and you must tap the attachment to download the rest of it. This behavior helps both to avoid filling the iPad with large files you may not want and to keep down the amount of data you transfer.

View Files Attached to Incoming E-Mail Messages

1 Press the Home button.

The Home screen appears.

2 Tap **Mail**.

The Mailboxes screen appears.

3 Tap the inbox you want to open.

The inbox opens.

A A paperclip icon (𝒜) indicates that a message has one or more files attached.

4 Tap the message you want to open.

The message opens.

5 If the attachment appears as an outline with a Download button (↓), tap to download the attachment.

A button for the attachment appears.

6 Tap the attachment's button.

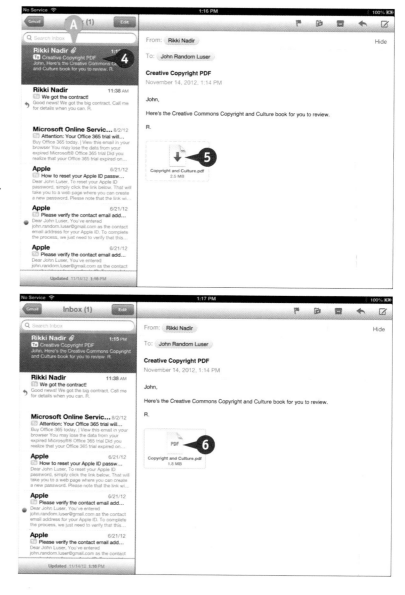

The attached file opens in the Viewer app.

Note: The Viewer app provides basic features for viewing widely used document types, such as PDF files, Microsoft Word documents, and Microsoft Excel workbooks. If the Viewer app cannot open the file you try to open, your iPad tries to suggest a suitable app.

 Tap **Open Attachment** (📤).

A dialog showing apps for opening or using the attachment appears.

⑧ Tap the app in which you want to open the document. For example, tap **Open in iBooks**.

Ⓑ The file opens in the app you chose.

⑨ Depending on the app, you may need to tap the file to open it.

Note: After you open an attached file in an app, your iPad stores a copy of the file in that app's storage. You can then open the file again directly from that app.

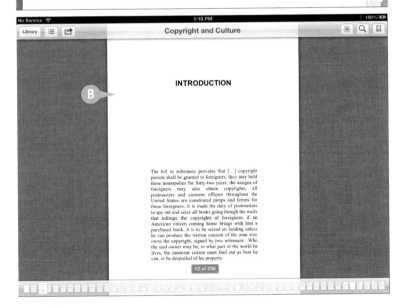

How can I delete an attached file from an e-mail message?

You cannot directly delete an attached file from an e-mail message on the iPad at this writing. You can delete only the message along with its attached file. If you use an e-mail app such as Apple Mail to manage the same e-mail account, you can remove the attached file using that app. When you update your mailbox on your iPad, the iPad deletes the attached file but leaves the message.

Search for E-Mail Messages

To find a particular e-mail message, you can open the inbox for the account that contains it and then browse for the message. But often you can locate a message more quickly by searching for it using a name or keyword that you know appears in the message's From field, To field, or Subject field. You cannot search the bodies of messages at this writing.

You can search either in a single inbox or in all your inboxes at once. Searching all inboxes is useful when you are not sure which e-mail account contains the message.

Search for E-Mail Messages

1 Press the Home button.

The Home screen appears.

2 Tap **Mail**.

The Mailboxes screen appears.

3 Tap the inbox you want to open.

A Tap **All Inboxes** if you want to search all your inboxes for the message.

The inbox opens.

4 Tap in the Search box.

The Search controls appear.

 Type your search term.

A list of search results appears.

 Optionally, tap a different item in the bar under the search box: **From**, **To**, **Subject**, or **All**.

Note: Selecting **All** in the Search bar makes Mail search the From, To, and Subject fields, not the full content of messages.

Mail updates the search results.

 Tap the message you want to open.

The message appears.

Is there another way to search for e-mail messages?

Yes. You can use the iPad's general search functionality to return e-mail matches along with other search results. Press the Home button to display the Home screen, and then press again to display the Search screen. Type your search term, locate the Mail search results, and then tap the message you want to see.

CHAPTER 8

Working with Contacts and Calendars

Your iPad can manage your contacts, keep your schedule, and track your commitments.

Explore Ways of Syncing Your Contacts and Calendars

Your iPad is great for carrying your contacts and calendars with you so that you can keep in touch and on schedule wherever you go. To fully exploit these features, you must sync your contacts and calendars among your iPad, your computer, and your other devices — and you must make sure you do not get duplicate data by syncing the wrong way.

If you have an iCloud account, the best way to sync your contacts and calendars is through iCloud. If you do not have an iCloud account, you can sync your contacts and calendars directly with your computer.

Sync Contacts and Calendars through iCloud

If you have an iCloud account, sync your contacts and calendars through iCloud rather than syncing directly with your computer. Your iOS devices and computers then automatically upload changes to your contacts and calendar to iCloud, download the changes from iCloud, and integrate them.

To sync your contacts and calendars through iCloud, you set up iCloud on each computer and device. For example, on your iPad, tap **Settings** on the Home screen, and then tap **iCloud** on the Settings screen. Sign in to your iCloud account if you have not already done so. Then set the **Contacts** switch (Ⓐ) and the **Calendars** switch (Ⓑ) to the On position to turn on syncing.

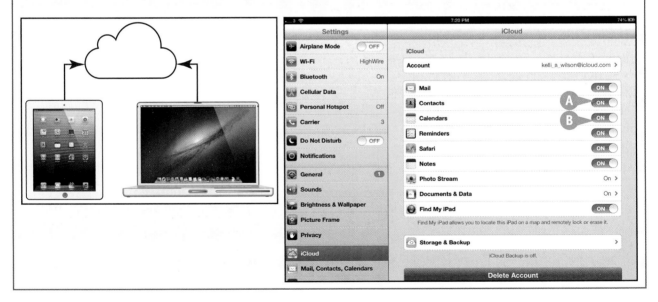

Sync Contacts and Calendars Directly with Your Computer

If you do not have an iCloud account, you can sync your contact and calendar data directly between your computer and your iPad using iTunes.

First, connect your iPad to your computer using the USB-to-Lightning cable. If you have set up Wi-Fi sync, you can connect your iPad via wireless instead. Launch iTunes on your computer if iTunes does not launch automatically.

Next, click the iPad's entry in the Devices category in the Source list (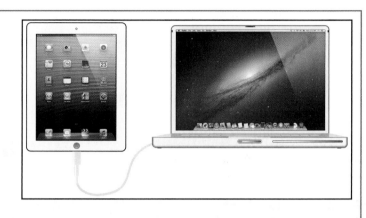) in iTunes to display the control screens. Click **Info** to display the Info screen, click **Sync Contacts** (☐ changes to ☑) and **Sync Calendars** (☐ changes to ☑) and choose which contacts and calendars to sync. Click **Apply** to apply the changes and run the sync.

After you specify the contacts and calendars to sync, you can keep them synced by connecting your iPad to your computer. If the sync does not run automatically on connection, click the iPad's entry in the Devices category in the Source list to display the control screens, and then click **Sync**.

Browse or Search for Contacts

To see which contacts you have synced to your iPad, or to find a particular contact, you can browse through the contacts.

You can either browse through your full list of contacts or choose to display only particular groups — for example, you can display only your business-related contacts by selecting the appropriate group. You can also search for contacts to locate them.

Browse or Search for Contacts

Browse Your Contacts

1 Press the Home button.

The Home screen appears.

2 Tap **Contacts**.

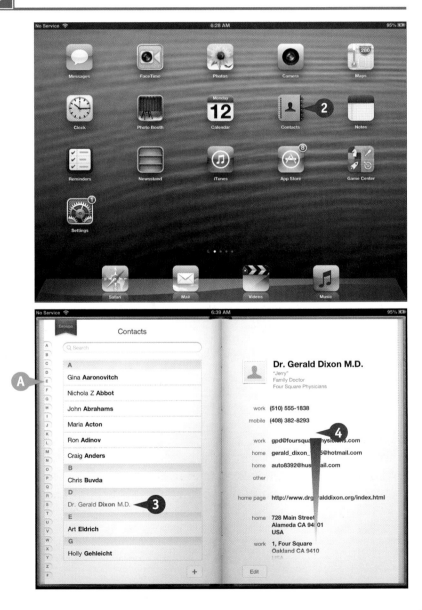

The Contacts screen appears.

Ⓐ To navigate the screen of contacts quickly, tap the letter on the left that you want to jump to. To navigate more slowly, scroll up or down.

3 Tap the contact whose information you want to view.

The contact's details appear.

4 If necessary, tap and drag up to scroll down the screen to display more information.

Choose Which Groups of Contacts to Display

1 From the Contacts list, tap **Groups**.

2 In the Groups list, tap **Show All Contacts**.

Contacts displays a check mark next to each group.

Note: When you tap **Show All Contacts**, the Hide All Contacts button appears in place of the Show All Contacts button. You can tap **Hide All Contacts** to remove all the check marks.

3 Tap a group to remove its existing check mark or apply a check mark.

4 Tap **Done**.

The Contacts list appears, showing the contacts in the groups you selected.

Search for Contacts

1 From the Contacts list, tap **Search**.

2 On the Search screen, type the name you want to search for.

3 From the list of matches, tap the contact you want to view.

The contact's information appears.

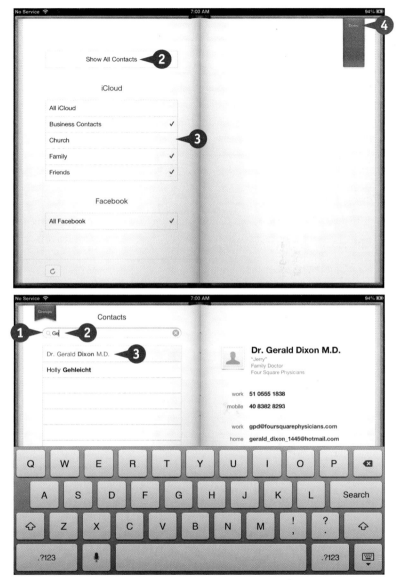

How do I make my iPad sort my contacts by last names instead of first names?

Press the Home button. Tap **Settings** and then **Mail, Contacts, Calendars**. In the Contacts box, tap **Sort Order**. Tap **Last, First**.

What does "Unified Info" mean at the top of a contact record?

Unified Info means that Contacts is displaying information drawn from two or more contact records for the same contact. Look at the Linked Contacts area of the screen to see which contact records are providing the information.

Create a New Contact

Normally, you put contacts on your iPad by syncing them from existing records on your computer or on an online service such as iCloud. But when necessary, you can create a new contact on your iPad itself — for example, when you meet someone you want to remember.

You can then sync the contact record back to your computer, adding the new contact to your existing contacts.

Create a New Contact

1 Press the Home button.

The Home screen appears.

2 Tap **Contacts**.

The Contacts screen appears.

3 Tap **Add** (+).

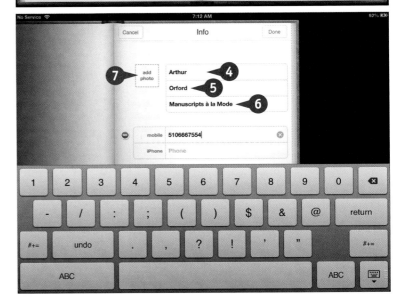

The New Contact screen appears, with the on-screen keyboard displayed.

4 Type the first name.

5 Type the last name.

6 Add other information as needed by tapping each field and then typing the information.

7 To add a photo of the contact, tap **add photo**.

The Photo dialog opens.

8 To use an existing photo, tap **Choose Photo** and follow this example. To take a new photo, tap **Take Photo** and see the tip.

The Photos dialog opens.

9 Tap the album that contains the photo you want to use.

The album's contents appear.

10 Tap the appropriate photo.

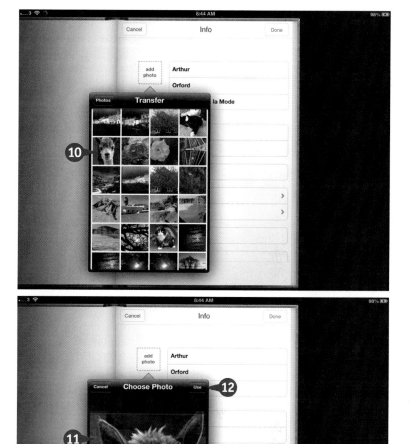

The Move and Scale screen appears.

11 Position the part of the photo you want to use in the middle.

Note: Pinch in with two fingers to zoom the photo out. Pinch out with two fingers to zoom the photo in.

12 Tap **Use**.

The photo appears in the contact record.

 TIP

How do I take a new photo of my contact?

1 In the Photo dialog, tap **Take Photo**.

2 In the Take Picture dialog, compose the photo, and then tap **Take Picture** (🔘).

3 On the Move and Scale screen, position the photo, and then tap **Use Photo**.

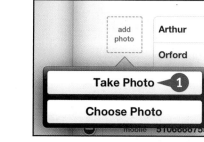

Share Contacts via E-Mail and Instant Messages

Often in business or your personal life, you will need to share your contacts with other people. Your iPad makes it easy to share a contact record either via e-mail or via Messages, Apple's instant-messaging service.

The iPad shares the contact record as a virtual business card in the widely used vCard format. Most phones and personal-organizer software can easily import vCard files.

Share Contacts via E-Mail and Instant Messages

Open the Contact You Want to Share

1 Press the Home button.

The Home screen appears.

2 Tap **Contacts**.

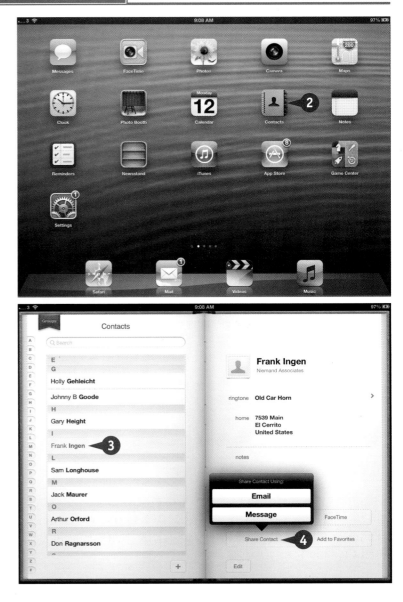

The Contacts screen appears.

3 Tap the contact you want to share.

The contact's details appear.

4 Tap **Share Contact**.

The Share Contact Using dialog opens.

Share a Contact via E-Mail

1. In the Share Contact Using dialog, tap **Email**.

   Ⓐ A new message titled Contact appears in the Mail app, with the contact record attached as a vCard file.

2. Address the message by typing the address or by tapping ⊕ and choosing a contact as the recipient.

3. Type a subject.

4. Type a message.

5. Tap **Send**.

   Mail sends the message with the contact record attached.

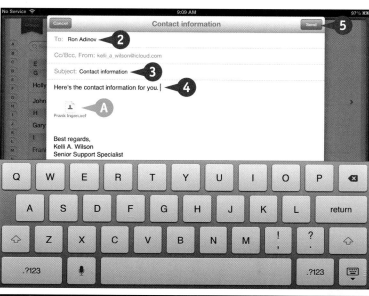

Share a Contact via Messages

1. In the Share Contact Using dialog, tap **Message**.

   Ⓑ The New Message screen appears, with the contact record attached to the message.

2. Address the message by typing the name or number or by tapping ⊕ and choosing a contact as the recipient.

3. Type a message.

4. Tap **Send**.

   iPad sends the message with the contact record attached.

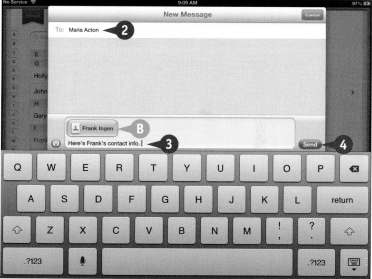

 TIP

How do I add a vCard I receive in an e-mail message to my contacts?
In the Mail app, tap the button for the vCard file. At the bottom of the dialog that opens, tap **Create New Contact**. If the vCard contains extra information about an existing contact, tap **Add to Existing Contact**, and then tap the contact.

Browse Existing Events in Your Calendars

Your iPad's Calendar app gives you a great way of managing your schedule and making sure you never miss an appointment.

After setting up your calendars to sync using iTunes, iCloud, or another calendar service, as described in Chapter 1, you can take your calendars with you everywhere and consult them whenever you need to. You can view all your calendars or only ones you choose.

Browse Existing Events in Your Calendars

Browse Existing Events in Your Calendars

1. Press the Home button.

   The Home screen appears.

2. Tap **Calendar**.

   The Calendar screen appears.

3. Tap **Month** to see Month view, in which each day appears in a box on a calendar chart.

Note: Month view shows a one-line entry with the time of each appointment that will fit in the box.

4. Tap an appointment to view a pop-up dialog showing its details.

5. Tap **Day**.

   The Calendar switches to Day view.

   A You can tap another day to display that day.

   B The left pane lists your appointments in order.

   C The right pane shows a vertical timeline for the day.

6. Tap **List**.

A list of upcoming appointments appears.

⑦ Tap an appointment to display its details.

⑧ To edit the event, tap **Edit**.

The Edit dialog appears, and you can make changes to the event. Tap outside the dialog to close it.

Choose Which Calendars to Display

① Tap **Calendars**.

The Show Calendars dialog appears.

② Tap to place a check mark next to a calendar you want to display, or tap to remove the check mark from a calendar you want to hide.

Ⓓ Tap **Show All Calendars** to place a check mark next to each calendar. Tap **Hide All Calendars** to remove all check marks.

Note: The Birthdays calendar in the Other category displays birthdays of contacts whose contact data includes the birthday.

③ When you finish choosing calendars to display, tap outside the dialog.

The calendars you chose appear.

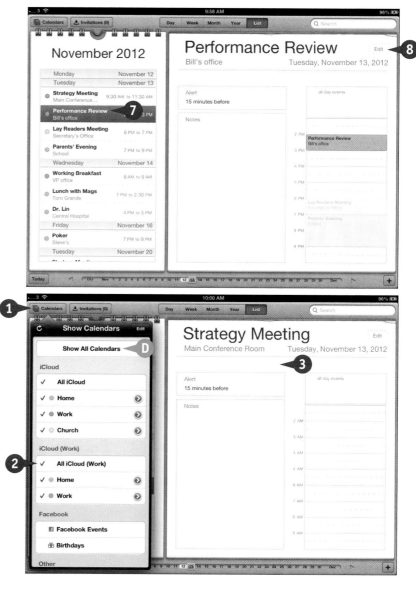

TIP

How can I quickly find an event?
Tap **Search** (Q) in the upper-right corner of the Calendar screen, and then type your search term. When Calendar displays a list of matches, tap the event you want to view.

Create New Events in Your Calendars

Normally, you will probably create most new events in your calendars on your computer, and then sync them to your iPad. But when you need to create a new event using the iPad, you can easily do so.

You can create either a straightforward, one-shot appointment or an appointment that repeats on a schedule. And you can choose which calendar the appointment belongs to.

Create New Events in Your Calendars

1 Press the Home button.

2 On the Home screen, tap **Calendar**.

3 In Calendar, tap **Week** to switch to Week view.

4 Tap and hold the time slot when you want to create the new event.

A New Event box appears where you tapped, and the Add Event dialog opens.

5 Type the title of the event.

6 Optionally, type the location of the event.

7 Tap **Starts, Ends**.

8 In the Start & End dialog, tap the date and time wheels to set the start time.

9 Tap **Ends**.

10 Set the end time.

Ⓐ If this is an all-day appointment, tap the **All-day** switch and move it to On.

Ⓑ If you need to change the time zone, tap **Time Zone**, type the city name, and then tap the time zone.

11 Tap **Done**.

The Add Event dialog reappears.

12 Tap **Alert**.

The Event Alert dialog appears.

13 Tap the timing for the alert — for example, **15 minutes before**.

14 Tap **Done**.

The Add Event dialog reappears.

Note: You can assign a second alert to the event by tapping **Second Alert** after choosing the first alert. A second alert can be a useful safety net for appointments you must not miss.

15 Tap **Calendar**.

The Calendar dialog appears.

16 Tap the calendar to which you want to assign the event.

17 Tap **Done**.

The Add Event dialog reappears.

18 Tap **Done**.

The event appears on your calendar.

TIP

How do I set up an event that repeats every two weeks?
On the Add Event screen, tap **Repeat**. In the Repeat dialog, tap **Every Two Weeks** (Ⓐ), placing a check mark next to it, and then tap **Done**.

Work with Calendar Invitations

As well as events you create yourself, you may receive invitations to events that others create. When you receive an event invitation attached to an e-mail message, you can choose whether to accept the invitation or decline it. If you accept the invitation, you can add the event automatically to a calendar of your choice and set an alert for it.

Work with Calendar Invitations

Deal with an Invitation from an Alert

 When an invitation alert appears, tap **View**.

The Calendar app appears.

A pop-up dialog opens showing brief details of the invitation.

Ⓐ If the pop-up dialog shows you all you need to know, tap **Accept**, **Decline**, or **Maybe** to deal with the invitation.

2 Tap **Details**.

The Event Details dialog appears.

③ To choose which calendar to assign the event to, tap **Calendar**, tap the calendar in the Calendars dialog, and then tap **Done**.

④ To set an alert, tap **Alert**, tap the button for the alert interval — for example, tap **15 minutes before** — and then tap **Done**.

⑤ To control how the calendar shows the event's time, tap **Availability**; tap **Busy** or **Free**, as appropriate; and then tap **Done**.

⑥ Tap **Accept**.

Deal with an Invitation from the Invitations Screen

Ⓑ In your calendar, the Invitations button shows an alert giving the number of invitations.

① Tap **Invitations**.

The Invitations pop-up dialog appears.

② To deal with an invitation immediately, tap **Accept**, **Decline**, or **Maybe**, as needed.

Note: To see the detail of an invitation, tap its button in the Invitations pop-up dialog. A pop-up dialog with the invitation's details appears where you can accept the invitation.

TIP

Why does an event appear at a different time than that shown in the invitation I accepted?

When you open the invitation, you see the event's time in the time zone in which it was created. If your iPad is currently using a different time zone, the appointment appears in your calendar using your time zone's time, so the time appears to have changed.

Keep Track of Your Commitments with Reminders

Your iPad's Reminders app gives you an easy way to note your commitments and keep track of them.

You can create a reminder with no due time, but to track your commitments, you may want to tie a reminder to a due time. When you create such reminders, your iPad can remind you of them at the appropriate time. If your iPad has cellular connectivity, you can also create location-based reminders. The iPad reminds you of such reminders when you reach or leave the specified location.

Keep Track of Your Commitments with Reminders

Open the Reminders App

1 Press the Home button.

The Home screen appears.

2 Tap **Reminders**.

The Reminders screen appears.

Note: When you complete a task, tap ☐ to the left of the reminder (☐ changes to ☑).

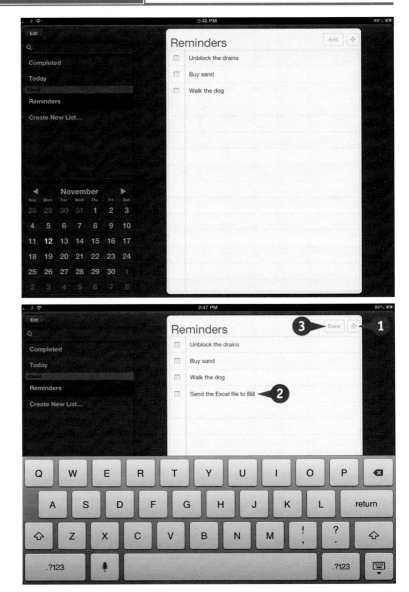

Create a New Reminder

1 In the Reminders app, tap ✛.

Reminder starts a new reminder beneath the last reminder, and displays the on-screen keyboard.

2 Type the text of the reminder.

3 Tap **Done**.

Note: To create a reminder using Siri, press the Home button for a couple of seconds until Siri bleeps, and then say the reminder aloud. For example, say "Remind me at 8 a.m. tomorrow to take the project files to the office."

The new reminder appears in the list.

④ Tap the new reminder.

The Details dialog appears.

⑤ Tap the **Remind Me On a Day** switch and move it to the On position.

A date and time button appears.

⑥ Tap the date and time button.

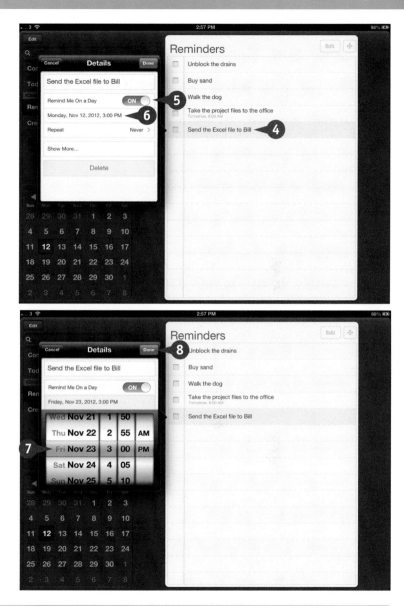

Date and time spin wheels appear.

⑦ Select the date and time for the reminder.

⑧ Tap **Done**.

TIP

How do I sync my iPad's reminders with my Mac's reminders?

Use your iCloud account to sync your iPad's reminders with your Mac's reminders.

On your iPad, press the Home button to display the Home screen, and then tap **Settings** to display the Settings screen. Tap **iCloud** to display the iCloud screen, and then move the **Reminders** switch to the On position.

On your Mac, click and **System Preferences** to open System Preferences. Click **iCloud** to display the iCloud dialog, and then select the **Calendars & Reminders** check box (changes to).

You can organize your reminders into different lists so that you can look at a single category of reminders at a time. For example, you may find it useful to create a Work list that enables you to focus on your work-related reminders.

After creating lists, you can easily switch among them. You can also move a reminder from one list to another as needed. And when you no longer need a particular reminder, you can delete it.

Keep Track of Your Commitments with Reminders (continued)

Create Different Lists of Reminders

1 On the Reminders screen, tap **Create New List**.

2 Type the name for the new list.

3 Tap **Done**. The Reminders app adds the new list to the Lists screen.

Switch among Your Reminders Lists

1 On the Reminders screen, tap the list you want to display.

A The list appears.

Change the List to Which a Reminder Is Assigned

1 In a Reminders list, tap the reminder.

The Details dialog appears.

2 Tap **Show More**.

Further controls appear, including the List button.

3 Tap **List**.

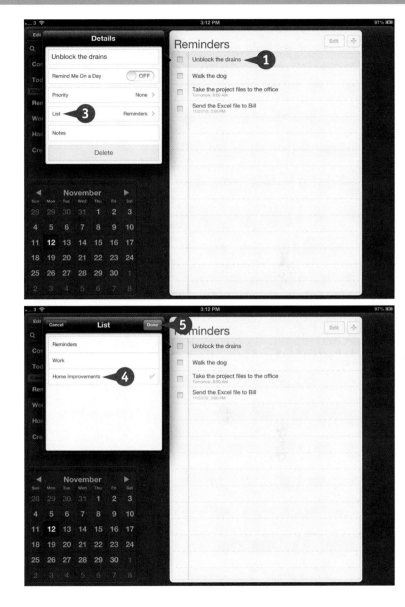

The List dialog appears.

4 Tap the list to which you want to assign the reminder.

5 Tap **Done**.

The Details dialog appears.

6 Tap **Done**.

The Details dialog closes.

The reminder moves to the list you chose.

Note: You can delete a reminder by tapping **Delete** on its Details dialog, and then tapping **Delete** in the confirmation dialog that appears.

TIP

Can I change the default list that Reminders puts my reminders in?
Yes. You can change the default list in the Settings app. Press the Home button to display the Home screen, and then tap **Settings** to display the Settings screen. Tap **Reminders** in the left column to display the Reminders screen, tap **Default List** to display the Default List screen, and then tap the list you want to make the default. On the Reminders screen, you can also choose how many reminders to sync — **2 Weeks**, **1 Month**, **3 Months**, **6 Months**, or **All Reminders**.

CHAPTER 9

Playing Music, Videos, and Games

As well as being a powerful handheld computer, your iPad is also a full-scale music and video player and gaming device.

Play Back Music Using the Music App

fter loading music on your iPad as described in the task "Choose Which Items to Sync" in Chapter 1, you can play it back using the Music app.

You can play music in several ways. You can play music by song or by album, as described in this task. You can play songs in exactly the order you want by creating a custom playlist, as described later in this chapter. You can also play by artist, by genre, or by composer.

Play Back Music Using the Music App

1 Press the Home button.

The Home screen appears.

2 Tap **Music**.

The Music screen appears.

3 Tap the button by which you want to sort. This example uses **Albums**.

The list of albums appears.

Ⓐ To see the music listed by other categories, such as Composers or Genres, tap **More**, and then tap the category by which you want to sort.

4 Tap and drag up to scroll down the screen if necessary.

5 Tap the album you want to play.

A screen opens showing the album's songs that are on your iPad.

6 Tap the song you want to play.

The song starts playing.

7 Tap and drag the slider to change the position in the song.

8 Tap 🔁 once to turn on repeating (🔁), again to repeat only the current song (🔂), and a third time to turn off repeating (🔁).

9 Tap 🔀 to turn on shuffling (🔀). Tap again to turn off shuffling (🔀).

10 Tap ⚛ to create a Genius automatic playlist based on this song.

Note: To use Genius, you must first enable it. See the task "Enable Genius Playlists in iTunes," later in this chapter.

11 If you want to change view, tap the thumbnail of the album cover.

The album cover appears full screen.

12 Tap 📋 if you want to see the song list. From here, you can rate the current song or tap another song to start playing it. Tap 📋 again to go back to the album cover.

13 Tap the thumbnail to return to the previous view.

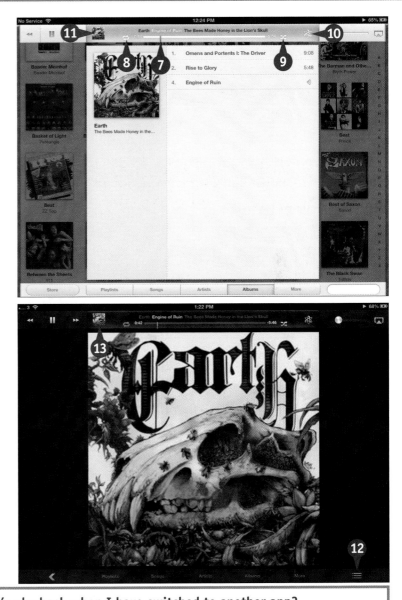

Is there a way to control the Music app's playback when I have switched to another app?
Yes. You can quickly control the Music app using the app-switching bar. Press the Home button twice in quick succession to display the app-switching bar, and then scroll left until you see the playback controls. Tap **Pause** (⏸) to pause the music, and tap **Play** (▶) to restart playback. Tap **Fast-Forward/Next** (⏭) to skip to the next track, or tap and hold to fast-forward. Tap **Rewind/Previous** (⏮) to go back to the beginning of the track, tap again to go to the previous track, or tap and hold to rewind. Tap **Music** (🎵) to display the Music app.

Play Back Videos Using the Videos App

To play videos — such as movies, TV shows, or music videos — you use the iPad's Videos app. You can play back a video either on the iPad's screen, which is handy when you are traveling, or on a TV to which you connect the iPad, or to a TV connected to an Apple TV box. Using a TV is great when you need to share a movie or other video with family, friends, or colleagues.

Play Back Videos Using the Videos App

1 Press the Home button.

The Home screen appears.

Note: You can also play most videos that are included on web pages. To do so, press Home, tap **Safari**, navigate to the page, and then tap the video.

2 Tap **Videos**.

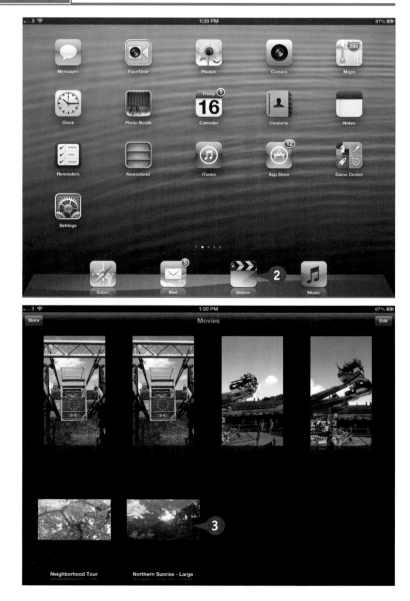

The Videos screen appears.

Note: Tap and drag up to scroll down the screen to see more videos.

3 Tap the video you want to play.

Note: Your iPad plays video in the orientation it was shot or produced — typically landscape orientation. So if you are holding the iPad in its upright, portrait orientation, turn it on its side for viewing the video.

The video's information screen appears.

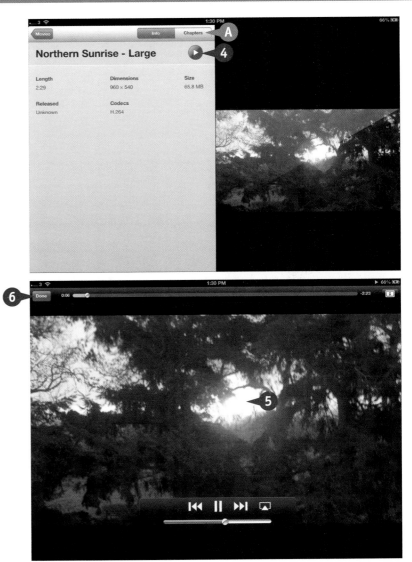

A Tap **Chapters** to see a list of the video's chapters.

Note: A chapter is a subdivision of a video — for example, a movie on a DVD is normally divided into chapters. You can skip forward to the next chapter or back to the previous chapter. Many videos have only a single chapter.

④ Tap .

The video starts playing.

⑤ When you need to control playback, tap the screen.

The playback controls appear, and you can pause the video, move forward, or take other actions.

⑥ Tap **Done** when you want to stop playing the video.

TIP

How do I play back videos on my television from my iPad?

First, check which connectors the television uses, and then get a suitable connector cable from the Apple Store (http://store.apple.com) or another supplier. For example, you may need the Apple Composite AV Cable or an equivalent for a standard TV. If possible, use a component connection for a standard TV, and use an HDMI connection for an HDTV.

Second, use the cable to connect the iPad's Lightning port to the television.

Third, tap **Settings**, tap **General**, and then tap **TV Out** to display the TV Out screen. Tap the **Widescreen** switch and move it to On or Off, as needed. To change the TV output, tap **TV Signal**, and then tap **NTSC** or **PAL**, as needed.

Create a Playlist with the Music App

Instead of playing individual songs or playing a CD's songs from start to finish, you can create a playlist that contains only the songs you want in your preferred order. Playlists are a great way to enjoy music on your iPad.

You can create either a standard playlist by putting the songs in order yourself, or use the Genius Playlist feature to have the Music app create the playlist for you. Before you can use the Genius Playlist feature, you must turn on Genius in iTunes and then sync your iPad.

Create a Playlist with the Music App

1 Press the Home button.

The Home screen appears.

2 Tap **Music**.

The Music screen appears.

3 Tap **Playlists**.

The Playlists screen appears.

Ⓐ The Genius symbol ( ) indicates a Genius playlist.

4 Tap **New**.

The New Playlist dialog opens.

5 Type the name for the playlist.

6 Tap **Save**.

The Songs screen appears.

7 Tap ⊕ for each song you want to add, or simply tap the song's button.

B The song button fades to gray to show you have added the song to the playlist.

C To browse by artists for songs to add, tap **Artists**. To browse by playlists, tap **Playlists**. To browse by albums, tap **Albums**.

8 Tap **Done**.

The screen for editing the playlist appears.

9 Tap ☰ and drag a song up or down to move it.

D To remove a song, tap ⊖ and then tap **Delete**.

E To add further songs, tap **Add Songs**.

10 Tap **Done** when you finish editing the playlist.

11 Tap a song to start the playlist playing.

F Tap **Shuffle** if you want to play the playlist's songs in random order.

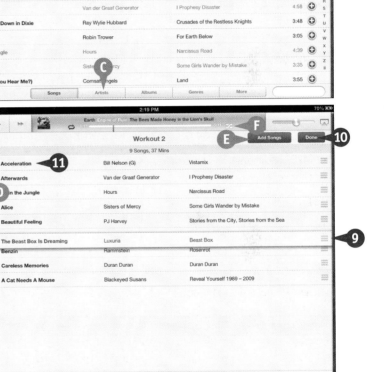

TIP

How do I delete a playlist?
In the Music app, tap **Playlists** to display the Playlists screen. Tap and hold the playlist you want to delete until ⊗ (**A**) appears, and then tap ⊗. The Music app deletes the playlist.

Enable Genius Playlists in iTunes

Creating a Genius playlist in the Music app is like having your own personalized radio station. Just play a song and tap the Genius icon. iTunes creates a playlist based upon the song you chose by selecting songs from your music library that have common features with the chosen song.

Before you can create a Genius playlist on your iPad, you must first turn the Genius feature. If you sync with a computer, you turn Genius on iTunes on the computer, and then sync. If you do not sync with a computer, you turn on the Genius feature in the iTunes app on the iPad.

Enable Genius Playlists in iTunes

1 Click **Genius** in the iTunes Source list.

2 Click **Turn On Genius**.

3 Type your iTunes Store account ID and password.

4 Click **Continue**.

5 Read the terms and conditions and then click the check box to select it (☐ changes to ☑).

6 Click **Agree**.

iTunes gathers information about your music library.

7 Sync your iPad to iTunes on your computer.

Note: Chapter 1 shows you how to sync your iPad to iTunes.

When the sync is complete, Genius playlists are enabled on your iPad.

Note: Genius chooses music using various separate pieces of information. For example, Genius uses tag information such as genre, beats per minute, and year to identify songs that have similarities. Genius also uses information drawn from the billions of songs purchased on the iTunes Store. For example, if many people who buy one song also buy another song, Genius factors this information into its mixes.

TIP

How do I turn on the Genius feature without using a computer?
If you do not use a computer, you can turn on Genius within the iTunes app on your iPad. Press the Home button to display the Home screen, tap **iTunes**, tap the **Genius**, and then tap **Turn On Genius**.

Create a Genius Playlist

Once you have enabled Genius in iTunes on your computer and then synced your iPad, creating a Genius playlist on your iPad is very simple. All you need do is play the song on which you want to base the Genius playlist and then tap the Genius icon.

Once the Genius list is created, you have very little manual control over the process. But if you are unhappy with the song list that Genius provides, you can edit that playlist.

Create a Genius Playlist

1 Tap the song on which to base the Genius playlist.

The song begins to play.

2 Tap ⚛ in the Now Playing pane.

iTunes builds a Genius playlist that appears in your music library's Playlist section as the song you picked is playing.

3 Tap **Playlists**.

The Playlists screen appears, showing all your playlists.

4 Tap **Genius Playlist**.

The contents of the Genius Playlist appear, and you can see the list of songs that Genius has picked.

Ⓐ If you want Genius to try again, tap **Refresh**. You can do this multiple times if needed.

5 Tap **Save**.

Ⓑ The Genius playlist takes on the name of the song from which you started.

6 If you want to edit the playlist, tap **Edit**. You can then edit the playlist using the techniques explained in the task "Create a Playlist with the Music App" earlier in this chapter.

7 When you are ready to return to the Playlists screen, tap **Playlists**.

TIP

Why does Genius tell me to try again when I pick a song to start a Genius playlist?
The less popular the artist, song, or genre, the more likely that Genius cannot compile a suitable playlist from that song. The bigger the music library you have, along with an eclectic mix of artists and genres, this becomes less of an issue. You should already have a good idea of what kind of music is in your library. For best results with Genius playlists, pick an artist or genre that you know you have sufficient content for Genius to pull from.

Use the Shuffle, Repeat, and AirPlay Features

Your iPad's Music app gives you several convenient playback options for enjoying your music. This task shows you how to use the Shuffle feature to mix up your music into a random order and the Repeat feature to repeat either an entire selection — such as an album or a playlist — or a single song.

When playing music on your iPad, you may want to use the AirPlay feature to transmit the music to an AirPort Express, an Apple TV, or AirPlay-enabled speakers.

Use the Shuffle, Repeat, and AirPlay Features

Use the Shuffle Feature

1 Open the item you want to play. For example, tap **Albums** and then tap the album you will listen to.

The Music app displays the album's songs in the album's order.

2 Tap the **Play/Pause** button (▶).

3 Tap  to turn the Shuffle feature on.

The Music app starts playing songs from the library, or playlist, in a randomized order.

Use the Repeat Feature

1 Open the item that contains the songs you want to play. For example, tap **Artists**, tap the artist, and then tap the album.

2 Tap the **Play/Pause** button (▶).

The song starts to play.

3 Tap to cycle through repeat modes: repeat all songs in order, repeat current song only, and no repeat.

TIP

How do I use the AirPlay feature?

If you have an AirPort Express wireless access point, an Apple TV, or an AirPlay-enabled speaker system, you can play music through it by using AirPlay. Tap to open the AirPlay dialog, and then tap the speakers (**A**) you want to use. When you are ready to switch back to the iPad, tap again, and then tap **iPad**.

Configure iPad Audio Settings

To make your music sound the way you want it, you can change the Equalizer, or EQ, preset. The EQ offers presets that help to accentuate music from a wide range of genres including Rock, Hip Hop, Jazz, Piano, and Vocal Latin. The EQ even includes Spoken Word and Vocal Booster presets for improving podcasts and audiobooks.

EQ presets change the sound quality as soon as you apply them. Some settings are more noticeable than others. Which EQ is best depends on your music, your speakers or headphones, and your ears.

Configure iPad Audio Settings

1 Press the Home button.

The Home screen appears.

2 Tap **Settings**.

The Settings screen appears.

3 Tap the left column and scroll down until iTunes & App Stores appears at the top.

4 Tap **Music**.

The Music settings appear.

5 Set the **Sound Check** switch to the On position to have iTunes play songs at the same level or to Off to play each song at its own level.

6 Tap **EQ**.

The EQ options appear.

Note: The EQ options are audio presets that you can choose to customize audio playback on your iPad.

7 Tap an EQ option to select it.

A A check mark appears next to the option you have chosen.

Note: Playing music with an EQ preset uses a little more battery power than playing without a preset.

 8 Tap **Music**.

The Music screen appears again.

9 Tap **Volume Limit** to set a maximum volume at which audio can be played back on your iPad.

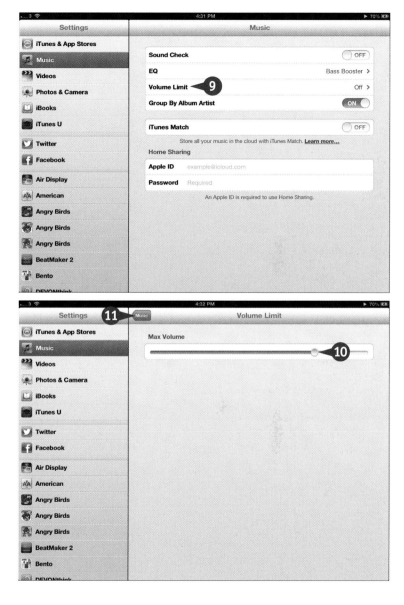

The Volume Limit slider appears.

10 Drag the slider to the desired level.

11 Tap **Music**.

The Music screen appears once more.

TIP

Can I keep the volume limit from being changed after I set it?

Yes. Set the volume limit as described in this task, and then apply restrictions. In the Settings app, tap **General**, tap **Restrictions**, and then enter a passcode to lock the restrictions. On the Restrictions screen, tap **Enable Restrictions**, and then tap **Volume Limit**. On the Volume Limit screen, tap **Don't Allow Changes**.

Enjoy Podcasts

Besides listening to music and watching videos, you can use your iPad to watch or listen to *podcasts*, which are video or audio programs released via the Internet. You can find podcasts covering many different topics by using Apple's free Podcasts app. Podcasts can be entertaining, educational, or both.

Before you can enjoy podcasts on your iPad, you must download and install Apple's Podcasts app from the App Store. See Chapter 6 for instructions on installing apps from the App Store.

1 Press the Home button.

The Home screen appears.

2 Tap **Podcasts**.

The Podcasts app opens, showing your library — the podcasts on your iPad.

A At first, when you have added no podcasts, you see an informational message.

3 Tap **Store**.

The Store screen appears.

4 Tap the category of podcasts you want to see.

The category's screen appears.

Note: You can also search for podcasts by tapping **Search Store** and then typing search terms in the Search box.

5 Tap a podcast that interests you.

6 Tap **Subscribe** if you want to subscribe to the podcast.

7 Tap ⬇ to download an episode of the podcast.

8 Tap **Library**.

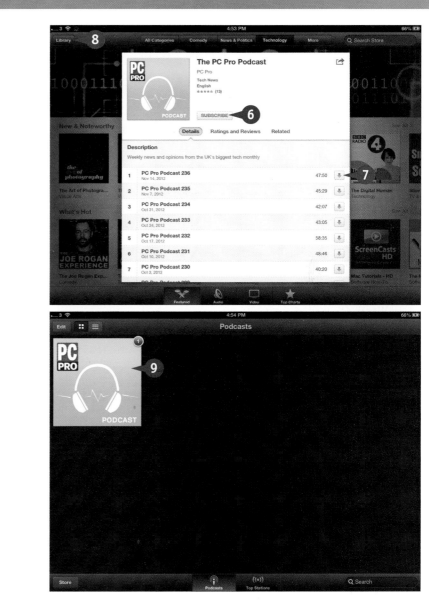

Your library appears, now showing the podcast or podcasts you have added.

9 Tap the podcast whose episodes you want to play.

10 Tap the episode you want to play.

TIP

Are there other ways to get podcasts?
If you sync your iPad with a computer, you can use iTunes to download podcasts and then sync them to your iPad. To access and subscribe to podcasts in iTunes, click **Podcasts** in the Library category in the Source list.

Learn with iTunes U

iTunes U is a free app for watching lessons and courses on your iPad or other iOS device. You can download a wide variety of lessons and courses for free from the iTunes Store and study them on your iPad. Schools and colleges can develop iTunes U content and distribute it via the iTunes Store.

Before you can watch iTunes U lectures on your iPad, you must download and install Apple's iTunes U app from the App Store. See Chapter 6 for instructions on installing apps from the App Store.

Learn with iTunes U

1 Press the Home button.

The Home screen appears.

2 Tap **iTunes U**.

The iTunes U app opens, showing your library — the iTunes U lessons on your iPad.

A At first, when you have added no lessons, you see an informational message.

3 Tap **Catalog**.

The Store screen appears.

4 Tap the category of content you want to see.

The category's screen appears.

Note: You can also search for courses by tapping **Search Store** and then typing search terms in the Search box.

5 Tap a course that interests you.

Tap **Subscribe** if you want to subscribe to the course.

 Tap ⬇ to download a lesson from the course.

 Tap **Library**.

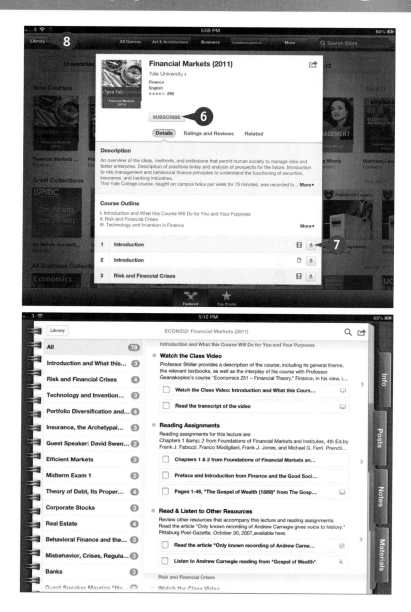

Your library appears, now showing the course or courses you have added.

 Tap the course whose lessons you want to view.

The lesson opens, and you can start working on it.

TIP

Are there other ways to get iTunes U courses?

If you sync your iPad with a computer, you can use iTunes to download courses and lessons and then sync them to your iPad. To access iTunes U content in iTunes, click **iTunes U** in the Library category in the Source list. To subscribe to iTunes U content in iTunes, click **iTunes Store** in the Store category in the Source list, and then click **iTunes U**.

Shop for Music and Videos at the iTunes Store

To find music and videos for your iPad, you can shop at Apple's iTunes Store by using the iTunes app.

When you buy music or videos from the iTunes Store using the iTunes app, the iPad downloads the files, so you can play them immediately. When you sync your iPad with your computer, iTunes copies the music or videos you have bought to your computer. If you use your iPad without a computer, you can sync the files to iCloud so that you can use them on your other devices — for example, on an iPhone.

Shop for Music and Videos at the iTunes Store

1 Press the Home button.

The Home screen appears.

2 Tap **iTunes**.

The iTunes screen appears.

3 Tap the appropriate button on the button bar to display the type of content you want. This example uses **Music**.

The screen you chose appears.

4 Tap the genre you want to display — for example, **Alternative**.

The genre's screen appears.

5 Tap the album or song you want to display.

The Info dialog for the album or song appears.

A Optionally, tap **Ratings and Reviews** or **Related** to see more information.

6 Tap a song title.

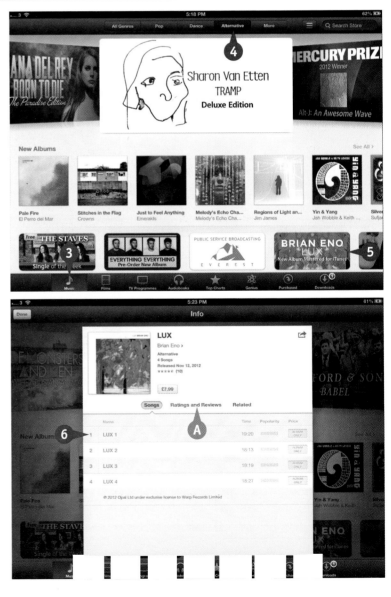

A preview of the song starts playing.

Ⓑ Tap **Stop** (▣) to stop the preview playing.

⑦ To buy the album, tap the price button.

The Buy Album button replaces the price button.

⑧ Tap **Buy Album**.

Note: Many albums have individual songs for sale. To buy a song, tap the song's price button, and then tap the **Buy Song** button that replaces it.

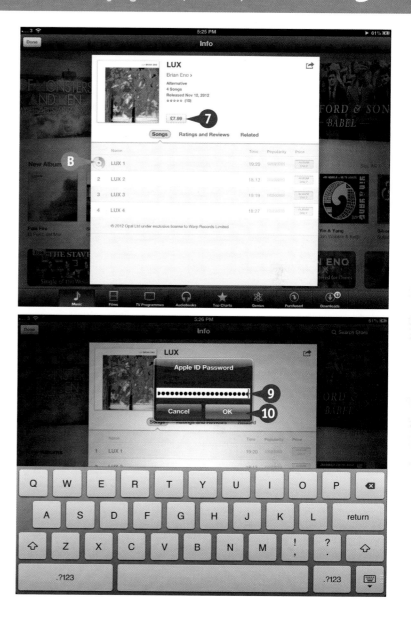

The Apple ID Password dialog opens.

⑨ Type your password.

⑩ Tap **OK**.

iTunes downloads the song, and you can play it using the Music app.

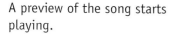

How can I find the music I want at the iTunes Store?
You can easily search for music within the iTunes app. Tap **Search Store** in the upper-right corner of the screen, and then type a search term. iTunes shows matching results as you type. Tap the result you want to view.

Get Genius Recommendations for Music, Video, TV, and Apps

Apple's Genius feature can recommend music, video, and TV shows you may like. Genius for these items is turned on by default, and you can easily view your recommendations in the iTunes Store app.

Genius can also recommend apps for you. This feature is not turned on by default, so you must enable Genius for Apps before you can use it.

Get Genius Recommendations for Music, Video, TV, and Apps

View Genius Recommendations for Music, Video, and TV

 Press the Home button.

The Home screen appears.

2 Tap **iTunes**.

The iTunes screen appears.

3 Tap **Genius**.

The Genius screen appears.

4 Tap the tab for the Genius category you want to see: **Music**, **Movies**, or **TV Shows**.

The list of Genius recommendations appears.

Turn On Genius for Apps and View Suggested Apps

1 Press the Home button.

The Home screen appears.

2 Tap **iTunes**.

The iTunes screen appears.

3 Tap and drag up to scroll down.

The bottom of the screen appears.

4 Tap the **Apple ID** button.

The Apple ID dialog appears.

5 Tap **View Apple ID**.

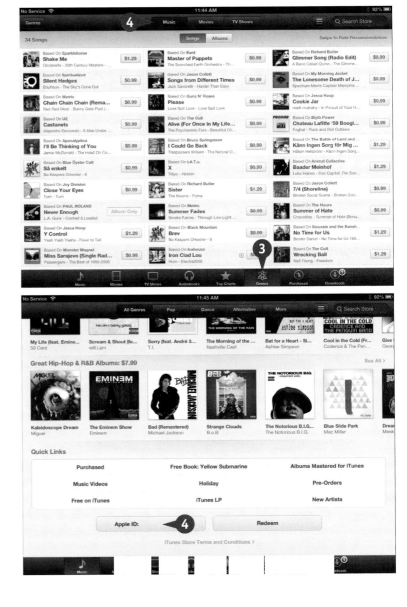

The Account dialog appears.

6 Tap **Turn On Genius for Apps**.

Genius for Apps appears and displays the Genius for Apps Terms and Conditions screen.

7 Tap **Agree**.

A confirmation dialog appears.

8 Tap **Agree** in this dialog, too.

Genius for Apps displays a message that you have successfully turned on Genius for Apps.

9 Tap **Done**.

Genius for Apps displays its suggestions for you.

A Tap **Not Interested** if you want to tell Genius for Apps that a particular type of app does not interest you.

10 Tap an app of interest to display its details.

TIP

How do I run Genius for Apps again?

To run Genius for Apps again, press the Home button, tap **App Store** on the Home screen, and then tap **Genius** on the bar at the bottom of the App Store screen.

Sign In to Game Center

Game Center is a social gaming feature built in to OS X 10.8, Mountain Lion, and in to iOS, the operating system for the iPhone, iPad, and iPod touch. Game Center enables you to take part in a wide range of single-player and multiplayer games.

To start using Game Center, you sign in using your Apple ID. If you do not yet have an Apple ID, you can create one for free within minutes.

Sign In to Game Center

1 Press the Home button.

The Home screen appears.

2 Tap **Game Center**.

Game Center opens, showing the Me screen.

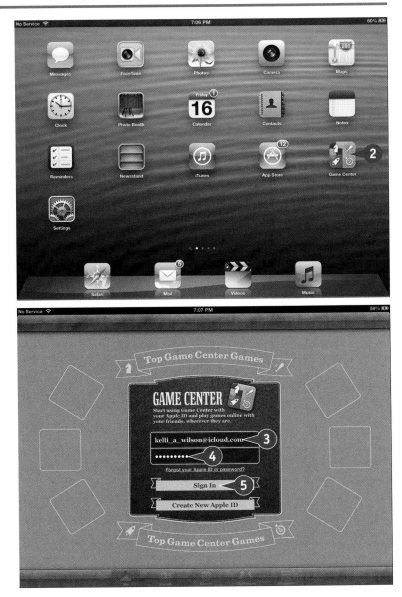

3 Type your Apple ID if your iPad has not filled it in for you.

Note: If you do not have an Apple ID, tap **Create New Apple ID**, and then use the New Account dialog to enter your details.

4 Type your password.

5 Tap **Sign In**.

The first time you sign in to Game Center, the Welcome dialog opens.

6 Type the nickname you want to use.

Note: Your nickname must be unique. When you click **Done**, Game Center warns you if it is not. You can then try another nickname.

7 Set the **Public Profile** switch to On if you want everyone to be able to see you. Set this switch to Off if you want to be hidden from other players.

8 Set the **Contacts** switch to On if you want to upload your contacts to Game Center so you can get personalized friend recommendations.

9 Tap **Done**.

The Me screen appears again.

You can start using Game Center as explained in the next task.

TIPS

Should I set the Public Profile switch and Contacts switch to On or Off?

This is entirely up to you, but generally it is better to err on the side of caution and set both the **Public Profile** switch and the **Contacts** switch to Off while you are coming to grips with Game Center. After you have explored Game Center, you can decide whether to make yourself publicly visible on it.

Can I add more than one e-mail address to my Game Center account?

You can add multiple e-mail addresses to your Game Center account either while setting it up or afterward. During setup, click **Add Another Email** in the Email section of the Create Profile window and follow the prompts. After setup, click **Account** on your home screen, click **View Account**, and then click **Add Another Email** and follow the prompts.

Add and Play Games with Game Center

After setting up your account, as explained in the previous task, you can play games with Game Center.

If your iPad already contains games that work with Game Center, the games will be ready to play when you launch Game Center. You can add further games by opening the App Store application from Game Center and downloading either free or pay games.

Add and Play Games with Game Center

1 In Game Center, tap **Games**.

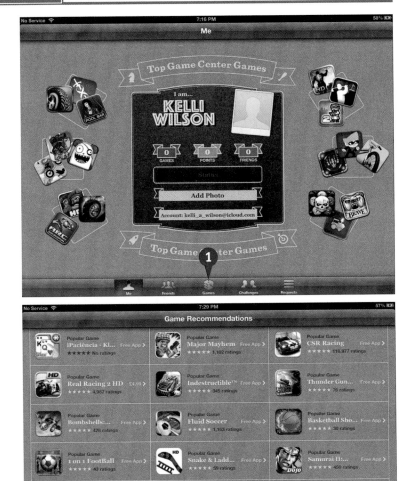

The Games tab appears.

If your iPad has no games compatible with Game Center, the Game Recommendations screen appears.

2 Tap a game that interests you.

The game's Info dialog appears.

3 Tap **Free** or the price button if you want to buy the game.

The Install App button appears in place of the Free button or price button.

4 Tap **Install App**.

The Apple ID Password dialog appears.

5 Type your password.

6 Tap **OK**.

Your iPad downloads and installs the app.

7 After the installation finishes, tap **Play Game**.

The game launches, and you can start playing.

TIP

How can I tell which games work with Game Center?
Each game that works with Game Center has a Game Center logo (Ⓐ) on its detail dialog. Make sure this logo appears on any game you plan to use with Game Center.

Information

Ⓐ   **Game Center**

Developer   Rovio Entertainment
Category   Games
Updated   Oct 26, 2012
Version   1.0.0

Add Friends and Play Games with Them

To get the most out of Game Center, you can add friends to your Friends list and invite them to play games with you. Similarly, other people can invite you to be friends and to play games. When other people send you invitations, you respond accordingly.

Add Friends and Play Games with Them

Send a Friend Request

1. In Game Center, tap **Friends**.

   The Friends screen appears.

2. Tap ➕.

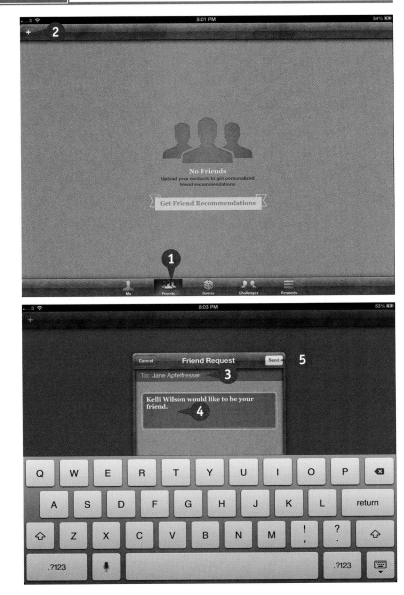

The Friend Request window opens.

3. Start typing your friend's Game Center nickname or e-mail address, and then pick the matching name from the list that appears.

4. Edit the canned message as needed. For example, you may want to make your identity clear by including personalized content.

5. Tap **Send**.

   Game Center sends the friend request.

Note: When your friend accepts the request, Game Center notifies you and adds the friend as a Game Center friend.

Accept a Friend Request

1 In Game Center, tap **Requests**.

The Requests screen appears.

2 In the left column, tap the request.

3 Tap **Accept** if you want to accept the friend request.

Game Center adds the friend to your Friends list.

Respond to Game Invitations

1 When an invitation appears on your screen or on the Challenges tab, tap to open it.

The Play Now button appears.

2 Tap **Play Now**.

The game begins.

TIP

How do I stop someone from being a friend?
If you have accepted the friend, tap **Friends** to display the Friends tab, tap the friend, and then tap **Unfriend**.

CHAPTER 10

Working with Photos and Books

In this chapter, you learn to use your iPad's Photos app to view photos. You also learn to use the iBooks app to read e-books and PDF files.

Browse Your Photos Using Events, Faces, and Places

You can use the Photos app to browse the photos you have taken with your iPad's camera, photos you have synced using iTunes or via your Photo Stream on iCloud, and photos you receive in e-mail messages or download from web pages.

You can browse by albums, by events, faces, and places. An *event* is a named collection of photos associated with a particular date or happening; a *face* is a person's face you teach your Mac to recognize; and a *place* is a geographical location. You can create events and identify faces in iPhoto or Aperture on the Mac.

Browse Your Photos Using Events, Faces, and Places

Open the Photos App and Browse by Albums

1 Press the Home button.

The Home screen appears.

2 Tap **Photos**.

The Photos app opens.

3 Tap **Albums**.

The Albums screen appears.

4 Tap the album you want to view.

Note: The Camera Roll album contains the photos you have taken using the iPad's camera, plus pictures you have saved from e-mail messages, instant messages, and web pages. If you capture screens from your iPad, those go in the Camera Roll too.

The album's screen appears.

5 Tap and drag up to scroll down the screen through the photos.

6 Tap the photo you want to view.

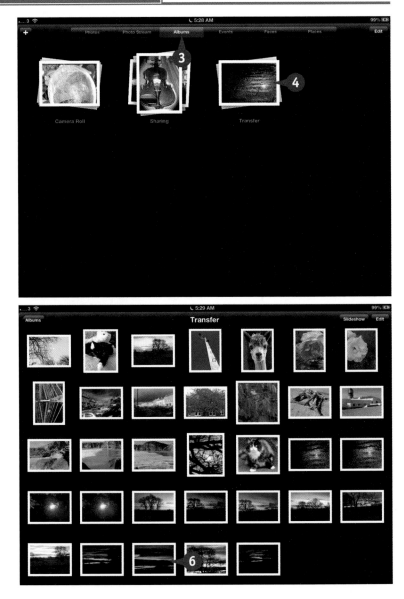

The photo appears.

Note: Swipe your finger to the left to display the next photo, or swipe to the right to display the previous photo.

⑦ Tap the button with the album's name to return to the album's screen.

Browse by Events

① In the Photos app, tap **Events**.

The list of events appears.

② Tap the event you want to view.

TIP

How can I move through a long list of photos more quickly?
You can move through the photos more quickly by using momentum scrolling. Tap and flick up with your finger to set the photos scrolling. As the momentum drops, you can tap and flick up again to scroll further. Tap and drag your finger in the opposite direction to stop the scrolling.

continued ▶

I f you allow the Camera app to access location information on your iPad, the Camera app automatically tags each photo with the GPS information or location information for where you took it. You can then sort your photos by using the Places feature.

Being able to identify photos by location can be great for finding the photos you want. But it means that anybody you share the photos with knows exactly when and where you took them.

Browse Your Photos Using Events, Faces, and Places (continued)

The photos in the event appear.

3 Tap the photo you want to see.

The photo appears.

Note: Swipe your finger to the left to display the next photo, or swipe to the right to display the previous photo.

4 Tap the event name when you want to return to the event.

Browse by Faces

1 In the Photos app, tap **Faces**.

The list of faces appears.

2 Tap the face you want to view.

The list of photos for the face appears.

3 Tap the photo you want to view.

The photo appears.

Note: Swipe your finger to the left to display the next photo, or swipe to the right to display the previous photo.

4 Tap the face's name button to return to the thumbnails of that individual's face.

5 Tap the **Faces** button to return to the Photo library.

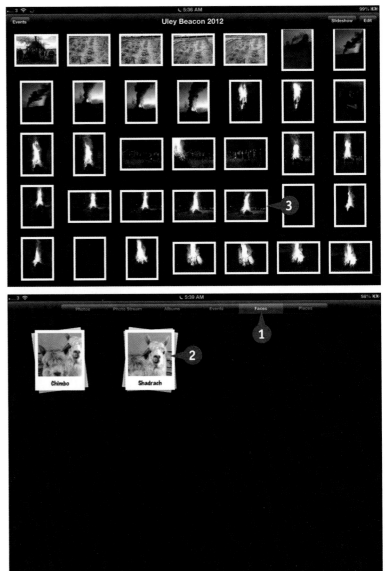

Browse by Places

1 In the Photos app, tap **Places**.

The Places map appears.

2 Pinch out to zoom in on what you want to view.

Note: You can also zoom in by increments by double-tapping the target area of the screen.

3 Tap the pinhead for the place you want to view.

A stack of thumbnails for the photos in the place appears.

4 Tap the top thumbnail.

The photos in the place appear.

5 Tap the photo you want to view.

The photo appears.

Note: Swipe your finger to the left to display the next photo, or swipe to the right to display the previous photo.

6 Tap **Map** to return to the Places map.

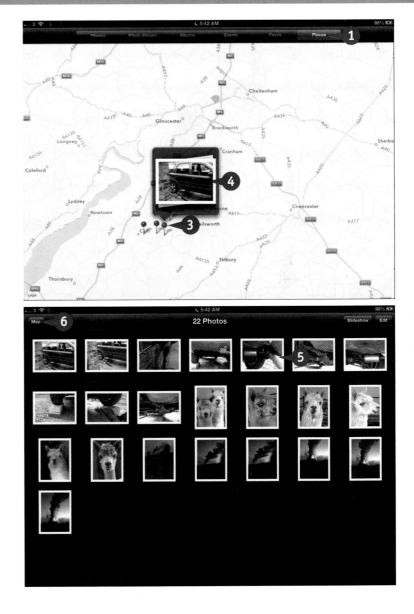

Why does the Photos button bar not show a Faces button?

The Faces button appears on the button bar in the Photos app only when you have synced photos with marked faces using iTunes. You must also have started using the Faces feature in iPhoto or Aperture; if you have not, none of your photos will have marked faces. The iPad does not normally recognize Face information or Place information you assign in an image-editing application in Windows.

Rotate Photos

The Photos application includes essential editing features like those you enjoy in iPhoto and other photo-editing applications, such as the ability to rotate a picture.

If you have a photo where the subject is sideways or upside down, you can use the Rotate feature to rotate the photo so it is the right way up. This works both for photos you take on the iPad and for photos you copy to the iPad. Launch the Photos app from your Home screen before beginning the following steps.

Rotate Photos

1 Open the photo that you want to rotate.

2 Tap **Edit**.

Note: You may need to tap the screen to reveal the controls at the top of the screen. These options disappear after a brief period of inactivity.

Photos opens the photo in Edit view.

3 Tap **Rotate** to rotate the image 90 degrees counterclockwise, until the photo is right side up.

Note: You can tap **Cancel** to abandon the edit.

4 Tap **Save**.

The Save dialog appears.

5 Tap **Save to Camera Roll**.

Note: When you rotate an image, the original image in the album is changed. You can revert the image back to its original state while in Edit view by tapping **Revert to Original**.

Note: There is scaled-down iPhoto app for the iPad that can provide more editing capabilities on your iPad.

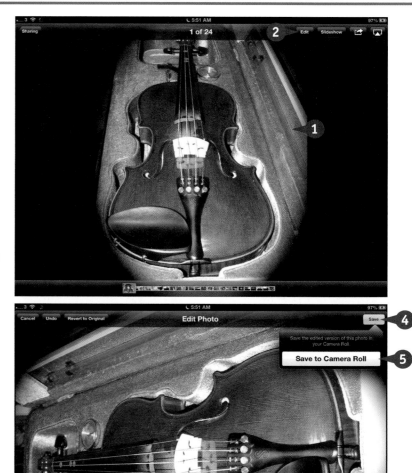

Enhance Photos

To instantly improve the appearance of a photo, use the Enhance feature. Enhance analyzes the brightness of the photo and attempts to improve the color balance by lightening or darkening the photo, raising the contrast, and boosting dull colors. You can use Enhance to toggle between before and after photographs to judge if the automatic enhancement really benefited a particular photograph. Launch the Photos app from your Home screen before beginning the following steps.

Enhance Photos

1 Open the photo that you want to enhance.

2 Tap **Edit**.

Note: You may need to touch the screen to reveal the menu options at the top of the screen. These options disappear after a brief period of inactivity.

Photos opens the photo in Edit view.

3 Tap **Enhance**.

Photos enhances the image.

Note: Tap **Enhance** to toggle Auto-Enhance off and on so you can judge the effect.

4 Tap **Save**.

The Save dialog appears.

5 Tap **Save to Camera Roll**.

Note: When you enhance an image, the original image in the album is changed. You can revert the image back to its original state while in Edit view by tapping **Revert to Original**.

Reduce Red-Eye

Red-eye is a photographic effect that occurs when the camera's flash reflects off the back of the subject's eyes, causing the eyes to glow red. You can use the Red-Eye feature in the Photos app to reduce or remove red-eye. Launch the Photos app from your Home screen before beginning the following steps.

Reduce Red-Eye

1 Open the photo for which you want to reduce red-eye.

2 Tap **Edit**.

Note: You may need to tap the screen to display the controls.

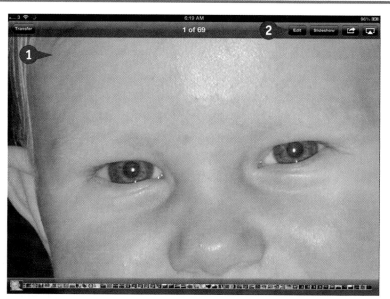

Photos opens the photo in Edit view.

3 Tap **Red-Eye**.

4 Tap each red eye in the photograph.

Photos tries to remove the red-eye.

Note: You can tap each red eye again to undo.

5 Tap **Apply**.

6 Tap **Save**.

The Save dialog appears.

7 Tap **Save to Camera Roll**.

Note: When you remove red-eye from an image, the original image in the album is changed. You can revert the image back to its original state while in Edit view by tapping **Revert to Original**.

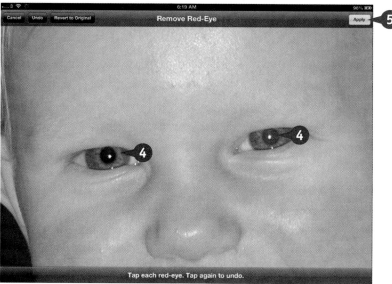

Crop and Straighten Photos

Often, photos you take will include unwanted areas at the edges. To tighten up a photo and emphasize its subject, you can use the Crop feature to remove these unwanted areas. Launch the Photos app from your Home screen before beginning the following steps.

Crop and Straighten Photos

1 Open the photo that you want to crop.

2 Tap **Edit**.

Photos opens the photo in Edit view.

3 Tap **Crop**.

A rectangular grid appears around the photo.

Note: You can tap **Constrain** at the bottom of the interface to choose a specific aspect ratio for the cropping.

4 Drag the top, bottom, corners, or sides of the rectangle to frame the composition of the photo.

Note: To straighten the photo, place two fingers on the screen and rotate them clockwise or counterclockwise.

Note: You can tap **Reset** to undo your crop instructions.

5 Tap **Crop** to crop the actual image.

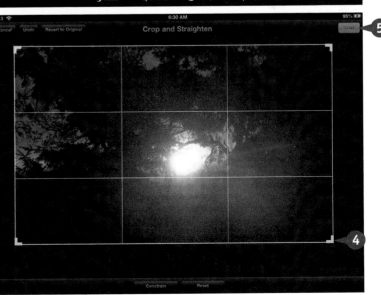

Create Albums

Not only can you sync photo albums you have created on your computer to your iPad, but you can also create albums directly on your iPad. The process is similar to creating a playlist within the Music app, in that you start a new album, name it, and then select the photos you want to include in it. You can create albums to store a collection of photos with a similar theme and include only the photos that you want to view.

Create Albums

1. Select the **Albums** category from within the Photos app.

2. Tap .

The New Album dialog opens.

3. Type the name for the new album.

4. Tap **Save**.

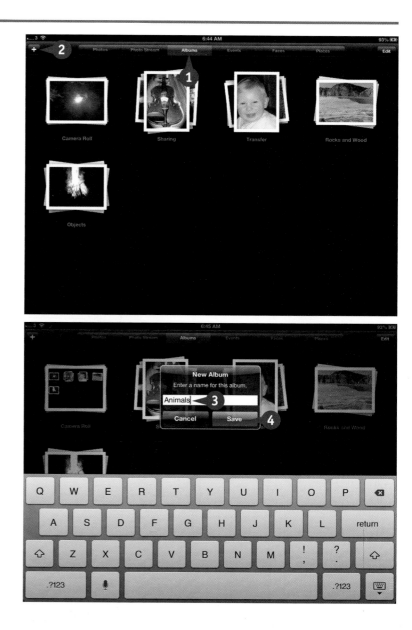

The Photos category automatically opens.

Note: Tap a different photo category to open it. For example, if you prefer to browse by events, tap **Events**.

5 Tap each photo that you want to add to the album.

A check mark appears in the bottom-right corner of each photo that you pick.

Note: Tap **Select All Photos** to add all photos to the album. This may not be a practical option if you have many photos in your library.

6 Tap **Done**.

Photos adds the selected photos to the album.

A The album appears on the Albums screen.

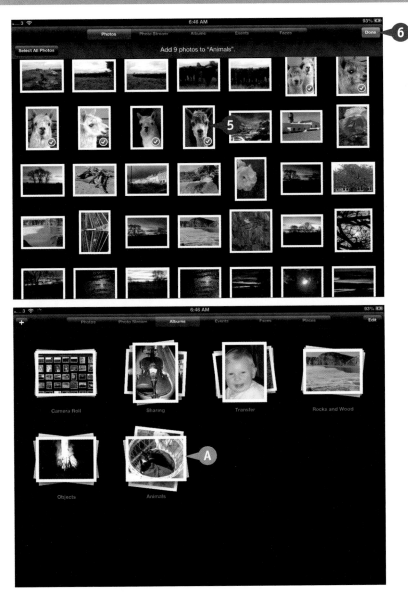

TIP

How do I delete albums from my iPad?
Tap the **Albums** category on the main Photos screen, and then tap **Edit**. An × appears in the upper-left corner of the albums you created on your iPad. You cannot delete albums that you have synced from your computer in this manner. To remove those albums, choose not to sync those albums to your iPad and then run another sync.

Share Your Photos with Your Computers and iOS Devices Using Photo Stream

If you have an iCloud account, you can use the Photo Stream feature to share your photos among your iOS devices and your computer.

After you turn on Photo Stream on your iPad, other iOS devices, and your Macs, Photo Stream automatically syncs your 1,000 most recent photos among the devices and your computers.

Share Your Photos with Your Computers and iOS Devices Using Photo Stream

Turn On Photo Stream on Your iPad

1 Press the Home button.

The Home screen appears.

2 Tap **Settings**.

The Settings screen appears.

3 Tap **iCloud**.

The iCloud screen appears.

4 Tap **Photo Stream**.

The Photo Stream screen appears.

5 Tap the **My Photo Stream** switch and move it to the On position.

6 Tap **iCloud**.

The iCloud screen appears again.

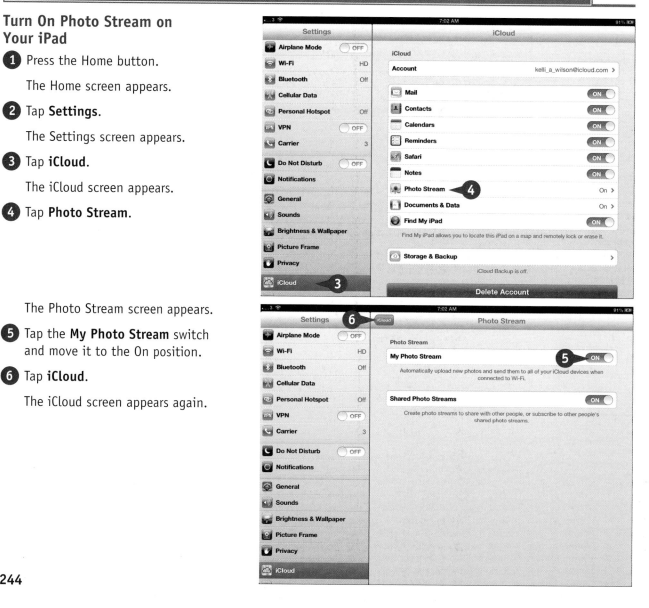

View Photo Stream on Your iPad

1 Press the Home button.

The Home screen appears.

2 Tap **Photos**.

The Photos screen appears, showing the previous screen you used — for example, the Albums screen.

3 Tap **Photo Stream**.

The My Photo Stream screen appears.

4 Tap the photo you want to view.

The photo opens.

Share Photos from Photo Stream

1 On the My Photo Stream screen, tap **Edit**.

The Select Photos screen appears.

2 Tap each photo you want to select.

⊘ appears on each photo you tap.

3 Tap **Share**.

The Share dialog appears.

4 Tap the means of sharing. For example, tap **Mail** to share via e-mail.

Note: You can also delete photos from your photo stream. Select the photos as described here, and then tap **Delete**.

TIP

How do I use Photo Stream on my computer?

On a Mac, click and **System Preferences**, and then click **iCloud** to display the iCloud pane. Click **Photo Stream** (☐ changes to ☑). Click **System Preferences** and **Quit System Preferences**. Next, click **iPhoto** (🖼) on the Dock, and click **Photo Stream** in the Recent list in the sidebar.

In Windows, click **Start** and **Control Panel**. Click **View By** and **Large Icons**, and then click **iCloud**. Click **Photo Stream** (☐ changes to ☑) and **Close**. Now click **Start** and **Computer**, navigate to the Photo Stream folder, and open it.

Share Photo Streams with Other People

When you have set up Photo Stream on your iPad, other iOS devices, and computer, you can not only share your photos among your computers but also share your photos with other people. Similarly, you can view the photo streams other people are sharing.

To share your Photo Stream, you turn on the Shared Photo Streams feature on your iPad. You can then create shared photo streams for specific people or groups of people.

Share Photo Streams with Other People

Turn On Shared Photo Streams

Press the Home button.

On the Home screen, tap **Settings**.

On the Settings screen, tap **iCloud**.

④ On the iCloud screen, tap **Photo Stream**.

⑤ On the Photo Stream screen, tap the **Shared Photo Streams** switch and move it to the On position.

⑥ Tap **iCloud**.

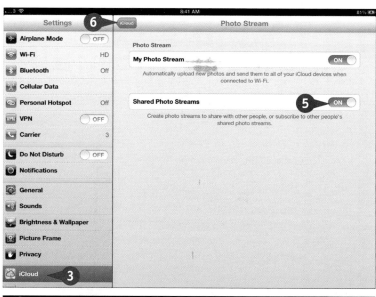

Create a Shared Photo Stream

Press the Home button.

Tap **Photos**.

Tap **Photo Stream**.

④ Tap ➕.

⑤ Tap ⊕ to display the Contacts dialog, and then tap the contact with whom to share the photo stream.

⑥ Tap **Name** and then type the name for the photo stream.

Set the **Public Website** switch to On if you want to make the photo stream public.

Tap **Create**.

246

9 Tap the new photo stream on the Photo Stream screen.

The screen for the photo stream appears.

10 Tap **Add Photos**.

The Add Photos screen appears.

11 Tap the source of photos you want to add. For example, tap **Photos**.

The item opens.

12 Tap each photo you want to add.

13 Tap **Done**.

The photos appear in the photo stream.

TIP

How do I view the Photo Streams other people are sharing?
Turn on Shared Photo Streams as described in this task by moving the Shared Photo Streams switch on the Photo Stream screen to the On position. Next, when you receive an e-mail message prompting you to join a shared photo stream, tap **Join this Photo Stream**. Then, in Photos, tap **Photo Stream**, and then tap the shared photo stream's name.

Share Photos via E-Mail and Messaging

From your iPad's Photos app, you can quickly share a photo either by sending it as an attachment to an e-mail message or by inserting it in a message in the Messages app.

Share Photos via E-Mail and Messaging

Select the Photo and Open the Share Dialog

1. Browse to the photo you want to share — see the preceding task.

2. Tap **Share** (icon).

   The Share dialog opens. You can now share the photo as described in the steps that follow.

Share the Photo via E-Mail

1. In the Share dialog, tap **Mail**.

   Your iPad creates a new e-mail message in the Mail app with the photo attached to the message.

2. Tap in the To box and address the e-mail message.

3. Tap in the Subject line and type the subject for the e-mail message.

4. Tap in the body area, and then type any text needed.

5. Tap **Send**.

Note: If the Photos Size dialog opens, tap the button for the size of photo you want to send.

   Mail sends the message.

Share the Photo via Messaging

1 In the Share dialog, tap **Message**.

Your iPad creates a new message in the Messages app with the photo attached to the message.

2 Tap in the To box and address the message.

3 Tap in the body area, and then type any text needed.

4 Tap **Send**.

The Messages app sends the message.

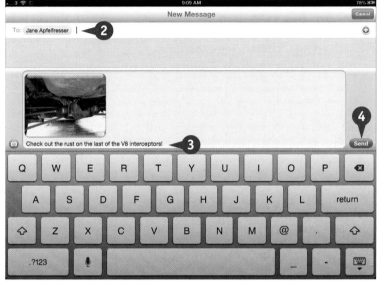

TIPS

How do I send multiple photos at once via e-mail?

From a screen that shows multiple photos, such as the Photo Library screen, tap **Edit**. The Select Photos screen appears. Tap each photo you want to send (**A**), placing a check mark, up to a maximum of five photos. Tap **Share** (**B**), and then tap **Mail** (**C**) in the dialog that opens.

What is the best size to use when sending photos via e-mail?

This depends on what the recipient will do with the photo. If the recipient needs to edit or print the photo, choose **Actual Size**. If the recipient will merely view the photo on-screen, choose **Large** or **Medium**. The **Small** size works for contact card images, but its picture quality is too low for most other uses.

Play Slide Shows of Your Photos

Your iPad can not only display your photos but also play them as a slide show. The slide show feature is limited to using existing groups of photos — you cannot create a slide show group on the iPad — but you can shuffle the photos into a different order. To make the most of your slide shows, you first choose the slide timing in the Photos screen in Settings. You can also choose to repeat the slide show or run the photos in random order. Then, when you start the slide show, you can choose which transition to use and add music.

Play Slide Shows of Your Photos

1 Press the Home button.

2 On the Home screen, tap **Settings**.

3 On the Settings screen, tap **Photos & Camera**.

The Photos & Camera screen appears.

4 To make the slide show repeat, tap the **Repeat** switch and move it to On.

5 To play the photos in random order, tap the **Shuffle** switch and move it to On.

6 Tap **Play Each Slide For**.

7 Tap the appropriate button — for example, **10 Seconds**.

8 Tap **Photos & Camera**.

9 Press the Home button.

10 On the Home screen, tap **Photos**.

11 On the Photos screen, locate the photos for the slide show. For example, tap **Events**, and then tap the event.

12 When the photos appear, tap the photo at which you want to start the slide show.

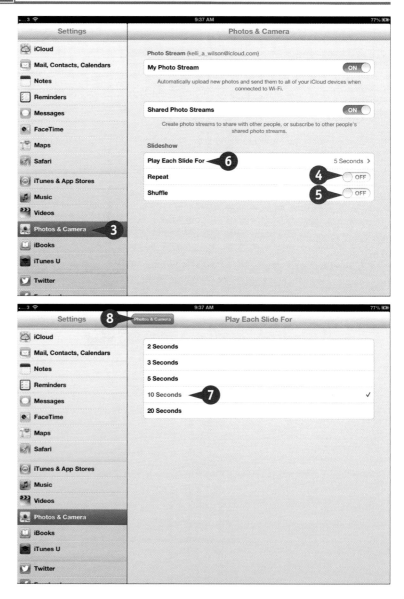

The photo appears.

13 Tap **Slideshow**.

The Slideshow Options dialog appears.

14 If you want to play music during the slide show, tap the **Play Music** switch and move it to On.

The Music button appears.

15 Tap **Music**.

The Music screen appears.

16 Tap the song, album, or playlist you want to play.

The Slideshow Options dialog appears.

17 Tap **Transitions**.

The Transitions dialog appears.

18 Tap the transition you want.

19 Tap **Slideshow Options**.

The Slideshow Options dialog appears.

20 Tap **Start Slideshow**.

The slide show starts.

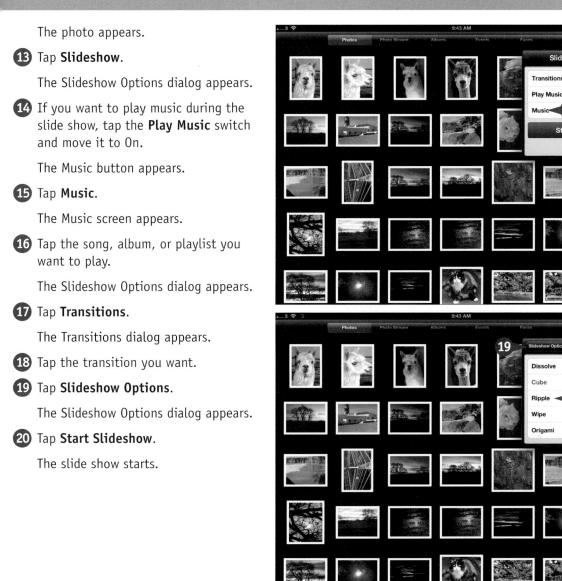

TIP

How can I play a custom slide show on the iPad?

You cannot create a custom slide show on the iPad at this writing, so you need to set up the custom slide show beforehand. In iPhoto on a Mac, create an album or an event that contains the photos you want to show; in Windows, place the photos in a folder or create an album in Photoshop Elements. Use iTunes to sync the photos to your iPad. You can then open the group of photos and set it playing as a slide show.

Play Photos from Your iPad on a TV

When you want to share your photos with other people, you can connect your iPad to a TV, and then display the photos on the TV screen. This is a great way to share the pictures at a size that a group of people can comfortably view.

To connect your iPad to a TV, you must get a cable with suitable connectors for the TV, such as the Lightning Digital AV Adapter. To play content, you must also set the iPad to provide the right type of video output for the TV.

Play Photos from Your iPad on a TV

Connect the iPad to the TV

First connect the Lightning connector on the TV cable to the iPad.

Note: To find the right kind of cable, check which type of input your TV uses.

Then connect the other end of the TV cable to the TV's port or ports.

Choose Video Output Settings

1 Press the Home button.

The Home screen appears.

2 Tap **Settings**.

The Settings screen appears.

3 Tap **General**.

The General screen appears.

4 Tap **TV Out**.

Note: The TV Out item appears only when you have connected the iPad to a TV.

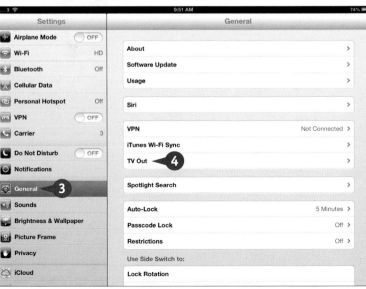

The TV Out screen appears.

5 Tap the **Widescreen** switch and move it to On or Off, as needed for the TV.

6 Tap **TV Signal**.

The TV Signal screen appears.

7 Tap **NTSC** or **PAL**, as needed for the TV. See the tip for advice on which to choose.

8 Tap **TV Out**.

9 Tap **General**.

The General screen appears.

Play Photos on the TV

1 Press the Home button.

The Home screen appears.

2 Tap **Photos**.

The Photos screen appears.

3 Locate the photos for the slide show. For example, tap **Albums**, and then tap the album.

The photos appear.

4 Tap the photo you want to display first.

The photo appears on the TV. You can then display further photos by swiping a finger to the left or right.

TIP

Should I choose NTSC or PAL on the TV Signal screen?
Normally, you need to choose the setting for the geographical area in which you are using the TV or from which the TV came. Most TV sets in North America use the NTSC format. Most TV sets in Europe use the PAL format. If in doubt, consult your TV's documentation.

Use Your iPad as a Digital Picture Frame

With its bright and beautiful screen, your iPad is great for displaying photos. iOS includes a feature for turning your iPad into a digital picture frame when you are not using it. When you turn on the Picture Frame feature, the iPad plays a slide show of the photos you choose.

To use Picture Frame, first choose settings in the Settings app. You can then turn on Picture Frame whenever you want.

Use Your iPad as a Digital Picture Frame

Choose Settings for Picture Frame

1 Press the Home button.

2 On the Home screen, tap **Settings**.

3 On the Settings screen, tap **Picture Frame**.

4 On the Picture Frame screen, tap a transition.

5 Set the **Zoom in on Faces** switch to On or Off, as needed.

6 Set the **Shuffle** switch to On if you want to show the photos in random order.

7 Choose which photos to use by tapping **All Photos**, **Photo Stream**, **Albums**, **Faces**, or **Events**. You can select only one button at a time.

Note: When you select Photo Stream, Albums, Faces, or Events, another box appears on the Picture Frame screen. Place a check mark on each photo stream, album, face, or event to include.

8 Tap **Show Each Photo For**.

9 On the Show Each Photo For screen, tap a length — for example, **3 Seconds**.

10 Tap **Picture Frame**.

Start Picture Frame

1 If your iPad is unlocked, press the Sleep/Wake button to lock it.

2 Press the Sleep/Wake button.

The lock screen appears.

3 Tap .

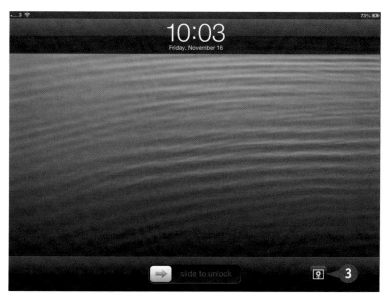

Picture Frame starts displaying your photos.

Note: Picture Frame works best if you have a stand you can use to prop the iPad up at a suitable angle for viewing.

4 When you want to stop the show, tap the screen.

The lock screen controls appear.

5 Tap .

Picture Frame stops showing the photos.

Note: You can also stop Picture Frame by unlocking the iPad.

TIP

What is the difference between the Dissolve transition and the Origami transition?
The Dissolve transition is a subtle effect that gradually replaces one photo with the next. The Origami transition displays multiple photos at once, folding the "page" to reveal other photos.

Read Digital Books with iBooks

To enjoy electronic books, or *e-books*, on your iPad, download the free iBooks app from the App Store. Using iBooks, you can read e-books that you load on the iPad from your computer, download free or paid-for e-books from online stores, or read PDF files you transfer from your computer.

If you have already loaded some e-books, you can read them as described in this task. If iBooks contains no books, see the next task, "Browse and Buy Digital Books with iBooks," for instructions on finding and downloading e-books.

Read Digital Books with iBooks

① Press the Home button.

The Home screen appears.

② Navigate to the Home screen that contains the iBooks icon. For example, tap and drag left to scroll to the right one or more times.

③ Tap **iBooks**.

The Books screen appears.

Ⓐ If Books does not appear in the upper-middle area of the iBooks screen, tap **Collections**. On the Collections screen that appears, tap **Books** to display the list of books.

④ Tap the book you want to open.

The book opens.

Note: When you open a book, iBooks displays your current page. When you open a book for the first time, iBooks displays the book's cover or first page.

⑤ Tap anywhere on the screen to hide the reading controls. Tap again to display them once more.

6 Tap the right side of the page to display the next page.

Note: To display the previous page, tap the left side of the page. Alternatively, tap the left side of the page and drag to the right.

7 To look at the next page without fully revealing it, tap the right side and drag to the left. You can then either drag further to turn the page or release the page and let it fall closed.

8 To jump to another part of the book, tap **Table of Contents** (≡).

Note: Alternatively, you can drag the indicator at the bottom of the screen.

9 When the table of contents appears, tap the part of the book you want to display.

Note: To search in the book, tap **Search** (Q). On the Search screen, type the search term, and then tap the match you want to display.

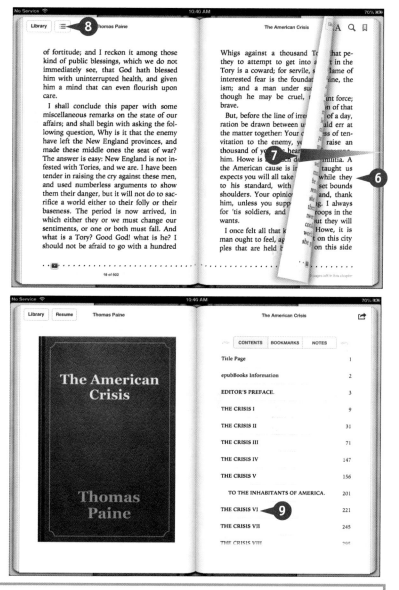

TIP

How do I change the font iBooks uses?
Tap the screen to display the controls, and then tap **Font Settings** (ᴀA). In the Font Settings dialog, tap **Small** (Ⓐ) or **Large** (Ⓑ) to change the font size. Tap **Fonts** (Ⓒ) to display the font list, and then tap the font you want to use. Finally, tap outside the Font Settings dialog to close it.

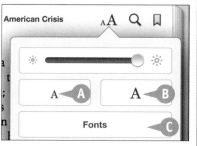

Browse and Buy Digital Books with iBooks

The iBooks app connects directly to Apple's online bookstore, which you can browse to find e-books. Some e-books are free; others you have to pay for, but many have samples that you can download to help you decide whether to buy the book.

After you download an e-book, it appears on your iBooks bookshelf. You can then open it and read it as described in the preceding task, "Read Digital Books with iBooks."

Browse and Buy Digital Books with iBooks

1 Press the Home button.

The Home screen appears.

2 Navigate to the Home screen that contains the iBooks icon. For example, tap and drag left to scroll to the right one or more times.

3 Tap **iBooks**.

The Books screen appears.

4 Tap **Store**.

The Store screen appears.

5 Browse the store by scrolling the lists or tapping the buttons.

6 Tap a book whose details you want to view.

Note: You can also find books by searching. Tap **Search Store** in the upper-right corner of the screen, type your search term, and then tap a result.

The book's details appear.

Note: Tap **Ratings and Reviews** to see reader ratings and reviews of the book.

7 Tap **Sample** to get a sample of the book, or tap the price button to buy the book.

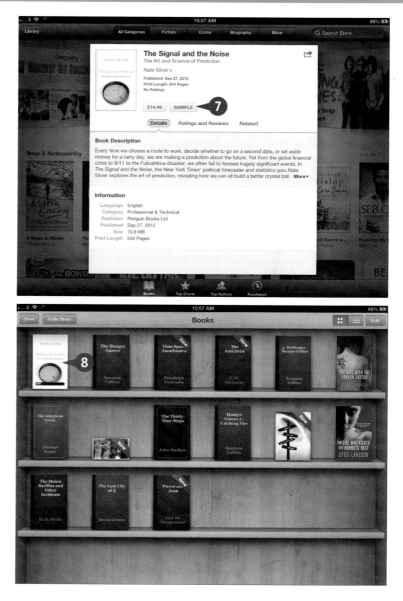

The sample or book appears on your iBooks bookshelf.

8 Tap the sample or book to open it.

TIP

Where can I find free e-books to read in iBooks?

In the iBooks Store, tap **Search Store** and type **free books** to display a list of free books.

Other sources of free e-books include ManyBooks.net (www.manybooks.net) and Project Gutenberg (www.gutenberg.org).

Add PDF Files to iBooks and Read Them

These days, many books, reports, and other documents are available as Portable Document Format, or PDF, files. You can load PDF files on your iPad and read them using iBooks. This is a great way to take your required reading with you so that you can catch up on it anywhere.

Add PDF Files to iBooks and Read Them

Add PDFs to iBooks Using iTunes

1. Connect your iPad to your computer via the USB cable or Wi-Fi.

   The iPad appears in the Devices list in iTunes.

2. Click your iPad in the Devices list.

   The iPad's control screens appear.

3. Click **Books**.

   The Books screen appears.

4. Click the **File** menu.

   The File menu opens.

5. Click **Add to Library**.

   The Add To Library dialog opens.

6. Click the PDF file or select the PDF files you want to add.

7. Click **Open**.

   iTunes adds the PDF file or files to the Books list.

8. Click **Sync**.

   iTunes syncs the PDF files to the iPad.

9. Disconnect the iPad from your computer.

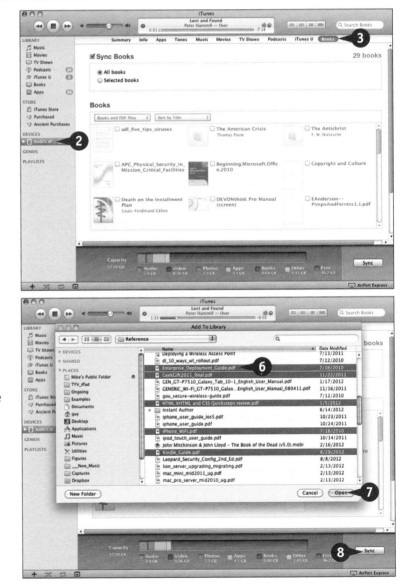

Read a PDF File Using iBooks

1 Press the Home button.

The Home screen appears.

2 Navigate to the Home screen that contains the iBooks icon. For example, tap and drag left to scroll to the right one or more times.

3 Tap **iBooks**.

The Books screen appears.

4 Tap **Collections**.

The Collections dialog appears.

5 Tap **PDFs**.

The PDFs screen appears.

6 Tap the PDF file you want to open.

The PDF file appears. You can then read the PDF file using the techniques described earlier in this chapter.

Note: If you open a PDF file while browsing the web in Safari, you can open the file in iBooks. To do so, tap the screen, and then tap **Open in iBooks** on the command bar that pops up.

TIP

How do I change the font size on the PDF file?

You cannot change the font size on the PDF file. This is because PDF is a graphical format — essentially a picture — instead of a text format. To make the PDF file more readable, place your thumb and finger on the screen and pinch outward to zoom the text to a larger size. You may find it easier to hold the iPad in landscape orientation rather than portrait orientation, so that you can view the page at a greater width.

CHAPTER 11

Using Maps and Clock

Your iPad includes a powerful Maps app for finding locations and directions and a Clock app that includes alarms, stopwatch, timer, and the ability to show clocks in multiple locations.

Find Your Location with the Maps App

Your iPad's Maps app can pinpoint your location by using either known wireless networks or the Global Positioning System, known as GPS, on cellular iPads. You can view your location on a road map, a satellite picture, or a hybrid that shows street annotations on the satellite picture. You can easily switch among map types to find the most useful one for your current needs. To help you get your bearings, the Tracking feature in the Maps app can show you which direction you are facing.

Find Your Location with the Maps App

1 Press the Home button.

The Home screen appears.

2 Tap **Maps**.

The Maps screen appears.

A A blue dot shows your current location. The expanding circle around the blue dot shows that Maps is determining your location.

Note: It may take a minute for Maps to work out your location accurately. While Maps determines the location, the blue dot moves, even though the iPad remains stationary.

3 Tap and pinch in with two fingers.

Note: You can tap and pinch out with two fingers to zoom in.

The map zooms out, showing a larger area.

4 Tap the curled map corner.

The map options appear.

5 Tap **Satellite**.

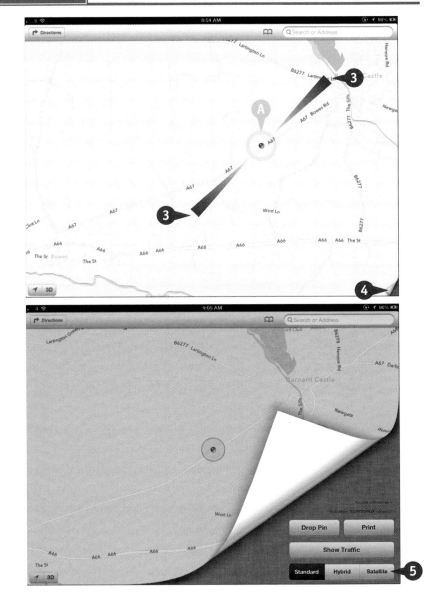

The Satellite view appears.

6 Tap the curled map corner.

The map options appear.

7 Tap **Hybrid**.

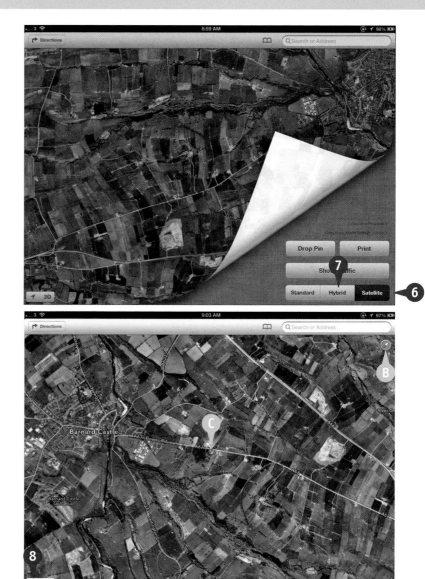

The satellite map appears with road names and place names overlaid on it.

8 Tap **Location** (changes to).

Ⓑ The Compass arrow appears (). The orange arrow indicates north.

Ⓒ The map turns to show the direction the iPad is facing, so that you can orient yourself.

TIP

Which is the best view to use in Maps?
That depends on what you are doing. When navigating on roads, you will probably find Standard view most helpful. When you want to check out the landscape, use Satellite view. And when you want to identify features on the landscape, use Hybrid view.

Find Directions with the Maps App

Your iPad's Maps app can give you directions to where you want to go. Maps can also show you current traffic congestion to help you identify the most viable route for a journey.

Maps displays driving directions by default, but you can also display walking directions.

Find Directions with the Maps App

1 Press the Home button.

The Home screen appears.

2 Tap **Maps**.

The Maps screen appears.

3 Tap **Directions**.

The Directions panel appears.

4 Tap **Start**, and type the start location for the directions.

Note: If the starting location or ending location is an address in the Contacts app, start typing the name, and then tap the match in the list.

5 Type the end location.

A Tap **Switch Places** () if you need to switch the start location and end location.

6 Tap **Route**.

B A screen showing the driving directions appears. The green pin marks the start, and the red pin marks the end.

Note: If multiple routes are available, tap a button to view a different route. For example, tap **Route 2** (Route 2 changes to Route 2) to view it.

7 Tap **Start**.

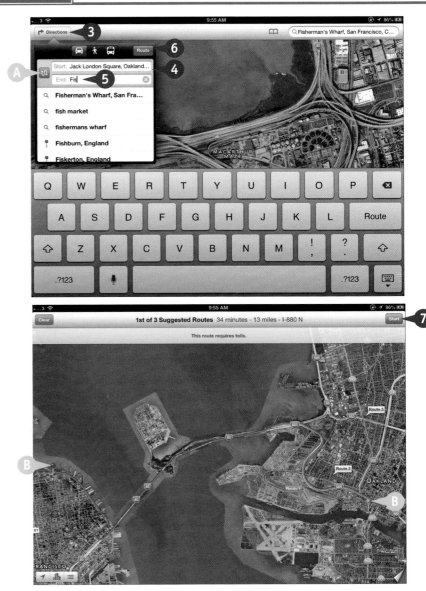

The first screen of directions appears.

 Tap and scroll as needed to follow the directions.

The next screen of directions appears.

9 Tap **Overview**.

The overview screen appears.

10 Tap **Directions** (≣).

C The Directions panel appears, showing a complete list of the directions.

11 Tap **Resume** to return to step-by-step directions.

TIP

How do I get directions walking?

Tap 🚶 to display the distance and time for walking the route.

Be aware that walking directions may be inaccurate. Before walking the route, check that it does not send you across pedestrian-free bridges or through rail tunnels.

Explore with 3D Flyovers

Maps is not only great for finding out where you are and for getting directions to places, but it can also show you 3D flyovers of the places on the map.

After switching on the 3D feature, you can zoom in and out, pan around, and move backward and forward.

Explore with 3D Flyovers

 Press the Home button.

The Home screen appears.

 Tap **Maps**.

The Maps screen appears.

3 Display the area of interest in the middle of the screen. For example, tap and drag the map, or search for the location you want.

4 Tap ![icon] (![icon] changes to ![icon]) in an urban area or **3D** (**3D** changes to **3D**) outside urban areas.

The screen switches to 3D view.

5 Pinch out with two fingers to zoom in.

Note: You can pinch in with two fingers to zoom out.

6 Tap and drag to scroll the map.

7 Place two fingers on the screen and twist clockwise or counterclockwise to rotate the view.

 The Compass arrow () appears. The orange arrow indicates north.

Note: You can tap 🧭 to return the screen to its original orientation.

8 Tap 🏛 (🏛 changes to 🏛) or **3D** (**3D** changes to **3D**), depending on which button appears on-screen.

The standard view reappears.

TIP

What does Flyover do with the Standard map?
When you tap **3D** to switch on Flyover with the Standard map displayed, Maps tilts the map at an angle, as you might do with a paper map. For most purposes, Flyover is most useful with the Satellite map and the Hybrid map.

Use Maps' Bookmarks and Contacts

When you need to be able to return to a location easily in the Maps app, you can place a bookmark at the location. Similarly, you can add a location to your contacts, so that you can access it either from the Contacts app or from the Maps app. You can either create a new contact or add the location to an existing contact.

You can also return quickly to locations you have visited recently but not created a bookmark or contact for.

Use Maps' Bookmarks and Contacts

1. Press the Home button.

   The Home screen appears.

2. Tap **Maps**.

   The Maps screen appears.

3. Find the place you want to bookmark. For example, tap and drag the map, or search for the location you want.

4. Tap and hold the place you want to bookmark.

   The Maps app drops a pin on the place.

5. Tap 🛈 on the pin's label.

   The Location dialog appears.

6. At the bottom of the dialog, tap **Add to Bookmarks**.

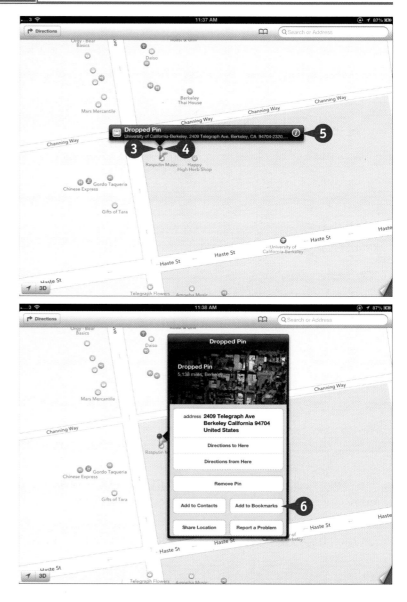

270

The Add Bookmark dialog appears.

7 Type the name for the bookmark.

8 Tap **Save**.

The Add Bookmark dialog closes.

9 Tap the pinhead.

The pin's label appears.

10 Tap ⓘ.

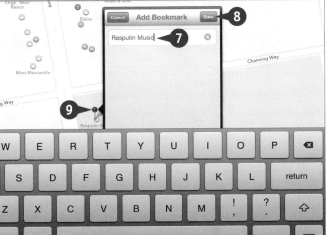

The Location dialog appears.

11 Tap **Add to Contacts**.

The Contact dialog opens.

12 To create a new contact, tap **Create New Contact**.

The New Contact dialog appears.

To add the location to an existing contact, tap **Add to Existing Contact**, and then tap the contact in the Contacts dialog.

13 Type the details for the contact.

14 Tap **Done**.

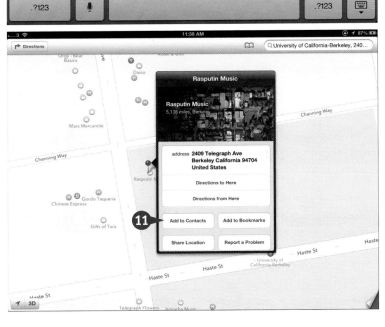

TIP

How do I go to a location that I have bookmarked or created a contact for?

In the Maps app, tap **Bookmarks** (📖). In the Bookmarks dialog, tap **Bookmarks** or **Contacts**, and then tap the location.

You can also go back to a recent location by tapping **Recents**, and then tapping the location.

Share a Location with Others

Often, you will find it useful to share a location with other people. The Maps app enables you to share a location in moments via e-mail, instant messaging, Twitter, or Facebook.

You can share your current location, a location you have bookmarked or created a contact for, or a location on which you drop a pin.

Share a Location with Others

1 Press the Home button.

The Home screen appears.

2 Tap **Maps**.

The Maps screen appears.

3 Find the location you want to bookmark.

4 If the location does not already have a bookmark or contact, tap and hold it to drop a pin on it.

5 Tap the pin.

The pin's label appears.

6 Tap 🔵.

The Info dialog appears.

A If you have just dropped a pin, you may want to name it rather than leaving the default name, Dropped Pin. Tap **Add to Bookmarks**, type the name, and then tap **Done**.

7 Tap **Share Location**.

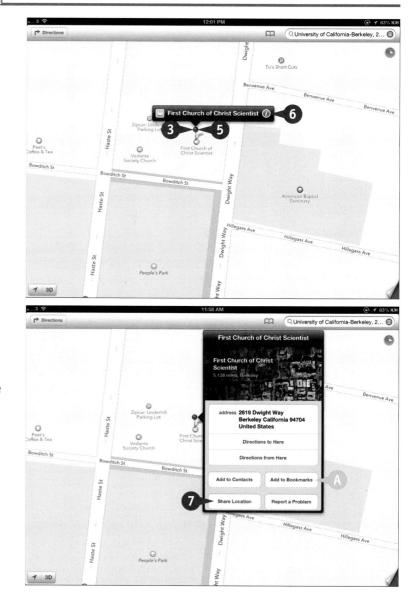

The Share dialog opens.

8 Tap the means of sharing you will use. For example, tap **Mail** to share via e-mail.

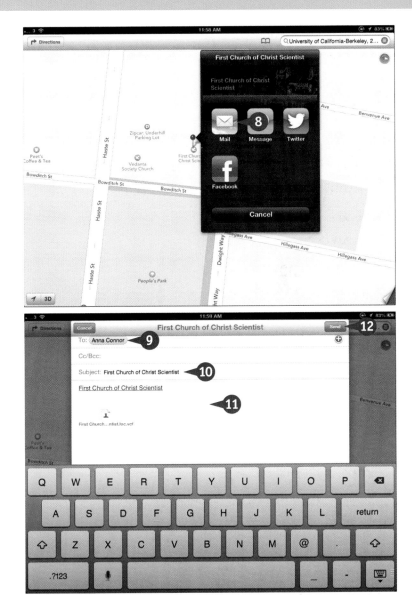

Your iPad creates a new e-mail message in the Mail app with the location's link inserted in the message.

9 Tap in the To box, and address the e-mail message.

10 Tap in the Subject line, and change the default subject line as needed.

11 Optionally, tap in the body area, and type any text needed.

12 Tap **Send**.

How else can I share a location?

If you have created a contact for the location, you can share the contact from the Contacts app. Tap the contact's entry to display the Info dialog, and then tap **Share Contact**. In the Share Contact Using dialog, tap **Email** or **Message**, as needed. You can then complete the message and send it.

Set Alarms

Your iPad's Clock app includes full Alarm features. You can set as many alarms as you need, and create different schedules for the alarms. For example, you can set an alarm to wake you each weekday but not on the weekend. You can make an alarm play an alarm tone or music.

Set Alarms

1 Press the Home button.

The Home screen appears.

2 Tap **Clock**.

The Clock screen appears.

3 Tap **Alarm**.

The Alarm screen appears.

4 Tap ➕.

The Add Alarm dialog appears.

5 Tap the time controls to set the alarm time.

6 To set a repeating alarm, tap **Repeat**.

The Repeat dialog appears.

7 Tap to place a check mark next to each day you want the alarm to sound.

8 Tap **Back**.

The Add Alarm dialog appears again.

9 Tap **Sound**.

The Sound dialog appears.

10 Tap a sound to preview it.

A check mark appears next to the sound.

11 When you have chosen the alarm sound, tap **Back**.

The Add Alarm dialog appears again.

12 If you want to use the Snooze function, tap the **Snooze** switch and set it to On.

13 Tap **Label**.

The Label dialog appears.

14 Type the name for the alarm.

15 Tap **Done**.

The Add Alarm dialog appears again.

16 Tap **Save**.

The Alarm screen appears.

Ⓐ The alarm appears at the top of the screen.

Ⓑ The grid shows a graphical representation of when the alarm occurs.

17 Move the alarm's switch to On or Off, as needed.

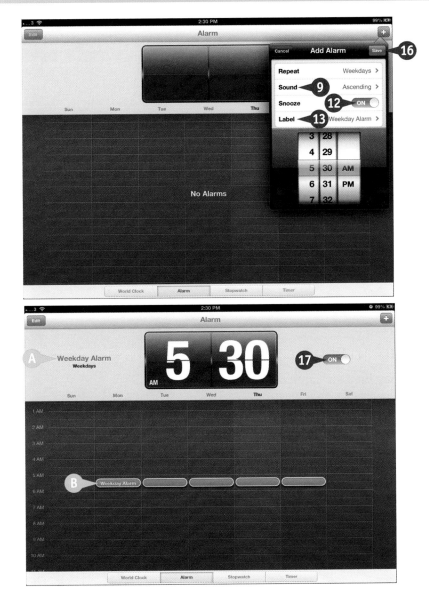

Is there an easy way to tell whether an alarm is set?
Yes. The alarm icon () appears in the status bar when an alarm is set.

Use the Stopwatch and Timer

Your iPad's Clock app includes a Stopwatch feature and a Timer feature. Stopwatch provides a handy way of timing events such as races. Timer enables you to count down from a set time and sound an alarm when the time elapses.

Use the Stopwatch and Timer

Use the Stopwatch

1. Press the Home button.

   The Home screen appears.

2. Tap **Clock**.

   The Clock screen appears.

3. Tap **Stopwatch**.

   The Stopwatch screen appears.

4. Tap **Start**.

The stopwatch starts running.

5. Tap **Lap** to mark a lap time.

   Ⓐ The lap time appears in the list.

   Ⓑ The upper readout shows the total time elapsed.

   Ⓒ The lower readout shows the time since the last lap mark.

6. Tap **Stop**.

7. Tap **Reset** when you need to reset the stopwatch.

Use the Timer

1 Press the Home button.

The Home screen appears.

2 Tap **Clock**.

The Clock screen appears.

3 Tap **Timer**.

The Timer screen appears.

4 Tap the time controls to set the number of hours and minutes.

5 Tap **Sounds**.

The When Timer Ends panel appears.

6 Tap a sound to preview it.

A check mark appears next to the sound.

7 When you have chosen the sound, tap **Set**.

The Timer screen reappears.

8 Tap **Start**.

The Timer starts running.

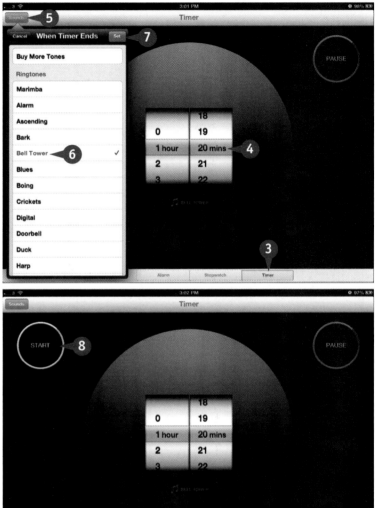

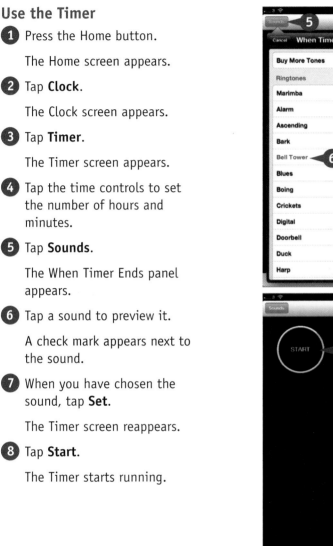

TIP

How can I make my iPad play music for a while as I go to sleep?

To play music and shut it off automatically after a set time, set the Timer feature to the interval you want. Tap **Sounds**, scroll down to the bottom of the When Timer Ends dialog, and tap **Stop Playing**. Then tap **Set**.

When you travel, or when you work with people in different parts of the world, you may need to track the time in different time zones. You can set up your iPad's Clock app with the different time zones you need so that you can instantly see the local time in each time zone you need to track.

Set Up Clocks in Multiple Locations

1 Press the Home button.

The Home screen appears.

2 Tap **Clock**.

The Clock app appears.

3 Tap **World Clock**.

The World Clock screen appears, showing a default selection of clocks in Cupertino and major cities around the world.

4 Tap **Add**.

The Choose a City panel opens.

5 Start typing the name of a city in the time zone you want to add.

Note: You can also select a city by scrolling down the list and browsing to the city.

A list of matches appears.

6 Tap the city you want to add.

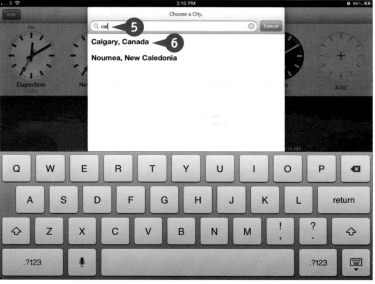

The World Clock shows the clock you added.

7 Tap **Edit**.

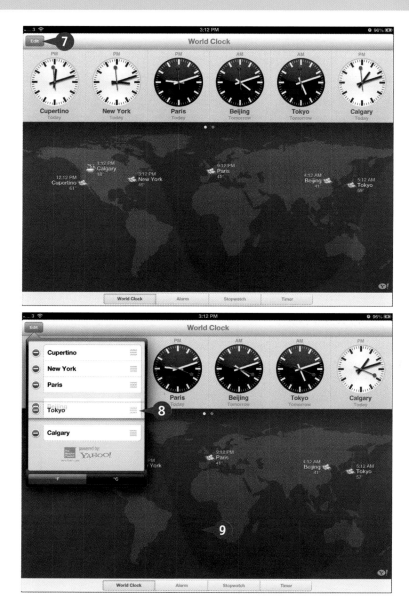

The Edit dialog appears.

8 Tap ≡ next to a clock, and drag it up or down the list as needed.

Note: To delete a clock, tap ⊖ next to it, and then tap **Delete**.

9 Tap outside the Edit dialog.

The clocks appear in your chosen order.

You can now easily see what time it is in each of the locations you are tracking.

TIPS

Why do some clocks have black faces and others white faces?
A black clock face indicates that it is currently between 6 p.m. and 6 a.m. in that time zone. A white clock face indicates that it is between 6 a.m. and 6 p.m.

How do I set the time on my iPad's main clock?
Normally, your iPad sets the time automatically, but you can set the time manually if you want. From the Home screen, tap **Settings**, and then tap **General**. Tap **Date & Time**, and then use the controls on the Date & Time screen.

CHAPTER 12

Taking Photos and Videos

In this chapter, you begin by using the Camera app to take both still photos and videos and using the Photo Booth app to take fun photos. You then learn to edit videos using the Trim feature, share your photos and videos with others, and create movies complete with titles and soundtracks by using Apple's iMovie app.

Take Photos with the Camera App

Your iPad includes a high-resolution camera in its back for taking still photos and videos, plus a lower-resolution camera in the front for taking photos and videos of yourself and for making video calls.

To take photos using the cameras, you use the Camera app. For the main camera, this app includes a digital zoom feature for zooming in and out, plus a grid that you can use for composing your photos.

Take Photos with the Camera App

1 Press the Home button.

The Home screen appears.

2 Tap **Camera**.

The Camera app opens. At first, the app shows a dark screen with shutter panels, which then open to display what is positioned in front of the lens.

3 Aim the iPad so that your subject appears in the middle of the photo area. If you need to focus on an item that is not in the center of the frame, tap the object to move the focus rectangle to it.

Note: If you need to take tightly composed photos, get a tripod that fits the iPad. You can find various models on eBay and photography sites.

4 If you need to zoom in or out, place two fingers together on the screen and pinch outward.

The zoom slider appears.

5 Tap ➕ to zoom in or ➖ to zoom out. Tap as many times as needed up to 5× zoom.

Ⓐ You can also zoom by tapping and dragging the zoom slider.

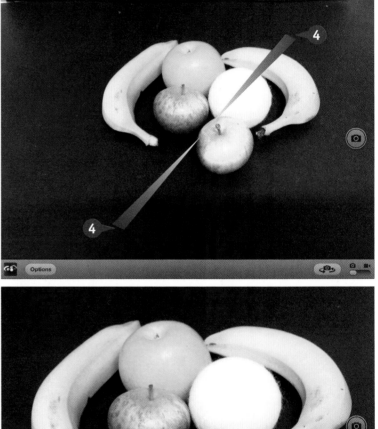

⑥ Optionally, tap where you want to focus.

Note: By default, the Camera app focuses on the middle of the screen, because that is where your subject is most likely to be. If what you see on screen appears blurred, try tapping the subject to change the focus.

⑦ Tap **Take Photo** (📷).

The Camera app takes the photo and displays a thumbnail.

⑧ Tap the thumbnail.

The photo appears.

Ⓑ From the photo screen, you can navigate as discussed in Chapter 10. For example, swipe your finger to the left to display the next photo, or swipe to the right to display the previous photo. Tap 🗑 to delete the photo.

⑨ Tap **Done** when you want to go back to the Camera app.

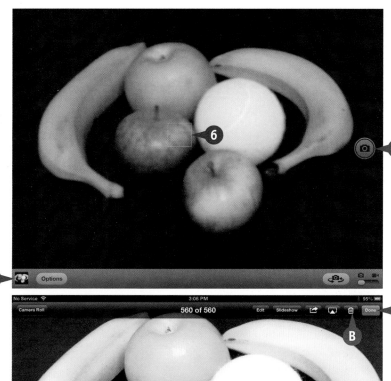

TIP

How do I switch to the front-facing camera?
Tap **Switch Cameras** (🔄) to switch from the rear-facing camera to the front-facing camera. The image that the front-facing camera is seeing appears on-screen, and you can take pictures as described in this task. Tap **Switch Cameras** (🔄) again when you want to switch back to the rear-facing camera.

Use the Grid to Compose Photos

The Camera app includes a Grid feature that you can turn on to help you compose your pictures.

You can display the Grid at any point when you will find it useful. Depending on the types of photos you take, you may find it helpful to leave the Grid displayed all the time.

Use the Grid to Compose Photos

1 Press the Home button.

The Home screen appears.

2 Tap **Camera**.

The Camera app opens. At first, the app shows a dark screen with shutter panels, which then open to display what is positioned in front of the lens.

3 Tap **Options**.

The Options pop-up dialog appears.

 Tap the **Grid** switch and move it to On to display the Grid.

Note: The Grid is helpful both for making sure your subject is positioned suitably and for checking that you are holding the iPad so that uprights run vertically and horizontal items run horizontally.

5 Tap **Done**.

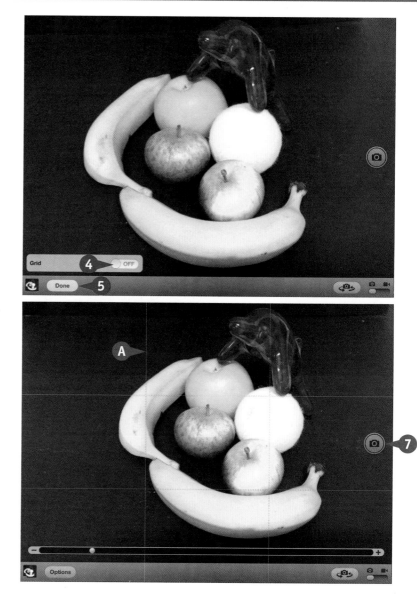

The Options pop-up dialog closes.

A The Grid appears.

6 Use the grid to position your subject and align the iPad.

7 Tap **Take Photo** ( ).

The Camera app takes the photo.

When the Camera app finishes taking the photo, it displays a thumbnail. You can tap the thumbnail to view the photo.

TIP

How does the Grid help with photo composition?
Apart from enabling you to align vertical lines and horizontal lines quickly and accurately, the Grid can help you implement the Rule of Thirds. This rule suggests placing the major point of interest on one of the dividing lines or intersections in the picture.

Take Fun Photos with Photo Booth

Your iPad includes the Photo Booth app, which you can use to take photos using special effects such as Thermal Camera, X-Ray, or Kaleidoscope.

You can use Photo Booth with either the iPad's front camera — the one on the screen side — or the main camera, so you can apply the effects to subjects other than yourself if you choose. After taking photos with Photo Booth, you can share them easily with other people.

Take Fun Photos with Photo Booth

1 Press the Home button.

The Home screen appears.

2 Tap **Photo Booth**.

Photo Booth opens, showing the iPad's front camera.

3 Tap the effect you want to use. This example uses **Thermal Camera**.

Photo Booth displays the camera's input full screen with the effect applied.

④ Compose your features to suit the effect.

Note: Tap 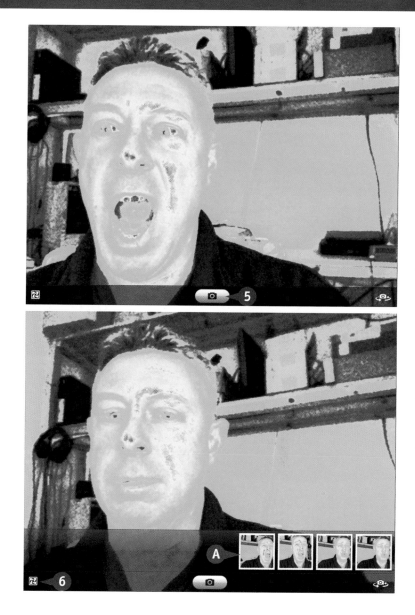 if you want to switch the view to the iPad's main camera.

⑤ Tap **Take Photo** (📷).

Ⓐ Photo Booth displays thumbnails of the photos you take.

⑥ Tap ⧉ when you want to go back to the screen for choosing effects.

TIP

How do I share the photos I take in Photo Booth?

Tap 🔄 in the lower-right corner of the Photo Booth window to display the Select Photos screen. Tap each photo you want to e-mail, and then tap **Email**. Photo Booth causes Mail to create a new message with the photos attached. You can then address the message, type a subject line, and tap **Send** to send it.

Capture Video

As well as capturing still photos, your iPad's cameras can capture high-quality, full-motion video. The rear camera records 1080p video, while the front camera records 720p video. A single video can use only one resolution.

To capture video, you use the Camera app. You launch the Camera app as usual, and then switch it to Video mode. After taking the video, you can view it on the iPad's screen.

Capture Video

1 Press the Home button.

The Home screen appears.

2 Tap **Camera**.

The Camera screen appears, showing the image the lens is seeing.

3 Tap the **Camera** switch and move it to Video.

The video image and video controls appear.

Note: If the still camera is zoomed out all the way when you switch to the video camera, the picture appears to zoom in. This is because the video camera uses a focal length longer than the wide-angle setting of the still camera.

4 Aim the camera at your subject.

5 Tap **Record** ( ).

A The camera starts recording, the Record button blinks, and the time readout shows the time that has elapsed.

6 To finish recording, tap **Record** (⏺).

The Camera app stops recording and displays a thumbnail of the video's first frame.

7 Tap the thumbnail.

The video appears.

8 Tap **Play** (▶).

The video starts playing.

9 Tap anywhere on the screen to display the video controls.

Note: If you want to trim the video, follow the procedure described in the next task before tapping **Done**.

10 When you finish viewing the video, tap **Done**.

The Camera app appears again.

TIP

What does the bar of miniature pictures at the top of the video playback screen do?
The navigation bar gives you a quick way of moving forward and backward through the movie. Tap the vertical playhead bar, and then drag to the right or to the left until the movie reaches the part you want. You can use the navigation bar either when the movie is playing or when it is paused.

Edit Video with the Trim Feature

When you capture video, you normally shoot more footage than you want to keep. You then edit the video to keep only the footage you need.

The Camera app includes a straightforward Trim feature that you can use to trim the beginning and end of a video clip to where you want them. For greater precision in editing, or to make a movie out of multiple clips, you can use the iMovie app, as described later in this chapter.

Edit Video with the Trim Feature

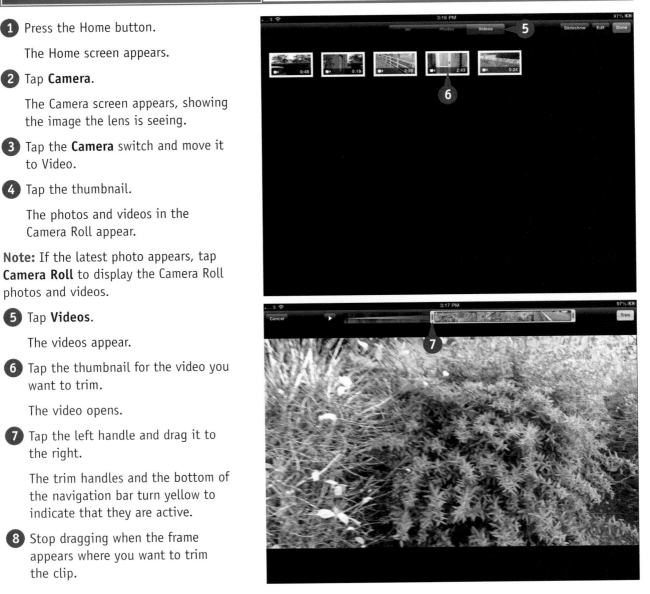

1 Press the Home button.

The Home screen appears.

2 Tap **Camera**.

The Camera screen appears, showing the image the lens is seeing.

3 Tap the **Camera** switch and move it to Video.

4 Tap the thumbnail.

The photos and videos in the Camera Roll appear.

Note: If the latest photo appears, tap **Camera Roll** to display the Camera Roll photos and videos.

5 Tap **Videos**.

The videos appear.

6 Tap the thumbnail for the video you want to trim.

The video opens.

7 Tap the left handle and drag it to the right.

The trim handles and the bottom of the navigation bar turn yellow to indicate that they are active.

8 Stop dragging when the frame appears where you want to trim the clip.

9 Tap the right handle and drag it to the left until the frame to which you want to trim the end appears.

10 Tap **Trim**.

The Trim dialog appears.

11 Tap **Trim Original** if you want to trim the original clip. Tap **Save as New Clip** to create a new clip from the trimmed content, leaving the original clip unchanged.

A The Trimming Video progress indicator appears while the Camera app trims the video.

12 Tap **Done**.

TIP

Is there an easier way of trimming my videos?

When trimming your videos, turn the iPad to landscape orientation. This makes the navigation bar longer and the trimming handles easier to use.

If you have a Mac, you can trim your videos more precisely, and make many other changes, by importing the clips into iMovie on the Mac, and then working with them there. In Windows, you can use an app such as Adobe Premiere Elements.

Share Your Photos and Videos

After taking photos and videos with your iPad's camera, or after loading photos and videos on the iPad using iTunes, you can share them with other people.

Chapter 10 explains how to share photos via e-mail and Messages. This task explains how to tweet photos to your Twitter account, assign photos to contacts, use photos as wallpaper, or print photos.

Share Your Photos and Videos

Select the Photo or Video to Share

1 Press the Home button.

2 On the Home screen, tap **Photos**.

3 On the Photos screen, tap the item that contains the photo or video you want to share. For example, tap an album.

4 Tap the photo or video you want to share.

5 Tap **Share** (📤) to open the Share dialog for photos or the Share dialog for videos.

6 Tap the appropriate button — **Twitter**, **Assign to Contact**, **Use as Wallpaper**, or **Print** — and then follow the instructions in the next sections. Videos have fewer options than photos.

Share a Photo on Twitter

1 In the Share dialog, tap **Twitter**.

2 Type the text of the tweet.

3 Tap **Add Location** if you want to add your location to the tweet.

4 Click **Send**.

Assign a Photo to a Contact

▶ In the Share dialog, tap **Assign to Contact**.

The Contacts dialog appears.

▶ Tap the contact you want to assign the photo to.

The Move and Scale dialog appears.

▶ Move the photo so that the face appears centrally.

4 If necessary, pinch in to shrink the photo or pinch out to enlarge it.

5 Tap **Use**.

Set a Photo as Wallpaper

▶ In the Share dialog, tap **Use as Wallpaper**.

▶ Move the photo to display the part you want.

▶ If necessary, pinch in to shrink the photo or pinch out to enlarge it.

4 Tap **Set Lock Screen**, **Set Home Screen**, or **Set Both**, as needed.

TIP

How do I print a photo?

Display the photo you want to print, and then tap **Share** (📷) to display the Share dialog. Tap **Print** to display the Printer Options dialog. If the Printer readout does not show the correct printer, tap **Select Printer**, and then tap the printer. Tap **Print** to print the photo.

Create Movies Using Apple's iMovie App

By installing Apple's iMovie app on your iPad, you can add the ability to create movies on the iPad itself. iMovie for iOS enables you to edit video clips created on your iPad or other iOS devices, but you cannot include video from other sources.

This task shows you how to create a movie project, trim movie clips to length and add them, add titles and a soundtrack, and change the project's theme and settings. Before you can follow these instructions, you must buy iMovie from the iTunes Store and install it as described in Chapter 6.

Create Movies Using Apple's iMovie App

Launch iMovie and Start a Movie Project

1. Press the Home button.

2. Navigate to the Home screen that contains the iMovie icon.

3. Tap **iMovie**.

   The iMovie screen appears.

4. Tap .

   The New dialog appears.

5. Tap **New Project**.

Note: From the New dialog, you can tap **New Trailer** to create a movie trailer.

   iMovie creates a new project.

Add Video Clips to Your Movie

1. Tap **Video** ().

   The Video pane appears.

Ⓐ You can also record video from the iPad's camera directly into iMovie by tapping 📷.

2. Tap the video clip you want to add.

   A selection border appears around the clip, and yellow cropping handles appear before and after it.

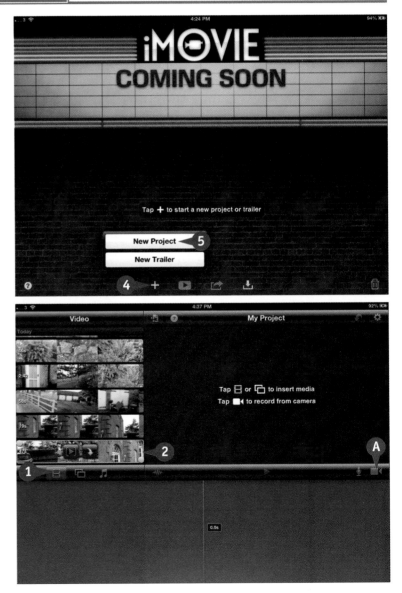

Note: If the clip is the right length, you do not need to crop it.

③ Tap the left cropping handle and drag right to where you want the clip to start.

Ⓑ The preview shows the current frame.

④ Tap the right cropping handle and drag left to where you want the clip to end.

⑤ Tap **Insert** (▶).

Ⓒ iMovie adds the video clip to the movie timeline.

Ⓓ To view the clip, tap **Play** (▶). iMovie rewinds to the beginning of the movie and plays it back. To view part of the movie, drag the timeline left or right so the playhead's red line appears where you want to start. Then tap **Play** (▶).

You can now add further clips as needed.

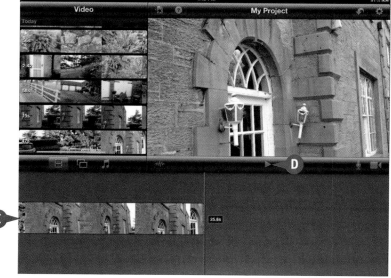

TIP

How do I remove a video clip from my movie?
Tap the clip in the timeline and drag it up to the top of the screen. The clip vanishes in a puff of smoke. If you find this move difficult, double-tap the clip to display the Clip Settings dialog, and then tap **Delete Clip**.

continued ▶

iMovie gives you impressively full features for composing and editing movies. For example, you can add a soundtrack of canned music or effects, pick the perfect playlist from the Music app, or record narration or other audio.

When you have finished creating your movie, you can share it directly from iMovie to online sites such as YouTube or Facebook.

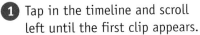

Add a Title

1 Tap in the timeline and scroll left until the first clip appears.

2 Double-tap the first clip.

The Clip Settings dialog appears.

3 Tap **Title Style**.

The Title Style dialog appears.

4 Tap a title style.

The opening title appears in the upper-middle part of the screen.

5 Tap the Title Text Here placeholder.

Note: Use the Ending title style to add a title to the end of your movie. Use the Middle title style to add a title to a clip in the middle. Use the None title style to remove the current title.

The on-screen keyboard appears.

6 Type the title text.

7 Tap **Done** on the keyboard.

The title appears.

Add a Soundtrack to the Movie

1 Tap .

The Audio pane appears.

2 Tap the music category you want. This example uses **Theme Music**.

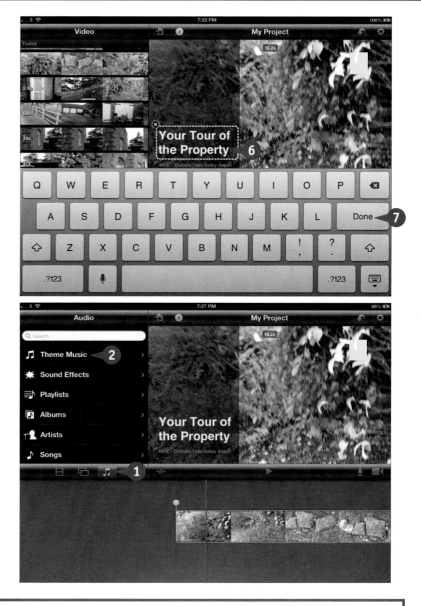

continued ▶

TIP

What other content can I use in my movies?

You can easily use your photos in your movies. Simply tap 🖼 to display the Photos pane, tap the photo source — for example, **My Photo Stream** — and then tap the photo you want to add to the movie. Double-tap the photo in the timeline to display the Photo Settings dialog, which lets you add a title or location to the photo.

Beyond the features covered here, iMovie offers many others. For example, you can adjust the transition between clips, record narration or vocal effects, and even add freeze frames. You can also record video directly into iMovie, which can help save time when you are working on a movie project.

Create Movies Using Apple's iMovie App (continued)

The pane for the music you chose appears.

③ Tap the music item to use.

Ⓐ iMovie adds the music as a green bar.

④ Double-tap the first clip.

The Clip Settings dialog opens.

⑤ To turn the clip's audio off, tap the **Audio** switch and move it to Off.

Ⓑ To mix the audio, tap and drag the volume slider in the Clip Settings dialog.

⑥ Tap outside the dialog to close it.

⑦ Double-tap the green music box below the first clip.

The Audio Clip Settings dialog opens.

⑧ To play the soundtrack, make sure the **Audio** switch is set to On.

⑨ Tap and drag the volume slider to set the volume level.

⑩ Tap outside the dialog to close it.

You can now repeat this procedure for the other clips in the movie.

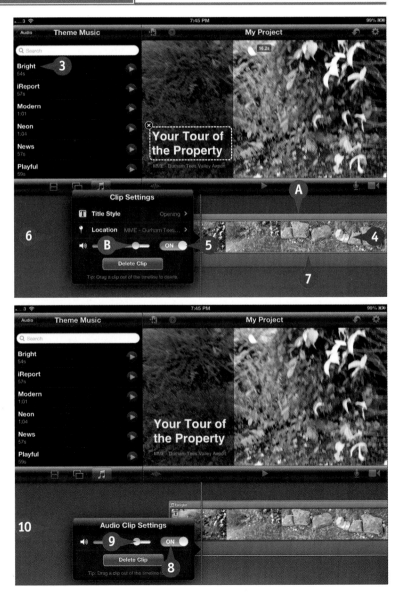

Change the Movie's Theme and Project Settings

1 Tap **Settings** (⬛).

The Project Settings dialog opens.

2 In the upper part of the dialog, tap the theme you want to apply. For example, tap **Simple** to apply the Simple theme.

3 Set the **Theme Music** switch to On or Off, as needed.

4 Set the **Loop Background Music** switch to On or Off, as needed.

5 Set the **Fade in from black** switch to On if you want to start with a black screen and then fade in the movie.

6 Set the **Fade out to black** switch to On if you want the movie to fade out to a black screen at the end.

7 Tap outside the Project Settings dialog.

The dialog closes.

TIPS

Where can I learn more information about what iMovie can do and how to use it?

You can learn more information about iMovie by tapping the **Help** icon (⬛) on the iMovie Home screen. You can also find information online by searching for "iMovie iPad."

How do I share a movie on YouTube?

After creating a YouTube account, tap **Share** (⬛) on the iMovie project screen, and then tap **YouTube** in the Share Movie To box on the screen that appears.

CHAPTER 13

Troubleshooting Your iPad

To keep your iPad running well, you should learn essential troubleshooting moves for the iPad itself and for iTunes. You can also update your iPad's software and track the device if it goes missing.

Normally, your iPad's apps run without problems — but like all software, they may sometimes suffer from bugs. When an app stops responding, you can force it to close so that you can regain control of your iPad.

Usually, you can easily tell when an app has stopped responding, because the screen does not change and your taps and gestures on the screen get no reaction. But if you are not certain that an app has stopped responding, it is a good idea to allow the app a few seconds to recover before you force it to close.

Close an App That Has Stopped Responding

① When an app stops
responding, press Home.

The Home screen appears.

② Press the Home button twice
in quick succession.

The app-switching bar appears.

Note: You can also swipe up the screen with four fingers to display the app-switching bar. For this to work, gestures must be enabled. From the Home screen, tap **Settings**, tap **General**, and then move the **Multitasking Gestures** switch to On.

3 Tap and hold the icon for the app that is not responding.

Note: You can tap and hold the icon for any app, but it is usually easiest to tap the icon for the app that is not responding.

The icons start to jiggle, and ⊖ appears at the upper-left corner of each icon.

4 Tap ⊖.

The app closes.

5 Tap above the app-switching bar.

The app-switching bar closes.

6 If necessary, tap the app's icon to start the app again.

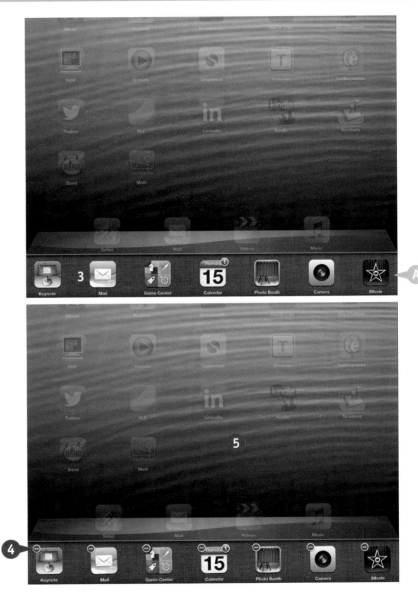

TIP

How else can I regain control of my iPad when it will not display the app-switching bar?
If your iPad does not display the app-switching bar when you press the Home button twice in rapid succession, shut down the iPad. Hold down the Sleep/Wake button until the Slide to Power Off slider appears, and then drag the slider across. If the Slide to Power Off slider does not appear, continue to hold down the Sleep/Wake button until the iPad shuts down. You can then press the Sleep/Wake button again to restart the iPad.

Update Your iPad's Software

Apple periodically releases new versions of the iPad's software to fix problems, improve performance, and add new features. To keep your iPad running quickly and smoothly, and to add the latest features that Apple provides, you should update the iPad's software when a new version becomes available.

iTunes and your iPad notify you automatically when a new version of the iPad's software is available. You can also check manually for new versions of the software.

Update Your iPad's Software

1 Connect your iPad to your computer via the USB cable.

The iPad appears in the Devices list in iTunes.

A dialog appears telling you that a new software version is available.

2 Click **Download and Update**.

Note: If iTunes has already downloaded the update for you, click **Update**.

iTunes downloads the new software, extracts it, and begins to install it.

The Summary screen shows the progress of the installation.

A If iTunes does not display the iPad's management screens, click the iPad in the Devices list to make the management screens appear.

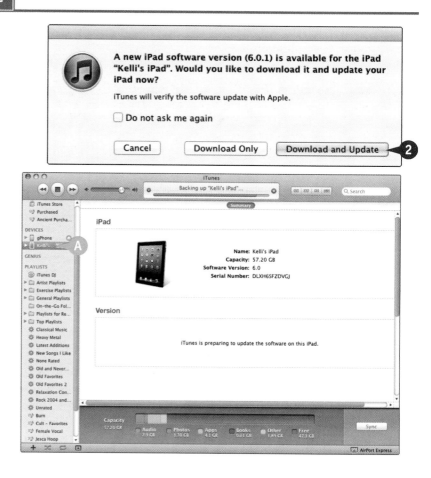

When the installation is complete, iTunes displays a dialog telling you that the iPad will restart in 15 seconds.

3 Click **OK**, or wait for the countdown to complete.

The iPad restarts, and then reappears in the Devices list in iTunes.

4 Click your iPad in the Devices list.

The iPad's management screens appear.

5 Verify the version number in the Software Version readout in the iPad box.

6 Disconnect your iPad from the USB cable. You can now start using the iPad as usual.

Your iPad has been updated, and is restarting. Please leave your iPad connected. It will appear in the iTunes window after it restarts.

This message will be dismissed in 4 seconds.

OK **3**

TIPS

How do I make iTunes check for a new version of my iPad's software?

Connect your iPad to your computer via the USB cable so that the iPad appears in the Devices list in iTunes. When the Summary screen appears, click **Check for Update** in the Version box.

Can I update my iPad's software without using a computer?

Yes. You can update your iPad "over the air" by using a wireless network. Press the Home button, tap **Settings**, tap **General**, and then tap **Software Update** to check for new software. If your iPad has cellular connectivity, you can also update using the cellular network, but because the update may involve transferring hundreds of megabytes of data, it is faster and less expensive to use a wireless network.

Extend Your iPad's Runtime on the Battery

To keep your iPad running all day long, you need to charge the battery fully by plugging the iPad in to a USB socket, the iPad Power Adapter, or another power source. You can extend your iPad's runtime by reducing the demands on the battery. You can dim your iPad's screen so that it consumes less power. You can set your iPad to go to sleep quickly. You can turn off Wi-Fi and Bluetooth when you do not need them, and you can turn off the power-hungry GPS feature on a cellular iPad when you do not need to track your iPad with the Find My iPad feature.

Extend Your iPad's Runtime on the Battery

Dim the iPad's Screen

1 Press the Home button.

The Home screen appears.

2 Tap **Settings**.

The Settings screen appears.

3 Tap **Brightness & Wallpaper**.

The Brightness & Wallpaper screen appears.

4 Tap the **Brightness** slider and drag it to the left to dim the screen.

A Move the **Auto-Brightness** switch to On if you want the iPad to adjust the brightness automatically to suit the ambient light conditions.

Turn Off Wi-Fi and Bluetooth

1 On the Settings screen, tap **Wi-Fi**.

The Wi-Fi screen appears.

2 Tap the **Wi-Fi** switch and move it to Off.

3 Tap **Bluetooth**.

The Bluetooth screen appears.

4 Tap the **Bluetooth** switch, and move it to Off.

Turn Off the GPS Feature

1 On the Settings screen, tap **Privacy**.

The Privacy screen appears.

2 Tap **Location Services**.

The Location Services screen appears.

3 Tap the **Location Services** switch and move it to Off.

4 If your iPad warns you that turning off Location Services will turn off Find My iPad, tap **Turn Off**.

5 Tap **Privacy**.

The Privacy screen appears.

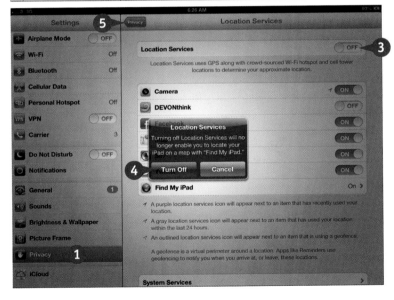

TIP

How can I make my iPad put itself to sleep quickly?
You can set a short time for the Auto-Lock setting. To do so, press the Home button. Tap **Settings**, tap **General**, and then tap **Auto-Lock**. Tap a short interval — for example, **2 Minutes** (Ⓐ).

General   Auto-Lock

2 Minutes ◀ Ⓐ

307

Troubleshoot the Inability to Charge the iPad Battery

I f your computer is a few years outdated and you are having problems charging your iPad, the USB ports on your computer may not supply enough power to meet the iPad's needs. If you ever experience a problem where you cannot charge the iPad, you can try several moves to troubleshoot the issue.

If you are having problems charging from your computer, use the USB power adapter to charge your iPad via an AC outlet to see if that solves the problem. Understanding essential troubleshooting methods can help you decide if the problem is minor or if you may need to get the battery replaced.

Check Your Cable Connections

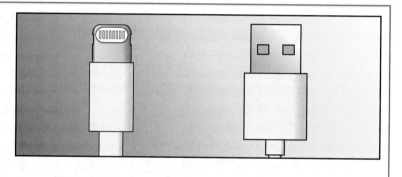

If your iPad does not charge, perhaps the first thing you should do is confirm that the cables are actually connected and secure. Make sure that the Lightning connector is attached firmly to the iPad and that the USB end is firmly attached to your computer or adapter. You should also make sure that the connectors are free of any dirt or dust that may hinder the charge. A faulty adapter also will not supply power to the iPad. Make sure you try another wall socket or another power supply if you have one.

Switch USB Ports

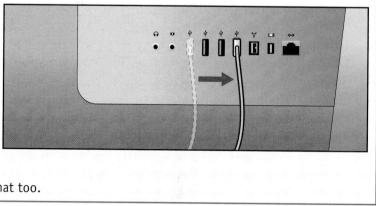

If you are using your USB-to-Lightning cable to connect the iPad to your computer, you can also try connecting to a different USB port. The USB port located on the keyboard may not transfer enough power to charge the iPad. If you are connected to this USB port, try disconnecting and connecting to a USB port located on the computer itself. If you have a powered USB hub, you can try that too.

Update to a New Computer

If your Mac or PC is out of date, and you have tried using a powered USB hub but found it unsatisfactory, you may want to consider purchasing a new computer. The built-in USB ports on a computer more than a few years old may not supply enough power to your iPad. In this case, the USB ports may be good only for syncing your iPad with iTunes. If so, Not Charging appears in the status bar next to the battery icon at the top of your iPad screen while connected.

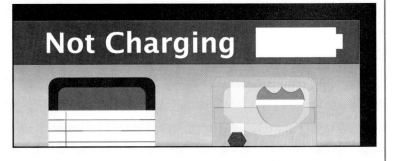

Wake Up Your Computer

Some computers do not charge the iPad when they are asleep; others do. If your computer does not charge the iPad when asleep, you can simply wake it up and configure your computer not to sleep while you are charging the iPad.

Set Up a Service Appointment

If you still cannot charge the iPad, you may need to replace the battery. One way to determine this is to schedule a service appointment at your local Apple Store or ship the iPad to Apple for inspection. Receiving technical support or setting up a service appointment is made very simple when you go to the Apple support site (www.apple.com/support/contact).

Genius Bar Service
Make an appointment at the Genius Bar in your state:

Indiana

iPad

Back Up and Restore Your iPad's Data and Settings with Your Computer

When you sync your iPad with your computer, iTunes automatically creates a backup of the iPad's data and settings. If your iPad suffers a software or hardware failure, you can restore the data and settings to your iPad. You can also sync your data and settings to a new iPad, an iPhone, or an iPod touch.

iTunes backs up the data that is unique on the iPad, such as the iPad's settings and notes you have created on the iPad, but does not back up music files, video files, or photos that you have synced to the iPad from your computer. For these types of files, which are still available on your computer, iTunes keeps a list of the files you have synced but does not keep extra copies of them.

Back Up and Restore Your iPad's Data and Settings with Your Computer

1 Connect your iPad to your computer via the USB cable or via Wi-Fi.

The iPad appears in the Devices list in iTunes.

2 Click your iPad in the Devices list.

The iPad's management screens appear.

3 Click **Summary**.

The Summary screen comes to the front.

4 (Control) +click (Mac) or right-click (Windows) your iPad in the Devices list.

The context menu opens.

5 Click **Back Up**.

iTunes backs up your iPad.

6 Click **Restore**.

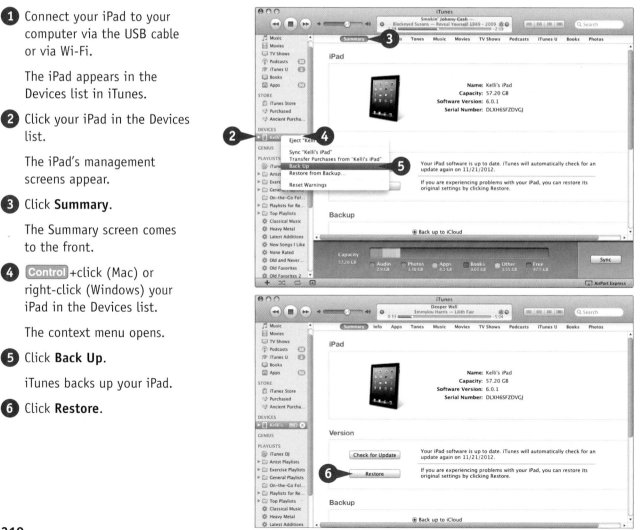

iTunes confirms that you want to restore the iPad to its factory settings.

7 Click **Restore**.

iTunes backs up the iPad's data, restores the software on the iPad, and returns the iPad to its factory settings.

Note: Do not disconnect the iPad during the restore process. Doing so can leave the iPad in an unusable state.

iTunes displays the Set Up Your iPad screen.

8 Click **Restore from the backup of** (○ changes to ⦿).

9 Click ⬍ , and choose your iPad by name.

10 Click **Continue**.

iTunes restores the data and settings to your iPad.

Your iPad restarts, appears in the Devices list in iTunes, and then syncs.

11 Disconnect the iPad.

TIP

How can I protect confidential information in my iPad's backups?

On the Summary screen in iTunes, click **Encrypt iPad backup** (☐ changes to ☑). In the Set Password dialog, type the password (**A**), and then click **Set Password** (**B**). iTunes then encrypts your backups using strong encryption.

Back Up and Restore Your iPad's Data and Settings with iCloud

When you sync your iPad with iCloud, you create a backup of the iPad's data and settings in your storage area on iCloud. If your iPad suffers a software or hardware failure, you can restore the data and settings to your iPad. At this writing, a standard free iCloud account gives you 5GB of data storage. This is enough to store your iPad's settings and your most important data and files. You can buy more storage if necessary, but even if you do, you must set your iPad to back up exactly those items you want to keep in iCloud. The iTunes Store lets you download again all the apps, media files, and games you have bought, so you do not need to back up these files.

Back Up and Restore Your iPad's Data and Settings with iCloud

1 Press the Home button.

The Home screen appears.

2 Tap **Settings**.

The Settings screen appears.

3 Tap **iCloud**.

The iCloud screen appears.

Ⓐ The Account button shows the e-mail address of your primary iCloud account.

4 Choose the data you want to synchronize with iCloud by moving the Mail, Contacts, Calendars, Reminders, Bookmarks, and Notes switches to On or Off as needed.

5 If you need to buy more storage, tap your account name.

The Account dialog appears, showing your storage amount in the Storage Plan area.

6 Tap the **Storage Plan** button.

The Change Storage Plan dialog appears.

7 Tap the storage plan you want, tap **Buy**, and follow the payment process.

8 Tap **Done**.

9 On the Account screen, tap **Photo Stream**.

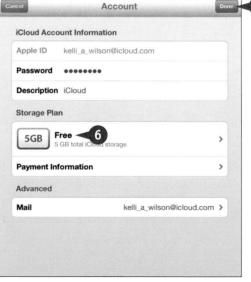

The Photo Stream screen appears.

10 Tap the **Photo Stream** switch, and move it to On or Off, as needed.

11 Tap the name of your iCloud account.

12 On the Account screen, tap **Documents & Data**.

The Documents & Data screen appears.

13 Tap the **Documents & Data** switch, and move it to On or Off, as needed.

14 Tap the **Use Cellular Data** switch, and move it to On or Off, as needed.

15 Tap **iCloud**.

16 Tap the **Find My iPad** switch, and move it to On or Off, as needed.

17 Tap **Storage & Backup**.

The Storage & Backup screen appears.

18 Tap the **iCloud Backup** switch, and move it to On.

19 If you want to back up your iPad now, tap **Back Up Now**.

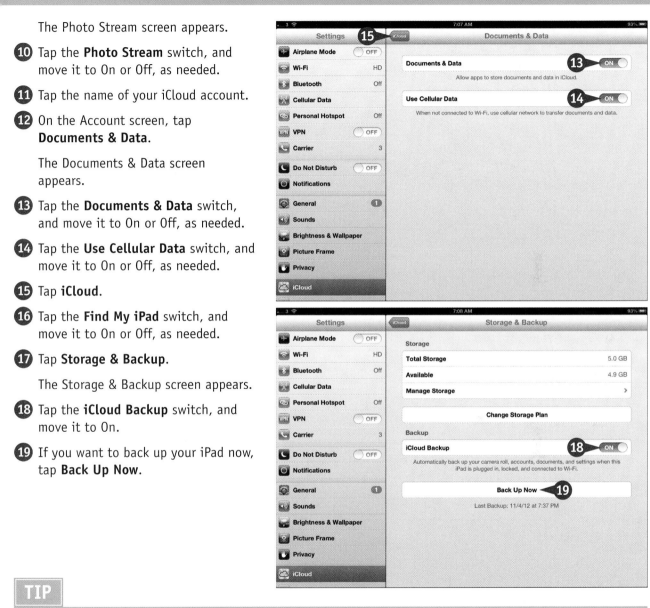

How do I restore my iPad from its iCloud backup?

First, reset the iPad to factory settings. Press the Home button, tap **Settings**, tap **General**, tap **Reset**, and tap **Erase All Content and Settings**. Tap **Erase iPad** in the confirmation dialog. When the iPad restarts and displays its setup screens, choose your language and country. On the Set Up iPad screen, tap **Restore from iCloud Backup**, and then tap **Next**. On the Apple ID screen, enter your Apple ID, and then tap **Next**. On the Choose Backup screen, tap the backup you want to use — normally, the most recent backup — and then tap **Restore**.

Reset Your Network, Dictionary, and Home Screen Settings

After experimenting with changes to your iPad's settings, you may want to restore the iPad to the default settings to undo the changes you have made. For example, you may want to restore your Home screen to its default settings to undo customizations.

From the Reset screen, you can quickly reset your network settings, your keyboard dictionary, your Home screen layout, or your location warnings. You can also reset all settings, as discussed in the next task.

Reset Your Network, Dictionary, and Home Screen Settings

1 Press the Home button.

The Home screen appears.

2 Tap **Settings**.

The Settings screen appears.

3 Tap **General**.

The General screen appears.

4 Scroll down all the way to the bottom.

The lower part of the General screen appears.

5 Tap **Reset**.

The Reset screen appears.

6 Tap **Reset Network Settings**, **Reset Keyboard Dictionary**, or **Reset Home Screen Layout**, as needed.

Note: Resetting the network settings deletes all network information you have entered, such as passwords for wireless networks. Resetting the keyboard dictionary deletes the custom words you have added to it. Resetting the Home screen layout puts the Home screen icons back in their default places.

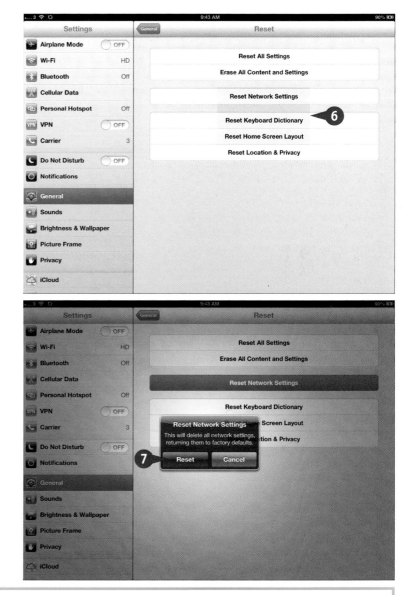

A confirmation dialog opens, showing a brief explanation of what the command will reset.

7 Tap **Reset**.

The iPad resets the item you chose.

TIP

What does the Reset Location & Privacy button on the Reset screen do?

When an app first requests location information, your iPad asks your permission. For example, when you first take a photo using the Camera app, the Camera app requests your location so that it can store it in the photo. After you tap **OK** (Ⓐ) for such a request, your iPad does not ask you again for the same app. Resetting the location warnings makes each app request permission again.

Restore Your iPad to Factory Settings

If your iPad starts malfunctioning and you cannot get iTunes to recognize it, you may need to restore the iPad to factory settings. This is an operation you perform on the iPad itself when severe problems occur with its settings, to get the iPad into a state where it can communicate with iTunes again.

If iTunes can recognize the iPad, use iTunes to restore the iPad instead of resetting the iPad as described here.

Restore Your iPad to Factory Settings

1 Press the Home button.

The Home screen appears.

2 Tap **Settings**.

The Settings screen appears.

Note: If your iPad is not responding to the Home button or your taps, press and hold the Sleep/Wake button and the Home button for about 15 seconds to reset the iPad.

3 Tap **General**.

The General screen appears.

4 Scroll down all the way to the bottom.

The lower part of the General screen appears.

5 Tap **Reset**.

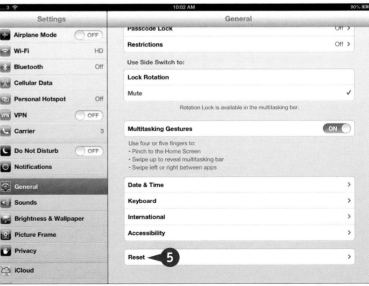

The Reset screen appears.

⑥ Tap **Reset All Settings**.

Note: If you have applied a restrictions passcode to the iPad, you must type the passcode after tapping Reset All Settings.

A confirmation dialog appears.

⑦ Tap **Reset**.

A second confirmation dialog appears, because resetting all settings makes such a serious change to your iPad.

⑧ Tap **Reset**.

The iPad resets all its settings.

Does resetting all the iPad's settings delete my data and my music files?
No, it does not. When you reset all the iPad's settings, the settings go back to their defaults, but your data remains in place. But you need to set the iPad's settings again, either by restoring them using iTunes or by setting them manually, in order to get the iPad working the way you prefer.

Troubleshoot Wi-Fi Connections

To get the most out of your iPad, use Wi-Fi networks whenever they are available, even if your iPad has cellular connectivity.

Normally, the iPad establishes and maintains Wi-Fi connections without problems. But you may sometimes need to request your iPad's network address again, a process called renewing the lease on the IP address. You may also need to tell your iPad to forget a network and then rejoin the network manually, providing the password again.

Troubleshoot Wi-Fi Connections

Renew the Lease on Your iPad's IP Address

1 Press the Home button.

The Home screen appears.

2 Tap **Settings**.

The Settings screen appears.

3 Tap **Wi-Fi**.

The Wi-Fi screen appears.

4 Tap ⊙ to the right of the network for which you want to renew the lease.

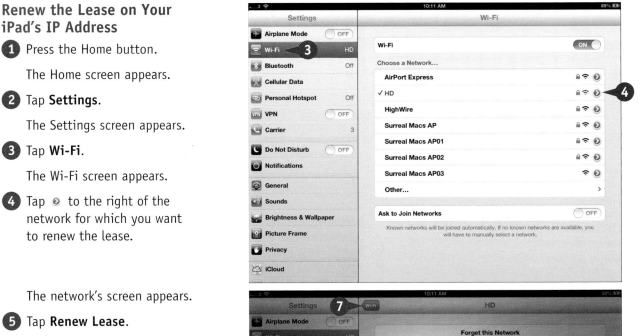

The network's screen appears.

5 Tap **Renew Lease**.

The Renew Lease? dialog opens.

6 Tap **Renew**.

7 Tap **Wi-Fi**.

The Wi-Fi screen appears.

Forget a Network and Then Rejoin It

 On the Wi-Fi screen, tap ⊘ to the right of the network.

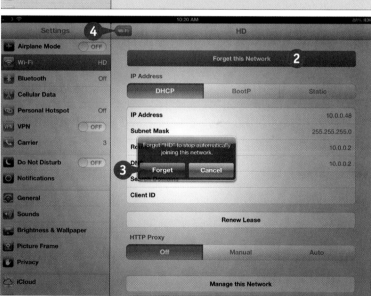

The network's screen appears.

② Tap **Forget this Network**.

The Forget this Network dialog opens.

③ Tap **Forget**.

The iPad removes the network's details.

④ Tap **Wi-Fi**.

The Wi-Fi screen appears.

⑤ Tap the network's name.

The password screen appears.

⑥ Type the password for the network.

⑦ Tap **Join**.

The iPad joins the network.

TIP

What else can I do to reestablish my Wi-Fi network connections?

If you are unable to fix your Wi-Fi network connections by renewing the IP address lease or by forgetting and rejoining the network, as described in this task, try restarting your iPad. If that does not work, reset your network settings, as described earlier in this chapter, and then set up each connection again manually.

Troubleshoot Connected Devices

Like any electronic device, the iPad and other connected devices may experience the occasional hiccup, where they do not do what they are supposed to do. You can connect devices to your iPad via a headset jack or the Lightning connector as well as Bluetooth. If you should have problems with any of these connection methods, you can try a few things to solve the issue.

If you should come across an issue that you just cannot seem to solve, try the Apple support site (www.apple.com/support/contact), which contains fixes and information.

Check Connections and Power Switches

When a problem occurs with a connected device, first make sure your physical connections are secure and that the power to your connected devices is on. Also, make sure your ports are clean. Lint and dirt can prevent connectors from connecting solidly. Use a can of compressed air to blow out lint, dirt, or smaller forms of wildlife from the ports and connectors.

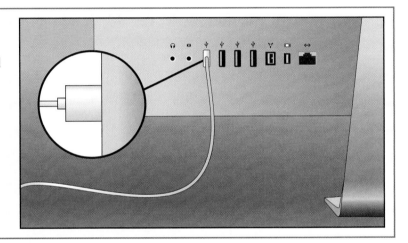

Replace Batteries

There is also a chance that the battery in your connected device may need to be replaced. If a device, such as a headset, is cutting in and out or does not work at all, try replacing the battery. Some wireless devices can really drain battery power. A faulty plug could also be the culprit.

Restart Devices

Another easy but effective troubleshooting move is to power-cycle the device in question — in other words, turn off the device and then turn it on again. When you turn off the device, leave it off for a few seconds to ensure that the insides of the device have actually powered down. If the device does not have an off and on switch, take the battery out. Often, simply turning a device off and then turning it back on again can solve minor issues.

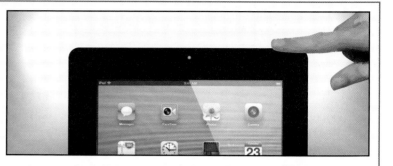

Reset Devices

It is possible that the device may have become confused because of a setting you have adjusted, which can happen when you configure a device. You can try resetting the device to its original factory settings to see if doing so fixes the issue.

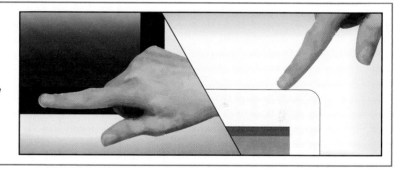

Upgrade Firmware

Some devices use software called *firmware* to run their internal functions. For example, routers and some video cameras have firmware. You can check with the manufacturer of the device to see if an upgrade is available for a particular device. A simple firmware upgrade may solve the issue.

Troubleshoot Why iTunes May Not See Your iPad

When you attach your iPad to your computer with the iTunes application running on your Mac or PC, the iPad should show up in the Devices list. If it does not appear in the Devices list, iTunes does not recognize your iPad.

Do you have the latest version of iTunes installed on your computer and firmware on your iPad? If you update and that still does not fix the issue, it may be a connection problem, so you can try another USB port on your computer. You can try a number of fixes to correct the problem of iTunes not recognizing your iPad.

Check Your Cable Connection

Start by ensuring that the cable to your iPad and your computer is connected securely. It can prove embarrassing to run through the entire litany of fixes, only to discover that the cables were not connected securely. You should also make sure that the ports and connector are free of dust and grime for a solid connection.

Restart Your iPad

You can try turning off your iPad and then turning it back on to see if that solves the problems. When you power-cycle your iPad, leave it off for a few seconds to ensure that the device has completely powered down. Turn the iPad on again to see if iTunes can now recognize it.

Switch to Another USB Port

The USB port in which you have the iPad connected simply may not work. If you are using a port on a USB hub to connect your iPad, remove the cable and connect it directly to a USB port on the computer itself.

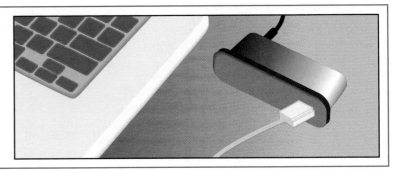

Restart the Computer

Try restarting the computer on which you have iTunes to see if iTunes then recognizes your iPad. Restarting the computer resets the operating system, the applications, and the USB ports, so it may enable iTunes to recognize your iPad. Restarting takes a few minutes but is well worth trying, because it can fix many minor problems.

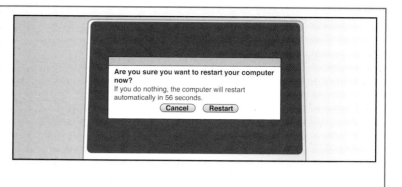

Check the iPad's Display

When connected to a computer, your iPad usually gives you a message alerting you to what it is doing. Occasionally, you may see a message that reads "Charging...please wait." In this case, the iPad may have to charge a few minutes before it has sufficient battery power to operate. If your iPad has suffered problems, you may see a message indicating that the device requires service.

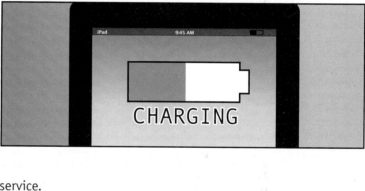

Verify Your Computer Meets System Requirements

If your computer does not meet the system requirements for your iPad, you will experience problems. Your iPad with Retina Display or iPad mini requires OS X 10.6.8 or later with iTunes 10.7 or later. On a PC, iPad requires Windows 7, Windows Vista, or Windows XP Home or Professional with Service Pack 2 or higher. iTunes 10.7 or later is also required for a PC. For iCloud, you must use Windows 7 or Windows 8; Windows Vista and Windows XP are not supported.

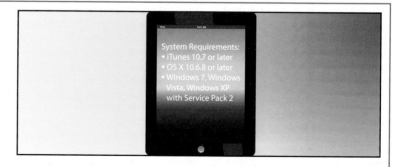

Troubleshoot iTunes Sync Problems

To keep your iPad charged and loaded with your current data and media files from your computer, connect it regularly to your computer and sync it using iTunes.

Connection and syncing are usually straightforward, but you may sometimes find that iTunes does not recognize your iPad when you connect it. When this happens, you will have to troubleshoot the physical connection and iTunes' settings. If iTunes is not set to sync automatically with your iPad, you must start the sync manually.

Troubleshoot iTunes Sync Problems

Check the USB Connection between Your Computer and Your iPad

① Check that the Lightning end of the cable is firmly plugged in to the Lightning port on the iPad. You may need to remove any case in order to make a good connection.

Note: Make sure the USB port you use is a full-power port rather than a low-power port. Use a USB port directly on your computer rather than a USB port on a peripheral device such as a keyboard. A USB port on a powered hub may deliver enough power, but one on an unpowered hub usually will not.

② Check that the USB end of the cable is firmly plugged in to a USB port on your computer.

Restart the iPad

① Press and hold the Sleep/Wake button on the iPad for several seconds.

② On the shutdown screen, tap and drag the slider to the right.

The iPad turns off.

③ Press and hold the Sleep/Wake button for 2 seconds.

The Apple logo appears on the screen, and the iPad restarts.

④ Connect the iPad to your computer via the USB cable.

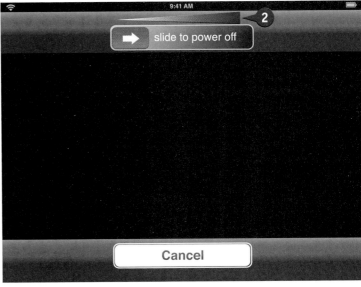

Restart iTunes

1 Close iTunes. In Windows, click **File** and then **Exit**. On a Mac, click **iTunes** and then **Quit iTunes**.

Note: If neither restarting your iPad nor restarting iTunes enables the two to communicate, try restarting your PC or Mac.

2 Restart iTunes. In Windows, click the **iTunes** icon on the Start menu or Start screen. On a Mac, click the **iTunes** icon on the Dock.

3 Connect the iPad to your computer via the USB cable.

Verify Automatic Syncing or Start a Sync Manually

1 If iTunes does not launch or become active when you connect your iPad, launch or activate iTunes manually.

2 Click your iPad in the Devices list.

3 On the iPad's management screen, click **Summary**.

4 Click **Open iTunes when this iPad is connected** (☐ changes to ☑).

5 Click **Apply**.

TIP

Why does nothing happen when I connect my iPad to my computer?
If your iPad's battery is exhausted, nothing happens for several minutes after you connect your iPad to your computer. This is because the iPad is charging its battery via the USB cable. After a few minutes, when the iPad's battery has enough charge to power the screen, the screen comes on, and syncing begins as usual.

Locate Your iPad with Find My iPad

If you have an iCloud account, you can use the Find My iPad feature to locate your iPad when you have lost it or it has been stolen. You can also display a message on the iPad — for example, to tell the person who has found the iPad how to contact you — or remotely wipe the data on the iPad.

To use Find My iPad, you must first set up your iCloud account on your iPad, and then enable the Find My iPad feature.

Locate Your iPad with Find My iPad

Turn On the Find My iPad Feature

1. Set up your iCloud account on your iPad as discussed in "Set Up Your E-Mail Accounts" in Chapter 4.

2. Press the Home button.

   The Home screen appears.

3. Tap **Settings**.

   The Settings screen appears.

4. Tap **iCloud**.

   The iCloud screen appears.

5. Tap the **Find My iPad** switch, and move it to On.

   A confirmation dialog appears.

6. Tap **Allow**.

   iCloud turns on the Find My iPad feature.

Locate Your iPad Using Find My iPad

1 Open a web browser, such as Internet Explorer or Safari.

2 Click the Address box.

3 Type **www.icloud.com**, and press **Enter** in Windows or **Return** on a Mac.

The iCloud Sign In web page appears.

4 Type your username.

5 Type your password.

6 Click ●.

The iCloud site appears, displaying the page you last used.

7 Click **iCloud** (☁).

The iCloud apps screen appears.

8 Click **Find My iPhone**.

continued ▶

TIP

Is it worth displaying a message on my iPad, or should I simply wipe it?

Almost always, it is definitely worth displaying a message on your iPad. If you have lost your iPad, and someone has found it, that person may be trying to return it to you. The chances are good that the finder is honest, even if he has not discovered that you have locked the iPad with a passcode. That said, if you are certain someone has stolen your iPad, you may prefer simply to wipe it, using the technique explained next.

Find My iPad is a powerful feature that you can use both when you have mislaid your iPad and when someone has deliberately taken it from you.

If Find My iPad reveals that someone has taken your iPad, you can wipe its contents to prevent whoever has taken it from hacking into your data. Be clear that wiping your iPad prevents you from locating the iPad again — ever — except by chance. Wipe your iPad only when you have lost it, you have no hope of recovering it, and you must destroy the data on it.

Locate Your iPad with Find My iPad (continued)

The iCloud Find My iPhone screen appears.

9 Click **Devices**.

Ⓐ The My Devices dialog appears.

10 Click your iPad.

The Info dialog appears, showing the iPad's location.

11 If you want to play a sound on the iPad, click **Play Sound**. This feature is primarily helpful for locating your iPad if you have mislaid it somewhere nearby.

Ⓑ A message indicates that the iPad has played the sound.

Lock the iPad with a Passcode

1 Click **Lost Mode** in the Info dialog.

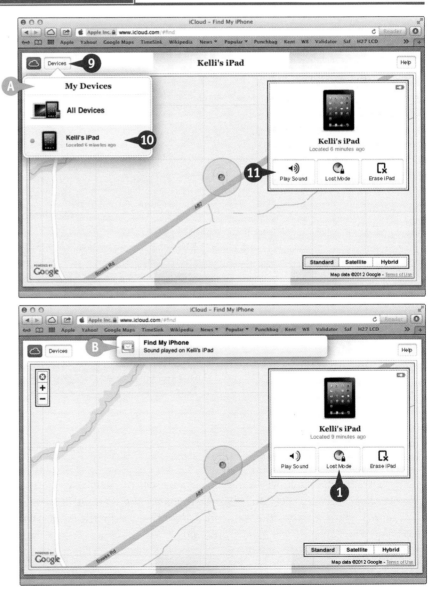

The Lost Mode dialog appears.

2 Click the numbers for a new passcode to apply to the iPad.

The Lost Mode dialog displays its Re-enter Passcode screen.

3 Click the passcode numbers again.

4 Optionally, type a contact phone number.

5 Click **Next**.

6 Optionally, type a message to whoever finds your iPad.

7 Click **Done**.

iCloud sends the lock request to the iPad, and then displays a dialog telling you it sent the request.

Remotely Erase the iPad

1 Click **Erase iPad** in the Info dialog.

The Enter Your Apple ID Password dialog appears.

2 Type your password.

3 Click **Erase**.

iCloud sends the erase request to the iPad, which erases its data.

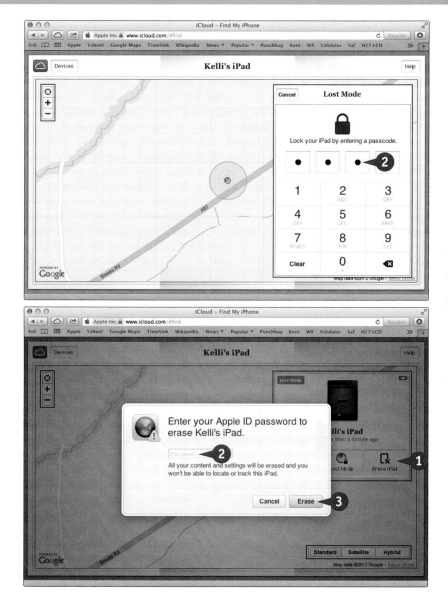

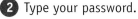

TIP

Can I remotely wipe the data on my iPad if I do not have an iCloud account?
You can set a passcode for the iPad as discussed in Chapter 2, and then move the **Erase Data** switch on the Passcode Lock screen to On. This setting makes the iPad automatically erase its data after ten successive failed attempts to enter the passcode. After five failed attempts, the iPad enforces a delay before the next attempt; further failures increase the delay.

Index

Index